African Perspectives on Adult Learning

Developing Programmes for Adult Learners in Africa

Other books in the Series

- *The Psychology of Adult Learning in Africa*
  Thomas Fasokun, Anne Katahoire and Akpovire Oduaran
- *Foundations of Adult Education in Africa*
  Frederick Nafukho, Maurice Amutabi and Ruth Otunga
- *Research Methods for Adult Educators in Africa*
  Bagele Chilisa and Julia Preece
- *The Social Context of Adult Learning in Africa*
  Sabo Indabawa, Stanley Mpofu

The Editorial Board for the Series

- Adama Ouane, UNESCO Institute for Lifelong Learning (Director)
- Martin Kamwengo, University of Zambia
- Rolene Liebenberg, Pearson Education South Africa
- Wolfgang Leumer, *dvv international*
- Christopher McIntosh, UNESCO Institute for Lifelong Learning
- Mantina Mohasi, National University of Lesotho
- Stanley Mpofu, Centre for Continuing Education, National University of Science and Technology, Zimbabwe
- Anthony Okech, Makerere University, Uganda
- Edward Turay, University of Sierra Leone
- Frank Youngman, University of Botswana (Series Managing Editor)
- Gabo Ntseane, University of Botswana (Assistant Series Managing Editor)

Photographs

All photographs in this book were provided by the authors, the UNESCO Institute for Lifelong Learning and *dvv international* with permission and free of charge.

African Perspectives on Adult Learning

Developing Programmes for Adult Learners in Africa

Mathew Gboku and Rebecca Nthogo Lekoko

Co-published by the UNESCO Institute for Lifelong Learning, Feldbrunnenstr. 58, 20148 Hamburg, Germany, and Pearson Education South Africa, corner of Logan Way and Forest Drive, Pinelands, Cape Town, South Africa, in collaboration with the *dvv international*, Obere Wilhelmstr. 32, 53225 Bonn, Germany, and the Adult Education Department of the University of Botswana, Private Bag 0022, Gaborone, Botswana.

First published 2007

ISBN 978 9282 011201

Published by Rolene Liebenberg with David Langhan
Project manager: Lenore Betts
Symbol research and selection: Sandie Vahl
Editor: Mark McClellan
Book design by Graham Arbuckle
Proofreader: Christine Didcott
Indexer: Stephen Anderson
Cover design and artwork by Toby Newsome
Typesetting by Robin Taylor
Printed by Creda Communications

The choice and the presentation of the facts contained in this book and the opinions expressed therein are not necessarily those of UNESCO and represent no commitments on the part of the Organization. The designations employed and the presentation of material throughout this publication do not imply the expression of any opinion whatsoever on the part of UNESCO concerning the legal status of any country, territory, city or area or of its authorities, or the delimitation of its frontiers or boundaries.

While every effort has been made to contact and acknowledge all copyright holders, this did not always prove possible. We would like to apologise for infringement of copyright so caused, and copyright holders are requested to contact the publisher in order to rectify the matter.

Contents

ADINKRA SYMBOLS

For the icons in this Series, we have chosen Adinkra symbols that are associated with learning and community in some way. These striking and expressive symbols are used by the people of Ghana and the Ivory Coast in textile and jewellery design, architecture, wood carvings, etc., and represent only one of a number of writing systems found in Africa.

	Symbol	Meaning	Interpretation
	bese saka	sack of cola nuts	abundance, plenty, affluence, power, unity, togetherness
	dame-dame	name of a board game	intelligence, ingenuity, strategy, craftiness
	dwennimmen	ram's horns	humility, strength, wisdom, learning
	mate masie	what I hear I keep	wisdom, knowledge, learning, prudence, understanding
	nkonsonkonson	chain link	unity, human relations, brotherhood, cooperation
	nsaa	hand-woven fabric	excellence, authenticity, genuineness
	sesa woruban	morning star inside a wheel	life transformation

The authors

Matthew Gboku
He holds a BSc in Agriculture from the University of Sierra Leone, an MPhil in Agricultural Extension and Rural Sociology from the Obafemi Awolowo University, and a PhD in Education from the University of Illinois. His teaching experience includes being a Lecturer in Agricultural Extension and Rural Sociology at Njala University College and a Senior Lecturer in Adult Education at the University of Botswana. He is currently a Training, Research and Monitoring Consultant for Agro-Business Consulting and Development (Pty) Limited. He wrote Chapters 2, 3, 5, 6, 8 and 9.

Rebecca Nthogo Lekoko
She holds a Doctor of Education from Pennsylvania State University. She is currently a senior lecturer in the Faculty of Education, Department of Adult Education of the University of Botswana and has previously been a Setswana language-lecturer at Teacher Colleges of Education. Her research and publication interests have been in the areas of programme planning, implementation and evaluation of adult and extension education programmes. She wrote Chapters 1, 4, 7, 10 and 11.

Foreword

The remedial strategy of borrowing text-books conceived in contexts of and for students from developed countries with well-established traditions of adult education is no longer viable. The present textbook series *African Perspectives on Adult Learning* represents the outcome of a venture initiated three decades ago by the Institute for International Cooperation of the German Adult Education Association (now known by its German abbreviation *dvv international*). Bringing together non-governmental and civil society organisations, the *dvv international* turned this venture into a creative partnership with academia aimed at building the training and research capacities of African universities serving the adult education community. It has become a means of fruitful cooperation with several leading African universities, all partners being commonly concerned with providing textbooks for university departments and institutes of adult education relevant for the African context.

The abiding interest, as well as the growing financial support and substantive input of the *dvv international*, has provided a key ingredient for the success of this project along with establishing its potential for expansion. Another major contributor from the beginning has been the University of Botswana. Its Department of Adult Education has given the academic and institutional support needed for such an ambitious undertaking, graciously shouldering the Editorial Secretariat of the Series. The third pillar of this endeavour – and a decisive one – was furnished by the UNESCO Institute for Education, now the UNESCO Institute for Lifelong Learning, an international centre of excellence in adult learning enjoying the full backing of UNESCO and boasting extensive publishing experience in the field. The Institute brought in vital international and inter-regional expertise, coupled with the vision of the Fifth International Conference on Adult Education (CONFINTEA V). The Institute has also mobilised sizeable financial resources of its own, led the Series Editorial Board and assumed responsibility for managing the often difficult matters entailed by such a complex venture.

The present Series recommends itself through other distinctive features reflecting the unique manner in which it has come about. One of these has to do with the professional guidance and scientific advice provided by the competent and sensitive Series Editorial Board, whose members have displayed the capability and wisdom required to steer a project of this kind. Their intellectual resources, experience and know-how made it possible for the Series to take on its actual form. We wish to express our deep gratitude to all of the members of the Editorial Board for their profound involvement and the optimism that they brought to the series and for their dedication to its successful completion.

The co-publisher with the Institute is Pearson Education South Africa, which has proven itself to be a partner highly committed to the goals of the project; one prepared to engage in a collaboration of a different order and take risks in exploring new paths in publication. As a full member of the Series Editorial Board, the co-publisher has offered invaluable assistance, especially in the writers' workshops and in coaching the authors throughout the composition of the volumes. The creative way in which Pearson Education South Africa has integrated the project into its work and its firm dedication to fostering editorial and authorial capacities in Africa deserves special mention. Without this sense of mission, the Series would not have seen the light of day.

The authors of the works in this Series have themselves been selected on the basis of proposals, which they submitted. We took pleasure in working with all of these devoted partners, and the project greatly benefited from their combination of individual conviction with teamwork and collective analysis and decision-making. We wish to thank all of the authors for their hard work as well as their adherence to a demanding schedule. Their professionalism and competence lie at the heart of this Series and were instrumental in its realisation.

Finally, and most importantly, special recognition is due Professor Frank Youngman, the Series Managing Editor, and his Assistant, Dr Gabo Ntseane, of the University of Botswana, who constitute the Editorial Board Secretariat. Frank Youngman initiated the idea of this series in 2001, and the Secretariat has been in the front line at all times, carefully guiding the process, monitoring progress, and ensuring the quality of the work at all stages without compromise.

This Series addresses the critical lack of textbooks for adult education and the alienating nature of those currently in use in Africa. We have sought to develop a new set of foundational works conceived and developed from an African perspective and written mainly by African scholars. An African perspective, however, is not mere Afrocentrism, although some degree of the latter is required to move beyond the reigning Eurocentrism and general Western domination of all scientific domains and adult education in particular. Injecting a dose of Afrocentrism without prejudice to universal values, elementary scientific knowledge, and other cultures; and without complacency in the face of retrograde and discriminatory values and traditions has proven to be a significant challenge. In essence, the African perspective has revealed itself to be both a renaissance of the continent and its manifold traditions as well as the birth of its own new vision and prospects in the context of a fast-growing, ever-changing and increasingly globalised world.

For the initial volumes in this evolving Series, the following five titles were selected: *The Psychology of Adult Learning in Africa*; *Foundations of Adult Education in Africa*; *Research Methods for Adult Educators in Africa*; *Developing Programmes for Adult Learners in Africa*; and *The Social Context of Adult Learning in Africa*. We will certainly judge the success of these volumes by taking into account the reactions and responses of their users; and we will make any necessary adjustments while striving to widen the scope of the venture to cover other linguistic areas of Africa and to explore new thematic fields for deepening the African perspective. There is no question but that *dvv international* and the UNESCO Institute for Lifelong Learning are committed to lending their intellectual and financial support to this endeavour. Furthermore, the University of Botswana is committed to providing the academic and administrative base for the Series, whilst Pearson Education South Africa foresees the on-going viability of the project. In opening up new approaches to adult education and learning in Africa, it meets the needs of governments, non-governmental and civil society organisations, and academia in an area of great importance to UNESCO and the community of nations.

Adama Ouane
Director, UNESCO Institute for Lifelong Learning, Hamburg

Preface

It became clear during the 1990s that adult learning must be an important part of all strategies for development. In a series of world conferences between 1990 and 1996, various agencies of the United Nations addressed the issues of education for all, the environment, human rights, population, social development, the status of women, human settlements and food security. Each of these conferences recognised that progress would be dependent on adult members of society transforming their life circumstances and gaining greater control over their lives. To achieve this change, adults require new knowledge, skills and attitudes. This significant insight was highlighted by the Fifth International Conference on Adult Education (CONFINTEA V), which was organised by UNESCO in 1997. CONFINTEA V affirmed that adult learning is potentially a powerful force for promoting people-centred development. It concluded that the education of adults is key to the twenty-first century.

The concept of adult learning articulated by CONFINTEA V is a broad one; embracing formal, non-formal and informal learning processes in all areas of people's lives. This concept is relevant in African contexts, where the learning of adults takes place across their various social roles, in the home, the community, and the workplace, as well as in formal educational and training institutions. Opportunities for learning are availed by a wide variety of providers. The state has a central responsibility to promote and facilitate adult learning. In some countries this responsibility has been diminished by the impact of structural adjustment policies. But in others, the state continues to play an important role, with a wide range of government departments organising programmes that involve adult learning. These programmes are multi-sectoral, including activities as varied as agricultural extension, health education, business training, consumer education, community development, and wildlife education. Also, the organisations of civil society are significant sites of adult learning, providing their own educational programmes, as well as a context in which adults acquire new competencies through their active involvement in running such organisations. For example, in many countries the trade union movement is an important source of adult learning.

Increasingly, the private sector is a major provider of learning opportunities for adults. Its role has two dimensions. Firstly, companies are expanding their training and development for employees as they respond to the challenges of technological change and global competition. Secondly, there is a rapid growth of commercial educational institutions, such as colleges, academies and institutes, which are responding to market demands for learning opportunities, especially in work-related fields such as computing, tourism, and business. These institutions are to be found in all the urban centres of Africa. Public and private universities also cater for many adult learners, especially through their part-time, evening, and distance learning programmes. The education and training of adults in Africa therefore takes place in many settings, embraces many content areas and modes of learning, and is provided by many different kinds of organisation. It is a complex and diverse field of activity.

The successful implementation of adult learning policies and programmes depends in large measure on the availability of knowledgeable, skilful, and socially committed educators of adults. Because they are key agents in the realisation of adult learning, the quality of their initial and continuing training is crucial. The educators of adults in Africa work in a wide variety of organisational and social contexts, from government bureaucracies to community-based projects. They have multiple roles as programme planners, organisers, teachers, researchers and counsellors. While this diversity of situations and roles reflects the reality of adult learning settings, it presents significant conceptual and practical problems in terms of the training of those who educate adults. One example is that not all who work with adults in learning activities identify themselves as adult educators. Rather, they identify themselves as health promoters or business advisors or community workers. Nevertheless, whatever the nomenclature of a particular cadre, it is important that they are proficient in their work of helping adults to learn. The development of their expertise includes a body of knowledge, skills and values that is centred on adult education as a field of study and practice.

The professional training of educators of adults in Africa takes place in institutions of tertiary education across the continent, primarily at diploma and degree level. For example, in every country there are agricultural colleges that prepare agricultural extension workers, health institutes that train community-based health workers, and technical colleges that train vocational teachers. In particular, many African universities have departments or institutes of adult education that train personnel for fields as varied as prison education and human resource development. Although the areas of content specialisation vary from agronomy to literacy, the curricula of the training programmes have many common topics, such as the psychology of adult learning, programme development, communication skills, and research methods. This is because all educators of adults require a common body of knowledge (such as awareness of the historical and philosophical dimensions of adult education practice) and a number of generic skills (for example, in teaching and research). A key learning resource in these training programmes is the prescribed course textbook. However, those who teach on these programmes often have difficulty in finding textbooks that are relevant to the work situations and social contexts of their students.

A review of English-language curriculum materials used in the professional training of adult educators in Africa reveals that the majority of textbooks for the courses are published in the United States of America or the United Kingdom. The content of these books seldom reflects issues of African development or the realities of adult education policy and practice in Africa. The social and organisational contexts, theoretical underpinnings, and practical examples are largely derived from the experience of adult education in the advanced industrialised countries of the West. Hence the textbooks currently being used in the training of adult educators in Africa are at best lacking in relevance and, at worst, actively promoting inappropriate models of adult education. Furthermore, because of the cost of these books, student access is often limited.

The post-colonial history of adult education as a field of study in African tertiary education institutions shows that very few indigenous textbooks have been produced over the years. Useful individual books, such as the *Adult Education Handbook* (ed. by the Institute of Adult Education, Dar-es-Salaam, 1973) and *A Handbook of Adult Education for West Africa* (ed. by Lalage Bown and Sunday Hezekiah Olu Tomori, London, 1979), have been one-off publications that were not followed up and were not widely available. When an institution in one country has consistently produce relevant materials, such as the Department of Adult Education at the University of Ibadan in Nigeria, they have been difficult to obtain in other countries. The problem remains of a lack of appropriate and accessible textbooks for use in the training of African adult educators.

There is therefore a need to develop relevant, affordable, and available textbooks that reflect African social realities, theoretical and cultural perspectives, policies and modes of practice. This is the need that the Series *African Perspectives on Adult Learning* seeks to meet. The books in the Series put the African context at the centre of their discussions of adult education topics. They take into account the impact of colonialism, liberation struggles, neo-colonialism, and globalisation. They show the importance to adult learning of African philosophies, indigenous knowledge systems, traditions and cultures. They demonstrate that the realities of class, gender, race and ethnicity in African societies shape the nature of adult learning activities. They provide examples of the policies and practices that characterise adult education across the continent. Whilst referring to international discourses on adult learning, their presentation of issues in adult education is Africa-centred. The Series therefore contributes to the endogenisation of education within the perspective of the African Renaissance.

The books in the Series *African Perspectives in Adult Learning* cover important subjects for the training of educators of adults in Africa. They are intended to be course textbooks that will be used in face-to-face teaching environments in a way that encourages interactive learning. Each book is designed to provide an overview of the subject, to introduce appropriate theory, and to provide discussion and examples rooted in professional practice, policies, and research from African contexts. Each chapter features clear learning objectives, practical examples, and activities for the reader to do individually or in a group, a summary and glossary, further questions to think about and further reading. It is hoped that the use of the books will promote the development of relevant curricula and interactive teaching approaches in adult education training programmes across the continent.

Each book in the Series provides an African perspective on an important area of knowledge and practice for the educator of adults. In *Developing Programmes for Adult Learners in Africa*, Matthew Gboku and Nthogo Lekoko consider the subject of programme development for adult learners in African contexts. The book promotes an approach to programme development that makes African ways of thinking and learning, beliefs and value systems, integral aspects of the planning process. It emphasises the need to involve learners themselves in planning learning programmes, thus guaranteeing relevance and cultural appropriateness. The book seeks to elaborate programme development approaches and models that are relevant to African contexts. Accordingly, the contents reflect the literature and practice of adult education in Africa. The discussion provides illustrations and examples that are based on empirical research findings, classroom experience, and field practice from Africa.

The aims of the book are:
- to provide a critical analysis of the fundamental concepts, principles, theories and models of programme development in the African context; and
- to provide an understanding of the processes and skills involved in programme development in different adult learning settings across Africa.

Chapter 1 provides the foundational frame of reference for understanding the concept of programme development. It provides a philosophical, historical and theoretical basis for planning, implementing and evaluating adult education programmes in an African way. The discussion in Chapter 1 lays the foundation for the issues discussed in the subsequent chapters. Chapter 2 describes types of adult education programmes, traditional approaches, and models of programme development. It provides a critical analysis of the approaches and models from an African perspective. The remaining chapters address important practical, personal and professional issues of programme development.

The ability to develop programmes is an essential skill for educators of adults, whose work centres on organising opportunities for adults to learn. *Developing Programmes for Adult Learners in Africa* provides an excellent resource for developing and enhancing this skill.

Frank Youngman
University of Botswana

African Perspectives on Adult Learning

Developing Programmes for Adult Learners in Africa

Chapter 1

Introduction to programme development

OVERVIEW

The content of this chapter reflects two main principles: i) that indigenous African philosophies should influence the way programme developers approach and carry out their duties; and ii) that programme development should address the practical realities of everyday African life.

In our discussion of programme development, we will consider the various factors that influence a programme developer's work, including environmental, human and resource factors, as well as the element of individual expertise and experience. We will also approach the philosophical nature of programme development work and the critical questioning that this entails. Africa's education history is addressed, with attention paid to the impact of colonialism on traditional education practices. We examine in some detail the important role indigenous African philosophies play in shaping education development programmes that are responsive to the needs and circumstances of the African adult learner.

LEARNING OBJECTIVES

By the end of the chapter, you should be able to:

1 Articulate reasons for using the concepts of programme development for African adult learners.
2 Make suggestions for developing programmes within an African context.
3 Articulate the importance of African philosophies in developing programmes for African adult learners.

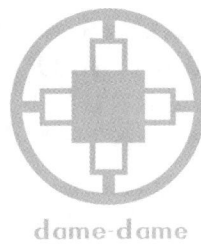

dame-dame

KEY TERMS

adult education   All adult educational activities provided to learners through a variety of channels, including face-to-face interactions and distance-learning education, using both print and non-print teaching and learning materials or aids.

programme   A time-bound plan that details the learning situation, what learners are to know, how they are to learn it, the learners' and teachers' roles; as well as the place, facilities and resources to be used.

programme development   A systematic and needs-driven process that consciously invites multiple voices to address the educational needs of a target learner group. It is the joint decision-making and negotiation process of people who contribute a number of things (expertise, finance, facilities and other resources) towards developing, implementing and evaluating programmes for learners in their African communities.

philosophy   The shared beliefs, thoughts and values that guide the development, implementation and evaluation of adult education programme practices.

indigenous African philosophies   Philosophies based on African beliefs, values and norms. These philosophies invariably stress the importance of unity/oneness; that is, the need to relate and work closely and co-operatively in a responsive and responsible manner.

principle   a commonly accepted rule of action

BEFORE YOU START

How many times have you used the word 'programme' or heard other people using it? What do you think is meant by a programme? How and why do people make and use a programme? As you consider these questions, remember that although there are different types of programmes the focus in this chapter is on adult education programmes.

PROGRAMME DEVELOPMENT VERSUS PROGRAMME PLANNING

Adult education, as an open and evolving field, has its share of debated or controversial concepts. It is important that we examine these concepts as far they relate to developing programmes in adult education. The concepts/debates usually centre on the issue of how an understanding of a particular concept influences the way that concept is actualised or used in practice. Two concepts are of particular concern: programme development and programme planning. These terms are sometimes used interchangeably in the literature of adult education and people seldom question or reflect on their use. A critical analysis of these terms is attempted here.

It has been realised that where the task of programming is necessarily participatory and democratic, as it is within an African context, the concept of programme development rather than programme planning is suitable. The general observation is that in instances where adult education practitioners are referred to as programme planners, they tend to use a frame of reference similar to that of prescriptive programming (Cervero, 1988; Dominick, 1990). Such a frame of reference gives the impression that programming is a task of producing a layout or a blueprint. This understanding, when applied to adult education programmes, tends to conceal some important processes of the act of developing programmes in an adult education setting.

Adult education practitioners do more than produce layouts that can be applied without failure in a number of contexts. It is for this reason that adult education practitioners are referred to as programme developers rather than programme planners. Using the concept of programme

development acknowledges the fact that programming in the African context, and perhaps in the entire field of adult education, is ever-changing, flexible and participatory. This approach recognises that social activities, such as programme development, cannot be reduced to some step-by-step production of blueprints.

Every instance of developing an adult education programme is different and has its own unique set of contextual requirements. However, what is common across all contexts is that the task of developing programmes brings different people from different sectors of society to work together, explore together, share ideas and make decisions together. More importantly, they will learn and act together according to the dictates of the prevailing environment.

Consider the situation today where the entire African continent faces the problem of HIV/AIDS. Ask yourself: When the issue of HIV/AIDS is discussed, who should be involved in the exploration, exchange and promotion of ideas? Also, think of other development programmes, for example, those addressing the problems of illiteracy, poverty and gender inequality and consider: Who gets involved?

The nature of problems addressed by adult educators presents programme development not as a neutral process but as an interactive process in which all involved are expected to contribute different opinions. Questions such as, 'Whose voice gets heard and why and how?' are asked (Cervero and Wilson, 1994). In the traditional African context too, for example, in the Setswana culture, developing programmes is the process of listening to multiple voices. Different perspectives are welcomed in an attempt to improve people's immediate well-being, as defined by their political, economic and cultural conditions. There is no moment during the process of developing programmes when programme developers perform the tasks without critically assessing and analysing their actions.

Questions that can help developers to reflect critically on their processes and progress include, 'What is the goal/purpose for doing what we are doing?', 'How does our work as programme developers impact upon the programme being developed?' and 'How will what we do improve the living conditions of the target population?' Many more questions can be asked to analyse the importance, authenticity and impact of all stages involved in programme design – needs-assessment, implementation, evaluation and post-evaluation. These stages (needs-assessment, implementation, evaluation and post-evaluation) are discussed in other chapters of this book.

The process of development can thus be explained as a reality-check activity that should enable programme developers to act responsibly and purposefully in response to authentic challenges and problems. Qualities such as critical thinking, reflection, flexibility and effective decision-making are central to the task of developing programmes. You will be introduced later on in this book to further issues of participatory and flexible approaches suggested for use in an African context.

Defining programme development

Developing programmes in adult education is like exploring a thick bush looking for a hidden treasure. It starts with a goal but no-one is sure of how the goal will be reached. Before carrying out the search, the explorers talk about and agree on how the exploration has to be carried out and other issues, such as the resources needed. The explorers will have to take into consideration a number of things, for example, knowing the place (the bush) where the search is going to be carried out; having an idea of the type of treasure they are looking for; understanding the difficulties involved in getting into the bush, and anticipating problems that they may encounter. Above all, the explorers have to be convinced that it is worth carrying out the exploration.

What is interesting is that when explorers decide upon their mission, they do this with the shared goal of looking for and bringing home the treasure. Prior to the expedition, discussions are held to establish a common ground for conducting the search and agreeing upon the relative importance of different factors involved in their quest. However, the actual search methods will differ and will offer up a number of unique experiences for the participating individuals.

Similarly, in developing adult education programmes, key individuals discuss and make decisions upon a number of issues. Thus, programme development is a means of keeping communication open between people who can contribute ideas, finance, facilities and other resources. These people may include experts in programme development, content specialists, evaluators, administrators, managers and potential learners. They talk about and take decisions on programme objectives, and they work out strategies to achieve the programme goals. This process involves discussion, debate, judgment and making conclusions. From this process, each programme developer accumulates unique experiences. A number of factors shape these experiences, including:

- The environment. Developers carry out the task in different environments. The environment influences the way things are run.
- Human interaction. Developing programmes means contributing individuals work and learn together. The ways these people interact will differ. The type of people involved and the purpose(s)

behind their coming together will shape the interaction pattern.

- Resources and logistical issues. The task of developing programmes is influenced by the availability of resources such as time, space, finances and other facilities.
- Experience and expertise. These qualities will also shape the development process and will depend upon the unique qualities of each individual. For example, a programme developer's planning expertise will influence their approach to the task, just as a lower-skilled individual will undertake the development in a manner that suits their expertise and experiences. So, developing programmes can mean different things to different people.

Programme development philosophy

Just as communication is a basis for building and maintaining relationships, the philosophical aspect of programme development provides the foundation for developing effective adult education programmes. Generally speaking, philosophy helps people to analyse a situation critically through asking a series of questions. These questions will not only address the situation but also ask questions of the enquiry process itself. This rigorous analytical process represents a basic principle that guides decisions and actions.

Programme developers often operate under certain assumptions. These assumptions are part of what is referred to here as programme philosophy and are most accurately described as 'best guesses'. They are 'best guesses' because they are based on some established ways of developing programmes in specific contexts. These guesses act as principles or philosophies for guiding the process of developing programmes. Such philosophies assume different forms. African proverbs, for example, embody important principles for development

practice. The proverb, '*It takes a whole village to raise a child*' is a good example here. This proverb carries the assumption that the proper upbringing and socialisation of children into productive and responsible citizens of African society is the responsibility of the entire community. Community members carry an individual and collective responsibility to educate, formally or informally, the young. The community imparts the relevant knowledge regarding the appropriate social skills and survival needs of the community, in order to equip the youth with a variety of skills that will enable them to fit into their respective societies.

The diversity of skills needed calls for different perspectives from everyone who can contribute in the community, which explains the reasoning behind the phrase, '*It takes a whole village to raise a child.*' This assumption has much to teach us today as we develop programmes for adult learners in an African context. We need to approach the task in a manner that respects indigenous ways of thinking and acting. Approaching our task in this manner allows us to operate under the guiding principle of, '*It takes a whole team to develop meaningful and relevant programmes for adult learners*', which means that participatory or collective approaches are necessary.

To illustrate this idea, we can think of how social problems are addressed in an African context. For example, endemic diseases that impede development are addressed through community-wide consultations. In the past, signals such as the blowing of the horn were used to alert community members. Hearing the sound, the people would know that they must assemble in the village meeting place for a matter that concerned them. The chiming of a large bell was another strategy used to summon people to a participatory meeting, as were house-to-house messages delivered by the chief messenger.

Although many of these traditional strategies no longer exist, in some African societies the village meeting place ('*kgotla*' in Setswana) remains a vibrant forum for community discussions. The meeting place creates an open and democratic environment where everyone may contribute. The exchange of ideas at this forum is not only open but also spontaneous.

Our starting point as programme developers should be at the point where we tap into traditional African ways of dealing with problems. Collective or communal action is an African tradition, and one that is especially relevant when it surrounds activities affecting a social group (family, community, nation or indeed any group of people).

Sadly, African traditional philosophy remains largely absent from the programme development guidelines currently in use. Thus, this book takes the bold step of addressing the issues of how African philosophies can inform current practices. This Afrocentric focus is reflected in the entire series of 'African Perspectives on Adult Learning'. For example, Chilisa and Preece's (2004) book *Research methods and indigenous knowledge systems* pays special attention to how such philosophies are an invaluable part of knowledge construction that is intended to benefit African learners. The authors address a number of different perspectives, including community-centred ways of knowing and the story-telling framework. These concepts are of special interest to us. Relevant ideas from the African philosophies will bring programming ideas closer to the thinking of the local people and, by achieving this, people may therefore relate and respond positively to and with the programmes.

One other important aspect of the programme philosophy that can be used as a guiding principle is that of beliefs. Beliefs refer to conceptual frameworks that help us interpret and respond to challenges and problems in a certain manner. You may have heard of the common saying, '*One good turn deserves another.*' This is an example of a statement that embodies people's beliefs. A belief shapes ways of thinking; it brings certain expectations and it also directs actions. A person with the belief '*One good turn deserves another*' anticipates a reward of some sort in response to what he or she does for other people. When applied to programme development, programme developers want to be satisfied with what they do. They expect and believe that when they direct their efforts into developing programmes, the result(s) should be satisfying to beneficiaries and other stakeholders, including themselves. Thus, they develop programmes for a purpose. Purpose is an important element of what is referred to here as a philosophy.

Reasoning is yet another integral aspect of the philosophy of developing programmes for adult learners. Viewed in this way, philosophy can be seen as a special kind of thinking and reasoning through which programme developers establish reasons for doing certain things in a specific manner. This act of reasoning is complex. It involves asking the question 'why?', making judgments, considering alternative means and offering convincing conclusions. Sound reasoning is therefore an essential attribute of programme developers. For example, when a programme is implemented to educate the youth about the impact of violence, such as in passion killings, there is reason for educating them. Perhaps you can suggest some of the reasons that may be involved.

Values and desires are further important aspects of philosophy. These values shape attitudes towards doing certain tasks. Consider this Setswanan value-laden statement: '*Mmua lebe o bua la gagwe.*' The statement implies that everyone has a natural instinct to voice or express his or her opinions, and that everyone has to be given an opportunity to do so freely – free from rejection, ridicule or humiliation. People who respect this value appreciate the importance of sharing information and respecting others' points of view. It is pleasing to see programme developers working within an African context taking this kind of value and applying it in their work, through a recognition of and respect for other people's points of view.

When people have come together with the common goal of developing relevant programmes, it is important that their views are heard and respected. As we mentioned earlier in this chapter, the task of developing programmes for learners in Africa should be a participatory one. This principle of participation encourages developers to welcome different perspectives, opinions and inputs from people who can make meaningful contributions to the programme.

We may conclude by saying that 'what we think and believe and feel [our philosophy] determines the way we act' (Ocitti, 1973: 91). Thus, our outlook on life shapes the way we develop programmes. Some of these philosophies are explicit, that is, they are clearly stated for each developer to know. In other cases, they are tacit (unstated). However, in all instances of developing programmes these philosophies shape the thinking and decision-making processes of programme developers.

Defining a programme philosophy

Against the background given in the preceding discussion, a programme philosophy may be viewed as a particular kind of thinking, reasoning, and decision-making used to address a prevailing problem. It is a set of guiding statements that gives programme developers direction to initiate, proceed and complete a task. Usually, a programme philosophy is in question-form, as shown in the following examples:

1 What beliefs do people hold about the way to develop adult education programmes for learners in Africa?
2 What do people think should be the goals for developing adult education programmes for learners in Africa?
3 What do people see as the right approach to addressing real-life challenges and problems of learners in Africa?
4 What should be the sources of ideas and decisions for developing adult education programmes for learners in Africa?

These questions help programme developers arrive at certain decisions, actions and conclusions. We suggest that programme developers formulate philosophies for developing programmes for adult learners in the African context and that these philosophies should be clear, meaningful and responsive to real-life challenges.

▨ ACTIVITY

1 **Imagine you pick up a newspaper and your attention is caught by the headline: 'Renewed commitment to family lives'. Reading the article, you learn that the government has set aside money for individuals who would like to establish programmes for the betterment or the strengthening of families of the twenty-first century.**
2 **What programmes do you think could best address the problems of African families in the twenty-first century?**
3 **What types of questions would you ask in this situation?**

Critical questioning in programme development

There is an extensive range of questions that applies to decisions on the right type of a programme as well as the right approach to adopt in developing such a programme. Several assumptions, values and beliefs influence the thinking and decision-making process. Below are several key questions that address the case presented in the previous activity. These questions frame the thinking, beliefs and values that apply to and influence programme implementation. This act of critical reflection and examination is essential if good decisions are to be made and relevant, responsive programmes developed. Thinking in this manner is, as mentioned earlier in this chapter, an integral aspect of the philosophical process. Critical questions include:

- Which programme should be given priority for families of the twenty-first century?
- What do people believe are the most pressing problems of these families?
- What should be the best approach to addressing the problems?
- Will families want to be included in the development of a programme intended to address their needs/problems?
- What likely support will there be for the proposed programme?
- Is it possible that some families will react strongly against the proposed programme?

These and other questions must be addressed before a convincing rationale for a proposed programme can be established and presented to potential funding organisations and the target group. It is essential that the programme is accepted by funders and families alike. This means that programme developers must make every effort to create workable proposals that address the real needs of families in the twenty-first century.

A critical question that underpins the work of programme developers is: 'How best should the needs of the target group(s) be determined and addressed?' There is, however, no single approach to assessing the needs of clientele. In Chapter 5 of this book you will look at some of the different needs-assessment techniques in use.

Participatory approaches have been cited as the most suitable for developing programmes for adult learners in Africa. Such approaches consider inputs from a number of people and convey the sense that programmes do not derive their relevance from a single person's perception. People who are, or might be, affected by the proposals should work with programmers. For example, a community may be hit by the HIV/AIDS pandemic, which devastates a number of families in the community. Although knowledge of these families' deaths may be widespread, an idea of what it takes to care for the sick and to recover from the loss of loved ones, as well as what could be done to help these families, can only be gained through talking and interacting with the affected families.

Families that have experienced the trauma of HIV/AIDS would know a great deal about their situations. Thus, authentic experiences must be taken into consideration when programmes intended to better the lives of people in the communities are developed. Values such as those of co-operation, consultation and mutual support are encouraged. By working collaboratively with the target group(s), programme developers increase the chance of programmes being accepted and supported by potential beneficiaries.

From the preceding discussion, you should realise that philosophy is more than simply asking questions. Philosophy greatly affects the way programme developers think, make decisions and carry out their tasks. Philosophy also helps reduce the chances of overlooking some important factors that, when addressed, may help solve an undesirable situation.

⊞ ACTIVITY

1 Think about a philosophy for developing a programme for learners in an African context. Consider a programme that you might be asked to take part in, for example, in your work environment.
2 Formulate three or four philosophical questions that can guide the development process of such a programme.

AFRICAN PHILOSOPHIES AND PROGRAMME DEVELOPMENT

African philosophies or ways of thinking can only be understood and appreciated when placed in an historical context.

The importance of African philosophies

Africa's experiences of slavery, imperialism, colonialism and apartheid have contributed much to changing African attitudes, values, ways of thinking and, ultimately, ways of acting. Nkrumah's Pan Africanism, Senghor's Negritude, Kaunda's African Humanism, Nyerere's *Ujamaa* and Biko's Black Consciousness Movement are prominent African philosophies that grew out of the continent's past. To Africanise programme development requires professionals to be knowledgeable about African experiences and how these experiences became integrated within our philosophies.

Teffo (2000) suggests that the African philosopher's starting point is the articulation of the African experience as the basis of the African's knowledge of all reality. Prah, quoted in Higgs, Vakalisa, Mda, and Assie-Lumumba (2000: 106), states:

When studying African society, Africa must take center stage. The center of gravity of knowledge of Africa must be based in Africa, and this must be steered by Africans themselves. We cannot in all seriousness study ourselves through other people's assumptions.

Several common assumptions on African life inform programme development for adult learners in Africa. These assumptions have their origins in traditional African practices. Traditionally, Africans are accustomed to acting in a co-operative and collaborative manner. From an early age, the African child is introduced to this way of life. In traditional African societies, a child lives with parents, siblings and/or relatives in a close-knit family unit. Family members interact and work closely with one another in a responsible manner. Thus, an African child is endowed with the spirit of collective endeavour from his or her infancy.

It is from this way of living that the proverb, '*Kgetse ya tsie e kgonwa ke go tshwaraganelwa*' ('The more hands, the easier to carry a [heavy] sack full of the locust') can be appreciated. Programme developers can learn a great deal from this proverb because it embodies certain principles of good practice and sound philosophical thought. The proverb reflects the following principles:

1 the principle of acting together as opposed to acting alone;
2 the principle of co-operation as opposed to fragmentation or competition;
3 the principle of unity as opposed to friction;
4 the principle of collectivism as opposed to individualism; and
5 a sense of belonging or connected-ness to a group as opposed to a sense of isolation.

These principles are used to guide a number of social activities in the African environment. They can likewise be used to guide the task of developing programmes for learners in Africa. For example, programme developers who utilise this philosophy ('The more hands, the easier to carry a heavy sack full of the locust') will engage in collaborative endeavours. In situations where local people are engaged in developing programmes, programmes become vehicles for enhancing cultural practices. When cultural practices are acknowledged, programmes become socially acceptable and responsive to the local community's needs and ways of life.

A passion for consultative approaches should not be regarded as just another habitual traditional adage. A study in four African countries by Oxenham and others found that, in the case of different approaches to literacy training and skills development for improved livelihoods, a greater emphasis was placed upon:

a programme that works with established groups of people who share a common purpose, rather than with individual applicants. In the absence of such groups, it would probably still be better to take the time to identify promising common purposes and to work on forming new purpose-driven groups than to resign programmes to unconnected individuals (Oxenham, et al., 2002: 3).

In the same study, the authors note that the team's experience:

produced a strengthening consensus that programmes that are well negotiated with their prospective learners in association with local authorities and leaders are likely to be more effective than programmes that are simply put to offer (Oxenham, et al., 2002: 3).

There is no question that consultative and participatory approaches to developing programmes are needed in an African context.

Basing programme development activities on African philosophies does not imply that other, non-African, perspectives should be ignored or rejected. Instead, it means that Africans should think for themselves, just as other peoples and races do elsewhere in the world. What Africa must avoid is the tendency to allow Western, and especially European, modes of thought to dominate our own experiences. As Seepe notes: 'by allowing the use of a Eurocentric approach, important interpretations key to the African experience are often ignored' (Seepe cited in Higgs, Vakalisa, Mda and Assie-Lumumba, 2000: 108).

Seepe also contends that, 'African experience be at the center of the programme developer's thinking, discourse and action. Programme developers must recognize the complementary nature of cultures and experiences. Programme developers must be informed first by their own context' (ibid: 108). This means that African societies should be at the centre of the way Africans view themselves in their social and cultural worlds. The approach requires programme developers to understand issues of Africanness, African culture and African languages.

This attitude brings with it the argument that Africa's indigenous knowledge systems (IKS) and other resources could be tapped into in order to revive the continent. The approach also seeks African solutions to African problems. This attitude is in marked contrast to the pessimistic view held by the programme developer identified by Seepe. According to Seepe (2000: 118), this developer has an image of Africa as:

a dark continent, dogged by ignorance, superstitions, poverty, unstable governments, underdevelopment, corruption, with nothing of value to be expected from her.

In the past, many African countries have invested their meagre resources in acquiring external knowledge systems, technology and resources in the areas of education, agriculture and manufacturing. Unfortunately, these investments have made little or no improvement to the lives of the African people. It is therefore important that programme developers maintain a positive attitude towards using what is in Africa for the benefit of Africans.

▦ ACTIVITY

1 You are assigned to develop a workplace literacy programme for the non-literate employees in an organisation of your choice (it may be in the public or private sector).
2 Select two or three principles that you learned from the topic 'African philosophies and programme development' and illustrate how these principles will influence and inform the way you develop your programme.

Historical trends in African education development

During the early stages of adult education in Africa, the need to make programmes responsive to local issues was accorded the highest priority. At that time, adult education was essentially education in and for the development of local communities. Traditionally, programmes were tailored to the immediate and pressing needs of local residents. We can consider the kind of education surrounding the issues of birth and childhood, and initiation and puberty rites. Here, people were educated and raised to believe that:

Nature brings the child into the world, but society creates the child into a social being,

a corporate person. It is the society that must protect the child, feed it, bring it up, educate it and in many ways incorporate it into the wider community. The child cannot be exclusively 'my child' but only 'our child' (Mbiti, 1998: 111).

Mbiti's observation illustrates the collective orientation of traditional African societies. Individualism was not promoted in the past and should not be promoted now or in the future, instead, collectivity should remain the key principle.

As more modern education systems began to dominate African culture and society, programme developers in Africa lost touch with these important traditional practices. It is not surprising that a critical analysis of these modern education systems reveals them to be flawed in a number of respects. For example, they are said to uproot and alienate the educated from African society (Goduka, 2000; Nkomo, 2000 and Teffo, 2000). Today, many Africans miss programmes that address, 'what local people know and can do and what local people have known and done for generations' (Warren et al., 1996).

There is a call for the reorientation of the programmes; to develop programmes that respect the indigenous conditions and eschew the Eurocentric foci (Semali, 1999). Thus, if programme developers truly want to develop meaningful and responsive programmes for learners in Africa, virtues such as the ones discussed here should not be ignored.

The discussion that now follows will give you an insight into the historical trends of our education system.

Pre-colonial era: Traditional African education

Education for Africa did not begin with the arrival of the colonists as some historians would want us to believe. Before colonialism, Africans were great educators and trainers of the local people. Under this traditional form of education, the need to train the young for adult life was given the highest priority. The young, for example:

were prepared for their social roles in the home, the village, or town, or tribe. They were constantly being made aware of the community to which they belonged, in and for which they were trained through work and play and religious rites, through songs and dance and folklore, through customary service received or given within [an] all-embracing network of family and kinship ties (Busla, 1968: 15).

Adulthood, on the other hand, was traditionally celebrated through non-formal education programmes that covered a number of issues, including marriage and procreation. As Mbiti observes: 'Marriage and procreation in African communities are in unity: without procreation, marriage is incomplete' (Mbiti, 1988: 133). Marriage and procreation programmes were considered very important because they were the foundation of strong families and communities. In some African societies, for example, if the wife did not bear children, it was arranged that the husband took her sister to be the wife; in other societies, when the wife died the husband married one of the dead wife's sisters (sororate marriage) (Mbiti, 1988). These practices remain in some societies, often in a modified or simplified form (Mbiti, 1988).

In the levirate and sororate institutions of marriage, we witness a philosophical awareness of the principle of collectivity – 'I am because we are; and since we are, therefore I am', where the existence of the individual is the existence of the corporate (Mbiti, 1988: 144). Because of this natural instinct to work together, a collective

approach was used to educate the community. Equally important was the belief that the education provided should directly relate to the immediate problems of the community, hence the principle of functionalism that also existed.

Functionalism implied that people were educated on, 'something that they would later find useful in day-to-day dealings within the society in which they lived' (Mgadla, 2003: 4). It was through education that people learned to adapt to the environment and to prepare for the eventualities of their future. Education thus enabled individuals to live a productive life within their society, as the main objective of the educational process was to prepare an individual to take his or her full place in the society (Matos, 2000). Organisers and developers were elders and leaders from the local communities who were respected for their knowledge of cultures and their integrity in preserving such cultures.

Education was therefore meant to inculcate a sense of belonging, which was, and still is, of crucial importance to Africans. Educational programmes were closely interwoven with the immediate and real challenges, problems and practices of the local people. Everything the young were taught had relevance to the life and culture of the community and to the kind of life they were expected to lead (Busla, 1968: 15).

In conclusion, we can say that education at that time was designed to help learners cope with the realities of life. As Mgadla observes, 'traditional education was realistic and purposeful; it was pragmatic rather than theoretical' (Mgadla, 2003: 106): the type of education that learners in modern-day Africa aspire to have. Learners need education programmes that prepare them for the current realities of their situation and for the challenges and opportunities of their future life. This is an essential principle that should be promoted when developing programmes for adult learners in Africa.

The colonial era: modern versus traditional education

The most commonly heard criticism levelled at the colonial system of education is that it did not deal with the realities of the African's environment (Nkomo, 2000; Mgadla, 2003). This criticism is the result of comparing modern education practices with the traditional practices of the past. The traditional system was functional in the sense that it sought to equip learners with the information, skills and competencies that would be useful in their daily lives. This functional aspect was destroyed with the introduction of the modern education system.

Traditional education was considered inappropriate by the colonisers, who introduced a new system that was designed to further their own interests as well as counter the lifestyles and cultural practices of the local people. The conventional approach to education implemented by the colonisers was entirely unfamiliar to Africans, while it was also completely ill suited to their own needs and interests. For example, the colonists' compensatory literacy programmes were intended to train local Africans, '[to fill] European positions and to serve the colonial system' (Matos, 2000: 13).

The colonisers had little interest in educating Africans for African citizenship, that is, to live productively in their own environments. Under colonial rule, local thinking, knowledge, practices and beliefs no longer guided Africans in their everyday lives.

The post-colonial era: a return to functionalism

It was not until after independence that deliberate efforts were made by newly formed African governments to redirect education to serve local needs (Matos, 2000). Shortly after many African countries obtained their independence, universities were challenged to train the cadres needed to replace the colonial administrator and to create indigenous capacity (Matos, 2000). It is this issue of indigenous capacity that interests us here.

Adult education needs to prepare African people to live in their societies and sensitise them to ways in which their societies can be developed. Thus, education should go beyond the rhetoric of the classroom environment and explore the practical world. Practicality and functionalism are principles that should nourish the minds of programme developers.

An important question posed by Busla (1968: 7) is: 'To what extent should the educational institutions of Africa meet the needs and aspirations of the society they seek to serve?' This question is particularly relevant for the twenty-first century adult education practitioners who are committed to developing meaningful and responsive programmes for adult learners in the African continent. Thus, Busla's question can act as an invaluable guiding principle.

Below, you are presented with a case study. Study it critically and answer the questions that follow.

CASE STUDY: THE ELDERS OF SOSO

Soso is one of the least economically developed and most educationally deprived settlements in Country X. The majority of the population is elderly, the youth having left the settlement to seek a more prosperous life in various urban centres.

According to a long-held cultural tradition, only the elders can discuss community issues with outsiders. When programme planners (strangers to the settlement) performed a needs-assessment exercise to address the severe problem of illiteracy in the community, only the youth were consulted. The elders were not invited to participate, which angered them considerably.

The day before a planned training workshop for literacy assistants, the village elders refused to let them use the *kgotla* (village meeting place) for this purpose. The programme planners had previously agreed with the youth that the *kgotla* would be used to conduct the workshop. When the literacy assistants arrived, some having travelled a considerable distance, they were told that they were not welcome in the settlement. Moreover, many parents had deliberately sent their children away from home, for example, to hunt, herd cattle, fetch firewood, etc., as a way of preventing them from attending the workshop.

- What was it that the programme planners did not do right in this case?
- What steps should programme planners take to avoid future occurrences of this type of problem with the village elders of this, or a similar, settlement?
- If you were an elder of Soso, how would you have acted in these circumstances?

SUMMARY

This chapter introduced a number of issues relating to developing adult education programmes in the African context. We began by differentiating between programme planning and programme development. In examining programme development, we looked at the various factors that influence a programme developer's task, which include environmental, human and resource factors, as well as the crucial factor of individual expertise and experience. We also examined the philosophical nature of programme development work, emphasising the guiding role African philosophies can play in this regard. An overview of Africa's education history considered the significance of traditional education practices in pre-colonial times, the impact of colonialism upon education development and the changing face of education in the post-colonial era. This historical perspective reminded us that the task of developing programmes is an ever-changing and complex process.

KEY POINTS

- The concept of programme development has been used instead of programme planning and this concept shall be used throughout this book.
- Programme development has been defined as a participatory process of sharing ideas, negotiating and learning together to address problems/needs that affect individuals, organisations, communities or the nation at large.
- Programme development for African learners has its roots in the African philosophies, such as the ones expressed in, 'It takes the whole village to raise a child.'
- Relevant African philosophies should act as guiding principles for developing adult education programmes for learners in Africa.

ACTIVITY

What were the concerns of some Africans regarding the programmes that were developed during the colonial era? What remedial suggestions applying to current and future practices of developing programmes for adult learners in Africa can you identify?

FURTHER QUESTIONS

1 Why are programme developers in the field of adult education considered critical decision-makers?
2 If you were to develop a programme for a certain group of adult learners in your area, what aspects would you select from the discussions in this chapter to guide the process?
3 How best can a programme harness and exploit the indigenous resources, values, cultures and diversity of Africans?

SUGGESTED READING

Busla, K. 1968. *Purposeful education for Africa*. The Netherlands: Mouton & Co.

Mgadla, P. 2003. *A history of education in the Bechuanaland protectorate to 1965*. New York: Oxford.

Ocitti, J. 1973. *African indigenous education: As practiced by the Acholi of Uganda*. Nairobi: East African Literature Bureau.

Semali, L. and Kincheloe, L. 1999. *What is indigenous knowledge: Voices from the academy*. New York: Falmer Press.

Chapter 2

Approaches for programme development in adult education

OVERVIEW

The chapter begins by exploring the nature of programmes from an international perspective, including a definition of adult education, a description of the types of adult education programmes and a discussion of the types of adult learners. This background information provides the reader with an understanding of the challenges posed to adult education practitioners when deciding how best to develop education programmes for the continent's diverse learner population. In the next section of the chapter, a typology of Eurocentric approaches to programme development is discussed. The inherent problems of each of these approaches are identified and attention is paid to how such problems could be avoided in the future. The chapter ends with a critique of the Eurocentric approaches in order to inform future practice.

LEARNING OBJECTIVES

At the end of this chapter, you should be able to:

1 Describe and analyse the different approaches used in programme development in adult education.
2 Discuss the nature and types of adult education programmes.
3 Critique the various programme development approaches currently used in the field of adult education.

nkonsonkonson

KEY TERMS

adult education programme   A programme designed on a full-time or
part-time basis to help the participants
acquire knowledge, skills and behavioural
change that will engage participants in
solving their problems.

adult learner   A participant in any adult
learning opportunity, whether special or
regular, who aims to develop new skills
or qualifications, or to improve existing
skills and qualifications, or to acquire
information.

participation   A process that consciously
applies collective undertakings to
examine a common concern or problem.
Participation is an empowerment process
in which people, in partnership with
those able to assist them, identify problems and needs and increasingly take
responsibility to plan, manage, control
and assess the collective actions that are
taken by the community.

BEFORE YOU START

List as many adult education programmes
in your country as you can, together with
their objectives. Also, identify the main
sources of funding for adult education programmes in your country. Compare your
national programmes with those presented
by students from other countries. What are
the main differences and similarities?

ADULT EDUCATION FROM AN INTERNATIONAL PERSPECTIVE

The meaning of adult education

The concept of adult education has been defined in different ways and according to the different perspectives of various scholars. The report of the First International Congress of University Adult Education (1969) defined adult education as:

a process whereby persons who no longer attend school on a regular and full-time basis undertake sequential and organized activities with the conscious intention of bringing about changes in information, knowledge, undertakings or skills, appreciation and attitudes or for the purpose of identifying and solving personal or community problem.

Early definitions of adult education such as this one tended to define the discipline in the context of literate societies that had comprehensive school systems. Over the years, however, emerging definitions have tried to resolve the lack of uniformity in defining adult education across cultures and nations. For instance, at the nineteenth UNESCO session convened in Nairobi in 1976, the definition of adult education proposed was:

the entire body of organized educational processes, whatever the content, level and method, whether formal or otherwise, whether they prolong or replace initial education in the schools, colleges, and universities as well as apprenticeship, whereby persons regarded as adults by the society to which they belong, develop their abilities, enrich their knowledge, improve their

technical or professional qualifications and bring about changes in their attitudes or behaviour in the twofold perspective of full personal development and participation in balanced independent social, economic, and cultural development.

Darkenwald and Merriam (1982: 9) define the concept of adult education as:

a process whereby persons whose major social roles are characteristic of adult status undertake systematic and sustained learning activities for the purpose of bringing about changes in knowledge, attitude, values, or skills.

A review of these early definitions, as well as more recent definitions proposed by authors such as Merriam and Caffarella (1999), Wilson and Hayes (2000), and Caffarella (2002), suggests that the overall purpose of adult education is to help individuals become knowledgeable, skilled and dedicated citizens who are willing to work, individually and collectively, towards achieving and maintaining an improved quality of life. This encompassing purpose of adult education can also be expressed by stating, as now follows, the range of activities it covers. We can therefore say that adult education:

1 provides relevant education of persons regarded by their communities or societies as adults;
2 may be organised in or out of school settings and other formal education institutions;
3 may represent a basic education or may expand or replace the package of knowledge, skills, attitudes, values and interests a person has acquired previously;
4 encourages the continuous growth and development of individuals;
5 aims to help people respond to practical

problems and issues of adult life;

6 prepares people for current and future work opportunities;

7 assists organisations in achieving desired results and adapting to change;

8 provides opportunities to examine community and societal issues, foster change for the common good and promote a civil society;

9 helps adults to develop new abilities or competences or enrich their knowledge or improve their technical or professional qualifications;

10 helps to give adults new directions in life by engaging them in what Fletcher and Ruddock (1986) called formation, deformation, reformation and transformation;

11 helps adults to change their behaviours, skills, interests, attitudes and values; and

12 aims in the end to lead on to full personal development and participation in the process of personal and community development, socially, culturally, economically and politically.

For a deeper understanding of the concepts of adulthood and adult education, you may want to read other books in this series, especially *The Psychology of Adult Learning in Africa* by Fasokun, Oduaran and Katahoire (2005), and *Foundations of Adult Education in Africa* by Nafukho, Amutabi and Otunga (2005). Both books are published by Pearson Education.

Types of adult education programmes

From the various definitions of adult education, it is generally accepted that effective adult education programmes enable people to develop new knowledge, attitudes and behaviours that will help to sustain improved quality of life for individual adults, groups, communities and society at large. In this regard, a programme can be viewed as a variety of activities designed to bring about the desired behaviour change in adult learners. 'Programme', according to Onyemunwa (1997), is an all-inclusive term covering a variety of activities on the part of an educational institution or agency with some of the activities either directed towards (i) the development of more or less explicit educational ends or tasks to be performed, or (ii) maintaining the viability of the agency or institution as a social entity. An adult education programme is primarily designed to bring about behavioural change of the participants or to enable them to solve some problems that have been identified.

In order to achieve the broader purposes of adult education, a variety of adult education programmes is available. Just like the adult learners they cater for, adult education programmes come in all shapes and sizes, as well as formats. They vary in their:

■ goals – the skill, knowledge, behavioural or attitudinal changes they are intended to bring about;

■ duration – day-long workshops and conferences to residential courses that may last for two years;

■ nature – formal or informal;

■ method of teaching: open discussion to structured courses;

■ size – individual, group of learners, community;

■ mode of delivery – distance or face-to-face; and

■ recognition – certification or non-certification.

Before we go on to look at the various types of adult education programme that exist, we should first define what we understand by the term 'programme'. A programme is defined as a time-bound plan that details the learning situation, what learners are to know, how they are to know it, the learners' and teachers' roles as well as the place, facilities and resources to be used. Thus, designs that include course descriptions, course outlines, outlines of educational events or any action plan for educational activities can be referred to as programmes. Our interest here is in the types of programmes offered in the field of adult education. Ehiametalor and Oduaran (1991: 7) identify a number of programmes in adult education, each with its own curriculum and objectives. The programmes include:

1 Adult Basic Education, including basic literacy, functional literacy, and numeracy;
2 Out of School Youth Programmes;
3 Income Generating Programmes;
4 Extension Programmes, including agricultural extension, community health extension, extra-mural studies, and continuing education;
5 Distance Learning Programmes, including correspondence schools and open universities;
6 Workplace Literacy Programmes;
7 Training and re-training programmes, including vocational/technical training, workers' education, and labour relations;
8 Civic education, including community development and political socialisation; and
9 Liberal education, including conscientisation and rural animation.

The above list is not exhaustive. We know of intergenerational programmes, citizenship education and others. Therefore, when the word 'programme' is mentioned in this chapter, remember that the examples noted above represent an inventory that can be added to and expanded as necessary.

⊞ ACTIVITY

Read the scenario below. What type of programme is being addressed here?

A rural area development officer (RADO) is leading a two-day programme on establishing a village poultry farm in a local community. The farm symbolises the residents' desire to integrate as a big family and to produce food for their own consumption. The villagers own the farm and retain the power to decide how the farm products can be distributed to people outside the 'big family'.

Types of adult learners

In order to develop relevant and useful programmes, there must be a match between the types of programmes and the types of adult learners and their educational needs. We can ask at this point: Who are these adult learners and where do they come from? The point-form summary presented below outlines the adult-learner scenario in many African countries and helps us to answer this important question. This summary of potential adult learners and their learning needs often guides professionals and practitioners in developing adult education programmes. In summary, adult learners are:

■ Young adults who have dropped out of school due to factors such as pregnancy, or the death of a parent(s) or relative(s). They live at home but have resumed their studies at places such as a non-government organisation centre, or by distance education with a local college.
■ Adults who have never had the opportunity to enter formal education. Despite their inability to read and write, these adults are part of the village community that has autonomy and jurisdiction over a wide range of local issues.
■ School leavers with different educational attainments who are working in various government ministries as accounting assistants, bookkeepers, office assist-

ants, and cleaners. In the evenings, many adults in this category engage in professional training and education.

- Diploma and degree certificate holders who have become less functional because of the introduction of new technologies (for example, computers, fax machines, printers, and photocopiers) in the workplace. This category of learners enrols in computer training literacy classes at the workplace to acquire the skills needed to remain relevant to their employing organisations.
- MSc and PhD holders at higher institutions of learning attending short courses and seminars on the use of Information Technology Systems (ITS), writing distance modules, attending book writers' workshops, and so on.
- Adults who attend driving schools, often requiring driving skills as part of their job or business duties.
- Retired employees learning to cope with life after work, either living alone, or in a nursing home or receiving home-based care. These learners attend counselling and therapy workshops organised by professional practitioners.
- Adults learning about survival skills as a worker at a National Health Centre, where they are overwhelmed by the numbers of HIV/AIDS patients.

The lesson to learn from the scenario given above is that adults vary greatly across the African continent in terms of their social, educational, economic and community situations. Despite the range of features that separate them, one similarity they all have in common is that they are all adults and they all have learning needs (Youngman, 1998). Their wide-ranging differences are an indication of the challenge that faces adult education in practice. Responding to the range of learning needs presented by a differentiated target group, in this case

adult learners, requires the development of relevant programmes to address situation-specific needs.

▦ ACTIVITY

1 Reflect on what you have learned from the preceding paragraphs, then give your own definition of adult education.
2 If you were to introduce an adult education programme in your community, what purposes and group of learners would it serve?

EUROCENTRIC APPROACHES TO PROGRAMME DEVELOPMENT

Adult educators have succeeded in identifying a number of approaches that have been used in programme development. There is, however, no agreement on the best approach. Consequently, individual programme developers are free to adopt any approach. However, the tendency and common belief among adult educators is that adult learners appreciate any programme approach if they are given the opportunity to participate in developing these programmes. The focus in this section is on four approaches: the top-down, bottom-up, participatory, and comprehensive.

The origin of the top-down approach in developing adult education programmes lies deep in the political past of most African countries. The approach is a legacy from the era of colonial administration, when development programmes were run centrally by the state with little or no involvement from the beneficiaries. In effect, the top-down approach is sponsor-centred. While the legacy of the top-down approach is still practised today, its failure to bring about significant improvement in the lives of the many people it was supposed to serve has led to change. Programme developers, project sponsors, policy makers and practitioners are keen to search for more learner-centred approaches.

The bottom-up and participatory approaches have emerged in response to the need to involve intended beneficiaries of adult education programmes in efforts to change and improve their lives.

The comprehensive approach strives to strike a balance between sponsor-centred and learner-centred approaches by regarding both the programme developer and the adult learners as important participants in the programme development process.

The top-down approach to programme development

In many Anglophone countries of Africa, adult education programmes are co-ordinated in a special department that forms part of the Ministry of Education. This department is responsible for developing adult education for the entire nation. Programme development under such structural arrangements is performed centrally on behalf of regional, district and community requirements. District and community staff may be involved but do not lead the process. The final programme that is passed on from the top to the bottom is rapidly implemented in and across all regions, districts and local communities. The critical factors here are how well the programme reflects the real needs of the beneficiaries and how effectively the programme development process itself captures the most recent and relevant knowledge and interests.

Top-down development of educational programmes for adults represents the concentration of the decision-making authority at the top of an organised hierarchy.

Programme development of this nature is an outcome of communication and the co-ordinated effort of a number of individuals operating vertically and horizontally at top management levels. With the top-down approach, adult education programmes are essentially formulated at central government level where policies are determined and decisions are taken regarding the allocation of resources.

In some cases, such as in Botswana, there is some consultation by the centre with lower-level organisations. However, according to Sharma (1992) this consultation generally takes the form of an explanation of policies and/or an elaboration of plans formulated at a higher level. While officials in the central government may consult lower-level personnel, the former decide on priorities. The lower-level officers receive communication about the contents of their local programmes from the top in the form of instructions.

Lauglo (1990: 27) identified four benefits that could be derived from the top-down approach. These are:

1 Costs are reduced by having one uniform programme serving the whole nation.
2 It helps the programme developers to uphold 'approved' practices. That is, programme developers can try out practices that are tested over time for adoption on a national scale.
3 It overcomes the problems of a decentralised process, and eliminates the barriers to learners' involvement.
4 The training and development of facilitators and management of other resources is easier.

In spite of the above comparative advantages, the top-down approach has been found to be particularly problematic. This has led to a shift towards more people-centred approaches, in an attempt to avoid

the shortcomings and subsequent programme failings of the top-down approach.
In an attempt to critique the top-down
delivery of non-formal education programmes, Maruatona (1998) alluded to adult
education in Sub-Saharan Africa as demonstrating the potential for political control to
be exercised by a powerful minority group.
A top-down approach to programme development leads to the delivery of programme
content as 'welfare' gifts by those in power to
potentially affected clients.

This perspective, according to Maruatona
(1998: 2), ignores gender, ethnic and political
power relations and ideological assumptions held and perpetuated by the providers
of such educational programmes. Giroux
(1988: 61) has also criticised the top-down
approach for being narrowly focused
on a few anticipated economic benefits.
Programmes developed via the top-down
approach expose the beneficiaries to content derived from the interests of the elite
class. The top-down approach represents
the cultural perspectives of the powerful,
while simultaneously marginalising or even
excluding the perspectives, experiences and
values of the less affluent societal groups.

CASE STUDY: THE
BOTSWANA NATIONAL
LITERACY PROGRAMME

An example of the top-down approach is
the Botswana National Literacy Programme
(BNLP). There is considerable evidence to
show that the initial efforts of the Botswana
Extension College to promote participatory
approaches were frozen when the BNLP
was introduced. The programme, as it is
now, stresses the contribution of experts in
material development and excludes the participants (Maruatona, 1998). The outcome
is a highly centralised literacy programme
with a top-down delivery arrangement

that does not reflect the local interests of
different ethnic groups. Recent studies
(Maruatona, 1997, 1998; Central Statistics
Office, 1997; Reimer, 1997) have identified
the following problems arising from the
top-down delivery nature of the BNLP:

1   It does not allow for multiple contex-
    tual and linguistic variations and tends
    to limit its capacity to accommodate
    the interests of different learners in
    Botswana.
2   There is a lack of learner participa-
    tion in deciding what to learn in the
    programme.
3   The learners are given limited oppor-
    tunity to decide even the type of skills
    they would need. They have to accept
    what is offered at a given time. For
    example, workplace literacy, according
    to Maruatona (1998), is based on mate-
    rials in the primers that were produced
    17 years ago. The five primers have
    nothing to do with workplace reali-
    ties and would therefore have a limited
    impact on their lives as workers.
4   The programme's innovations are lim-
    ited by its lack of flexibility.
5   The programme does not meet the
    practical and economic needs of the
    participants (Maruatona, 1996).
6   Other work and social commitments
    means participants drop out of the pro-
    gramme or cannot participate as fully
    as they would like (Central Statistics
    Office, 1997).
7   Learners used their own indigenous
    languages to discuss issues, though they
    are taught in the national language of
    Setswana.
8   The programme taught learners things
    that had a limited bearing on their com-
    munity life. Learners uniformly agreed
    that they did not use the skills from
    the programme for any community

activities. The learners also indicated that they were not taught practical skills, which they could use to improve their socio-economic status after completing the programme.

9   The programme lacks gender sensitivity and responsiveness to the differing needs of male and female participants. Most participants are women.
10 The programme does not meet the social development needs of the learners.
11 The programme fails to enable the learners to participate in decision-making; neither does it respond to Botswana's cultural diversity.
12 It does not cater for the rights of ethnic minorities and their identities (Youngman, 1997).

While the top-down approach has its merits, its major problem is that it is not people-centred. The approach limits its focus to a consideration of a few anticipated economic benefits derived from the interests of a powerful elite; the actual needs and interests of potential participants are often marginalised or ignored. This explains the reason behind the shift towards more people-centred approaches.

The bottom-up approach to programme development

Bottom-up programme development refers to the transfer of authority from the higher echelons of the state to the geographically dispersed agents of the central government system, thereby strengthening the regional and local staff of the civil service and civil society. The process empowers the local staff in terms of decisions affecting their work and enables them to learn more about the needs of local communities (Lauglo, 1990).

Bottom-up programme development has two main aims. Firstly, the approach seeks to ensure that people are involved in designing their own programmes. It therefore recognises the need for a high level of local participation to ensure programme impact and sustainability. Secondly, the bottom-up approach aims to provide a decentralised programme development and an implementation capacity that is sensitive and responsive to the needs, problems and priorities of local communities.

Bottom-up programme development addresses the problems, opportunities and priorities as identified by the communities benefiting from the programme. Using this approach, programme development is not seen as a process whereby programme developers prescribe what is 'best' for others and then simply provide resources in the hope that they will accomplish the prescribed goals. Bottom-up programme development demands that beneficiaries are brought into the decision-making process.

The bottom-up approach has the advantage of allowing people to participate in the programme development process. It can also be a means for bringing diverse groups of programme participants together in local communities, and for giving participants a sense of involvement in the decision-making process. The approach can promote unity as participants combine to share power, as well as foster a positive sense of autonomy for citizens who are directly involved in the programme's design and purpose.

Administratively, the decentralised nature of the bottom-up approach relieves the need for centrally based government staff to control and direct purely local issues. The bottom-up approach speaks to the needs and concerns of local people and gives great attention to the priorities of the targeted community. It also secures their commitment to the proposed programme(s) by actively encouraging their participation. Better use of locally available resources and self-help could also be promoted this way (Sharma, 1999).

The bottom-up approach, however, does have its limitations, which we will now consider.

The continuing influence of central government

Despite its stated advantages, the bottom-up approach is in reality more likely to be recognised as a top-down construct. Programmes, in essence, continue to be formulated at the centre, where policies are determined and decisions are taken regarding resource allocation. The major constraints at the local level arise from the local authorities' almost total dependence on central government for trained human resources and finance. There is some consultation by the centre with the local level organisations but this generally relates to an explanation of policies and/or an elaboration of plans formulated at higher levels.

The centre does consult the communities but the community officials sometimes assume that programme developers located in state headquarters never look at local plans. This view is not without justification. In Botswana, for example, 'many programme developers have never read a District Development Plan and some admit to not even know what they are. Some programme development officers have candidly reported that even if they did have district plans, in the end their ministry will proceed without reference to district plans' (Ellison, 1990: 114).

Poor co-ordination and communication links

Bottom-up programme development means integration of community plans with sectoral development plans at the centre. This requires effective co-ordination and satisfactory two-way communication between the centre and the local communities. Unfortunately, the co-ordination and communication link between the local communities and the headquarters of the sector ministry is weak in many African countries. In Botswana, for example, Sharma (1992: 108-111) discovered that the centre is not responsive to the problems, expectations and priorities of the government staff at the district and community levels. The district staff often feels frustrated, neglected, annoyed or lost, due to a vague, delayed, inadequate or unforthcoming response from the centre.

Organisation deficiency

Another limitation facing the bottom-up approach is organisation deficiency. Kenneth Ellison, in his report of the District Development Plan 4 consultancy, identified the following problems relating to the decentralised programme development process in Botswana:

(a) project implementation is adversely affected by infrequent and haphazard consultation with local staff and district staff; (b) implementation is frequently delayed by inflexible bureaucratic structures which require technical expertise and numerous reviews only available from centrally based authorities; (c) project implementation is not properly coordinated because of the exceedingly autonomous operations of sectoral ministries at the district level; (d) project implementation is delayed because districts have limited control of financial resources commensurate with their responsibilities; (e) district councils have experienced rapid growth in recurrent responsibilities without corresponding growth in qualified personnel; (f) personnel productivity, as distinct from personnel allocation, is emerging as a major constraint to effective programme development; (g) rapid development of

infrastructure has outpaced operational implementation capacity; (h) the structural linkage between extension staff and Village Development Committees rarely functions as a means of 'consultation with the people' resulting in poor sequencing of projects in relation to perceived needs; (i) some national policies and strategies need clarification and districts lack the authority, personnel, and support from central government to actually implement what these policies require; and (j) significant advances have been made in land use programme development in many districts, but implementation of land use plans is constrained by the lack of integrated development approach and project design capacity (Ellison, 1990: 28).

The bottom-up approach in practice

A concrete example of the bottom-up approach is the case of an FAO/UNDP (Food and Agriculture Organisation/United Nations Development Programme) project in Zambia. The project, which was operational from June 1989 to December 1992, provided technical support in improving agricultural extension methods and services in order to contribute to the development of the agricultural sector in Zambia's New Economic Recovery Programme. With a budget of US$1, 2 million for three and a half years, the project targeted 80 000 small-farm families in the Southern Province of Zambia.

The project adopted and advanced a programme development rather than a top-down technology delivery approach to extension, utilising a 'strategic extension campaign' system developed by the FAO. This approach emphasised the development of problem-oriented, area-specific agronomic, livestock and post-harvest practices. The end-of-project evaluation team found that this approach was highly suitable for the rain-fed, drought-prone, smallholder problems at hand, as it incorporated the bottom-up approach to extension message formulation.

The project's utilisation of KAP (Knowledge, Attitude, Practice) baseline surveys indicates that such surveys are imperative for the development of a bottom-up extension strategy and crucial in identifying problems that are relevant to extension and can be tackled by extension staff. This example, though specific to agricultural extension, has implications for other adult education programmes. The main implication is that adult education programme developers first need to know the indigenous knowledge systems of their adult learners and what the learners' attitudes and practices are with respect to new programmes that the programme developers want to implement (Adhikarya, 1994).

The bottom-up approach is a viable alternative to programme development because it recognises the need for the participation of people at all stages of programme development. Through this involvement, programmes that reflect the real needs, problems and priorities of local communities are possible. However, implementation and monitoring of the bottom-up approach could be a serious problem in many African counties, where a reliance of local communities on central government for financial resources and trained personnel may restrict its effectiveness.

The participatory approach to programme development

The concept of participation merges well with the principle of adult learning, which presumes that adults learn best when their own needs form the basis of programme design and they have the chance to participate actively in the design, development, and evaluation of the learning programme.

Active participation, as emphasised by Apel and Camozzi (1996), must be one of the cornerstones of programmes developed for adults. The participatory approach is important because it promotes programme flexibility; allowing the programme to adapt to the changing needs of the adult learners as they progress through their learning experience.

The participatory approach possesses a strong capacity-building component of practical and participatory workshops for training adult education personnel, subject matter specialists, trainers and community leaders. The skills learned include: programme development, strategy development, message design and positioning, multi-media materials development, pre-testing and production, as well as management, implementation, monitoring, and evaluation strategies. The programmer and the clients work together for the continuous improvement of the programme, through monitoring and ongoing evaluation as various components of the programme are implemented. The use of the participatory approach developed with a bias to extension programmes, such as the Strategic Extension Campaign developed by the FAO, fits well into programme development for other adult education programmes in Africa.

The participatory approach borrows from Freire's belief that the programme beneficiaries are not ignorant or empty objects requiring all the information to be provided to them (Freire, 1972). Rather, the approach relies on the beneficiaries' indigenous knowledge, values, belief systems and current practices. The participatory approach is a strategic campaign methodology developed by the FAO. It has now been introduced in Africa, the Near East, Asia and Latin America. This approach stresses the importance of people's participation in strategic programme development, systematic management and implementation of training programmes. The approach has ten operational phases (Adhukarya, 1994: 18):

1. problem identification and information-needs assessment;
2. objectives formulation;
3. strategy development and information positioning;
4. audience analysis and segmentation;
5. multi-media selection;
6. message design, development, pre-testing and materials production;
7. management planning;
8. training of personnel;
9. field implementation; and
10. process documentation and summative evaluation.

The above operational phases are similar to other models or ideas on programme development. However, this approach differs in the weight it places on the beneficiaries' participation during each stage of programme development. It also prioritises the importance of meeting the interests and needs of the target beneficiaries, as well as giving consideration to the human behaviours that may enhance or impede the programme development process. We can also note that the approach focuses on solving specific problems of beneficiaries based on relevant information or facts.

While participatory approaches to programme development have gained great credibility among programme developers of adult education programmes, they are still subject to criticism from an opposing school of thought that is strongly against citizen participation in programme development. Goldblatt and Aleshined (cited in Oduaran, 1994: 55) present seven reasons why people's participation in programme development should be limited or restricted. The reasons given are:

1 Those who are opposed to planned programmes may sabotage the efforts of the group.
2 The influential and powerful may either lobby for programmes that are not of immediate relevance to the majority or even impose their own interests to the disadvantage of the majority.
3 Those who are involved in final decision-making may not be truly representative of the people or even have a thorough understanding of the problem at hand.
4 Local citizens cannot improve the situation substantially in a direct, physical manner, because of a lack of knowledge or poor economic circumstances.
5 The involvement of the majority may not receive higher official support, which will limit or nullify their influence on the decision-making process.
6 The involvement of the majority may prolong and/or delay the programme development process and people may become impatient with this lack of progress.
7 The final implemented programme may differ widely from what was anticipated and this could give rise to goal conflict.

However, there are many concrete examples of the successful use of the participatory approach to programme development. Participatory techniques were used in the Aberdares Forest of Kenya to define forest values within the context of local people's own perceptions, needs and priorities, rather than according to categories of government officers. This was an attempt to move away from 'traditional' protection measures (for example, preventing human access by policing and legal bans) to a system that recognised the dependencies and needs of local communities and integrated them into forest conservation. The exercise used participatory tools such as scoring forest uses by allocating counters to timber, medicines, honey, building, foods, hunting, grazing, charcoal, fuel wood and radio (Emerton and Mogaka, 1996).

The participatory approach has also been used in the Natural Resource Management Project (NRMP). This project was initiated in Botswana in 1990 as part of the Southern Africa Development Community (SADC) regional programme to promote community-based natural resource management (CBNRM). The project also provided a means for implementing the 1986 Wildlife Conservation Policy. The four components of NRMP are: (i) demonstration projects in community-based resource utilisation; (ii) programme development and applied research; (iii) personal human resources development; and (iv) environmental education. Considerable achievement has also been registered in shifting control over wildlife quotas from central government to community enterprises. Another indicator of success of NRMP is the influence that it has had on other programmes, and positive attitudes concerning community-based initiatives, as expressed by other CBNRM projects, the Participatory Rural Appraisal Pilot Project, and the Community Based Programme Strategy Consultation (Reynolds, 1997).

Both the bottom-up and participatory approaches are people-centred. However, the essential difference between the two approaches is that the participatory approach identifies strategies for enhancing peoples' participation at each stage of programme development. In this way the tendency for the approach to be controlled by sponsors and affluent groups is avoided.

The comprehensive approach to programme development

The comprehensive approach conceptualises programme development as a multi-faceted process. Cookson (1998) views this process in two phases.

Phase 1: The steps in this phase relate to the self-examination and self-orientation of the programme developer. The steps enable the programme developer to seek assertive, self-directive and approved practice rather than to react to priorities of the moment. The steps include:

- Self-reflection – a focus on the nature of the multiple roles programme developers play within a non-formal adult education programme or a more formal adult education organisation and how the roles impact upon the programme development process. This examination of the varying expectations in programme development duties helps realise an individual's programming potentialities, as well as identifying areas of strengths and weaknesses.
- Self-examination – an assessment on an individual's philosophical orientation toward education and training. For example, whether the programme developer adopts a Eurocentric or Afrocentric approach, and which of the four approaches in this section is preferred or adapted. This helps the programme developer to identify and express a working philosophy and establish a positional relationship with the programme development process.
- A sense of professional responsibility – This can be manifested through continuous professional development and the collection and analysis of data relative to programme development activities.
- Awareness of contextual elements impacting on the programme development process – This includes the situational and organisational contexts as well as the parameters set by the learners' attributes and needs.
- Awareness of the community or organisational environment – This includes the conditions, relationships and policies outside the community or organisation that frequently interact with the conditions, relationships, and policies within the organisation.
- Knowledge of the internal conditions of the organisation impacting on the programme development process – This includes the administrative structure, policies, purposes, goals, objectives, restrictions and problems that a community or an organisation faces.
- Gaining a working knowledge of the kinds of adults participating in adult education programmes – This will include physical, psychological and mental characteristics of participants as well as their national, regional, cultural and ethnic backgrounds.

Phase 2: The second phase deals with the discrete activities intended to respond to given problem situations. It involves a comprehensive understanding of the contexts and a sound grasp of the characteristics of potential adult participants (Cookson, 1998). The steps therefore focus on the precise strategies needed in specific education and training programmes. A detailed discussion of the steps is provided in Chapter 3, but we can say here that the list includes:

- assessing learning needs;
- setting of the learning goals and objectives;
- designing the learning content;
- deciding on learning materials;
- promoting the programme;
- implementing the programme; and
- evaluating processes, inputs and outcomes.

It is worth letting the reader know at this point that the authors' beliefs and values are deeply rooted in the concept of participation. Our values and beliefs are, in turn, based on what is already known about adult learning. There is evidence to suggest that although adults learn in many ways, they learn best when they are given the chance to participate actively in the design, development and evaluation of the educational programme. The participatory approach is responsive to intended learners' development problems and information needs because it is specifically based on the learners' expressed learning needs. Since the learners are consulted during the programme development process, the approach increases the degree of relevance, and the acceptability of programme content by the beneficiaries (Adhikarya, 1994).

⊞ ACTIVITY

Reflect on the four types of approaches to programme development that you have read about in this chapter and complete the table below.

Approach	Features	Strengths	Weaknesses
Top-down			
Bottom-up			
Participatory			
Comprehensive			

A CRITIQUE OF EUROCENTRIC APPROACHES

Eurocentrism concerns the belief that European culture is qualitatively superior to other cultures. Consequently, programme approaches developed with a Eurocentric bias seek to impose Western models of programme design, purpose and administration on to what are perceived as inferior African versions.

Eurocentric approaches to programme development in African contexts generally displace the ideal of people-centredness and replace this with the notion (and practice) of a small number of elite individuals exercising control. Programme participants under the Eurocentric ethic are seen as passive recipients of development efforts who do not initiate efforts to develop themselves. The main failing of this approach is that it very often ignores or directly contradicts the actual needs, problems and aspirations of the programme participants.

With Eurocentric approaches, development is seen only in terms of physical output built around the participants who must have the right attitude, skills and understanding to generate, utilise and accommodate development on a more sustainable basis (Oduaran, 1989).

For Nyerere (1974), this rationale does not represent true development because it holds no place for the growth of participants' inner qualities; neither does it offer them an opportunity to become more self-reliant and more proficient in what they are doing. True development, Nyerere suggests, is summed up in the participants' capacity to expand their own consciousness and, therefore, their power over themselves, their environment and society. For Nyerere, the participants are the central core around which programme development must revolve.

CASE STUDY: THE PREVINOBA INTERVENTION PROJECT

The PREVINOBA intervention forms part of the larger North-West Groundnut Basin Village Reafforestation Project, and was formulated by the Water, Forest, Hunting and Soil Conservation Division (WFHSCD), supported by the Dutch embassy in Dakar and the FAO office in Senegal.

The first phase of the project (1986–1989) sought to re-establish the importance of trees in the maintenance of ecological equilibrium by improving and maintaining soil fertility, integrating trees into the agrarian system, and improving forest product supplies. From the outset, the project opted for an effective strategy of popular involvement. Thus its objectives called for:

- the design and implementation of a programme to increase the awareness, mobilisation and education of populations;
- a contribution to the planning of a rural area exploited in a rational and integrated manner (agricultural, pastoral and forestry speculation); and
- a contribution to the institutional reinforcement of the forestry service and the training of officers.

The participatory dynamic of dialogue and exchange with the population, as well as the results obtained during the first phase, highlighted the fact that the concerns of people in terms of forestry go beyond the simple framework of rural forestry.

The second phase of the project (1989–1995) provided the opportunity to situate the question of reintroducing trees into the agricultural system within the larger framework of land management. As a result, PREVINOBA put the emphasis on drawing up a land development and management plan where the programme activities would reconcile people's interests, policy orientations in the sector, restoration and conservation of the environment, and improved production under the concept of sustainable development. Within an increasingly favourable institutional context, WFHSCD moved toward an increased use of the participatory approach in the project's development.

It should also be noted at this point that the project strategy does not explicitly refer to the issue of gender and how this may affect development. However, the socio-demographic reality of the area, in which the stable project representatives were women, has opened up the dynamics of the project to the issue of gender.

The last phase (1995-1999) placed an emphasis on consolidating the lessons learned, extending activities, and setting up a working system of follow-up analysis. The overall aim is for the eventual transfer of the project to farmers' organisations, governmental structures and NGOs.

The PREVINOBA project demonstrates that the implementation of a participatory approach helps create the right conditions for planning that is grassroots-based and takes into account gender-related issues. Participatory approach tools, particularly those developed by the Research and Support Group for Farmer Self-Advancement (RSGFSA), the use of rural radio, and, above all, application of the Accelerated Participatory Research Method (APRM), have progressively given women the opportunity to participate fully in development planning, taking into account the priorities they themselves consider important.

The self-advancement of local development is a cyclical, repeated and continuous process which is, in the final analysis, in the hands of the beneficiaries themselves.

SUMMARY

The chapter started with a description of the types of programmes available for a range of adult learners. Several approaches and models that adult educators can use as a guide in developing their own programmes were presented and critiqued. The programme development process was specifically conceptualised from an African perspective so you could appreciate the integral importance of African ways of thinking, learning and value systems to the programme development process.

KEY POINTS

- There are many definitions of adult education. However, they all focus on such issues as education for continuous growth, responding to practical problems and issues of adult life, preparation for current and future work opportunities, change in behaviour, promotion of civil society, development of abilities and competencies, and personal and community growth.
- The different adult education programmes all respond to the goals and purposes of adult education, each with its own curriculum and objectives.
- Adult learners also vary across the African continent in terms of their social and economic situations.
- There are several approaches and models that can be used in developing adult education programmes.

- Programme development from an African perspective is flexible in the choice of previous models but stresses the adherence to the ten principles that form the pillars of African thinking, values and ways of doing.

ACTIVITY

What is the basis for having a programme development model from an African perspective?

FURTHER QUESTIONS

1 Discuss the ten critical practices a programmer can adhere to in developing an adult education programme from an African perspective.
2 List four types of adult learners in your community and prescribe specific adult education programmes for each type.

SUGGESTED READING

Higgs, P., Vakalisa, N. C. G., Mda, T. V. and Assie-Lumumba, N. T. (eds.). 2000. *African voices in education*. Cape Town: Juta.

Chapter 3

Models for programme development in adult education

OVERVIEW

The chapter starts with a description of the most common types of programmes available for a range of adult learners. These models mainly reflect Western perspectives that are used internationally in programme development. In the second section, a critique of these Western models is offered. The next section considers the educational rationale supporting the advance of a development model from an African perspective. This is followed by a proposed African-oriented development model and a summation of the critical practices that such a model should incorporate.

LEARNING OBJECTIVES

At the end of this chapter, you should be able to:

1 Identify the different models used in programme development.
2 Describe and analyse the different models used in programme development.
3 Critique the various programme development models currently used in the field of adult education.
4 Distinguish between existing Eurocentric models and a model from an African perspective.
5 Apply selected models in their own contexts.

sesa woruban

KEY TERMS

informal education   Spontaneous learning acquired through a person's day-to-day interaction with their social, physical and natural environment.

model   A schematic description of a system, theory or phenomenon that accounts for its known or inferred properties and may be used for further study of its characteristics; for example, an economic model.

prescriptive development theories   Theories originating from Western cultural practices that consider the development process in terms of a set of predetermined, rigid steps that the programme developer should follow.

programme development model   A model that comprises ideas from one or more persons about how programmes should be developed. It is a standard example of programme development that could be used as a guide by other programme developers in developing their own programmes.

✦ BEFORE YOU START

Why do you think it may be important to use modelling techniques in adult education programme development? Without using models, do you think programme development could be effective?

AN INTRODUCTION TO PROGRAMME DEVELOPMENT

There are numerous Western models of programme development for adult learners and to discuss them all is beyond the scope of this book. What we have done is to provide a brief account of some of the models. Special attention is paid to those models that emphasise people's participation, since the participatory approach forms the basis of our proposals regarding programme development from an African perspective.

Caffarella (2000) viewed programme models as consisting of ideas about how programmes should be put together and what ingredients are necessary to ensure successful outcomes. Most models are linear, that is, they follow specific steps in a particular sequence. However, some models are interactive. Interactive models allow programme developers to address a number of components simultaneously rather than following steps in sequential order (Caffarella, 2002). Unlike many other models, the interactive model acknowledges people and places as important elements of the programme development process and also takes into account cultural differences.

Whether linear or interactive, a programme model is a conceptual framework designed to guide programme developers on which technique to adopt to produce a good plan. It is a well-mapped-out procedure for producing a balanced adult education programme (Onyemunwa, 1997).

Linear programming models

The simplest and most common method used to plan adult education programmes is a prescriptive technique involving the use of a linear model. Linear methods provide a logical sequential path outlining the major steps to be followed in completing the programme development task. Following an already outlined structure is popular because it simplifies the task and provides a degree of perceived security for the programme developer. The activities begin with the identification of needs and conclude with the evaluation of the programme.

Figure 3.1 is an illustration of a seven-step linear model, each step specifying the particular activity involved. The illustration is not presented as an especially effective model. However, it does exhibit the sequential format common to linear models.

Linear models can be either integrated or non-integrated. When used in a non-

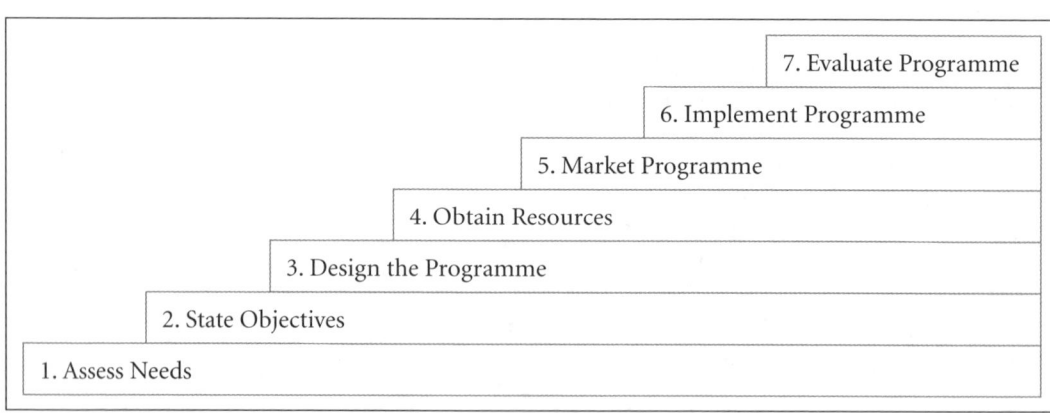

Figure 3.1 Illustration of a linear model for programme development.

integrated fashion, goals, procedures and other relevant components are formulated for adult education without interfacing them with other divisions or functions of the parent organisation. There is no conscious attempt to amalgamate the needs and values of the learners with the needs and values of the sponsoring organisation or the environment. The primary value of linear models is that they provide logical paths to creating educational experiences or achieving a specific educational goal. For example, it is logical for a programme developer to identify the needs a particular adult education programme must satisfy before defining programme and learning objectives.

Non-integrated linear models fail to account for the environmental and organisational contexts of programme development and this failing can create problems. The non-integrated linear model is therefore better suited, and less hazardous, when used in conjunction with a less complicated procedure, such as designing a training and development plan for an individual participant.

Non-linear programming models

Non-linear models attempt to provide greater flexibility in terms of time and resource allocation. They avoid presenting lock-step sequences to creating educational experiences. Instead, the non-linear model affords programme developers the opportunity to begin the programme development in any situation they find themselves. Figure 3.2 is an illustration of one type of non-linear model.

With the non-linear model, it is not a prerequisite for the programme developer to carry out a needs-assessment survey of the community or learners. Programme evaluation in this particular illustration is the main aim of the educational activity. Equally significant is the fact that the programmes obtained by non-linear models can be evaluated at any stage of implementation. By contrast, linear model programmes stress only summative evaluation. Onyemunwa (1997) argues that when programmes developed by non-linear models are adopted they tend to emerge satisfactorily, because formative evaluation

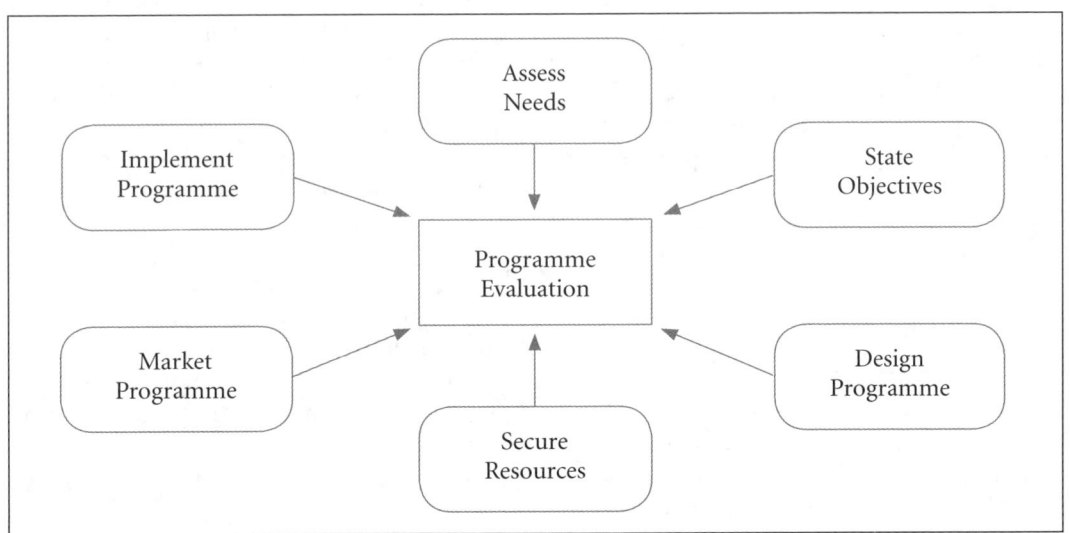

Figure 3.2 Illustration of a non-linear model for programme development.

takes place at any intermediate stage during programme development and implementation. Consequently, errors detected can be rectified; meaning programme effectiveness and efficiency is assured.

Advocates of this type of non-linear model cite the following advantages:

1   A non-linear model enables developers to execute programmes speedily because several programme components can be executed simultaneously.
2   The situation dictates which element will constitute the starting point for programme development. For example, where learner resistance is a possibility, such as in an adult education programme advocating the use of condoms to prevent HIV/AIDS transmission, marketing of the programme represents the best starting point, even before needs and objectives are identified.
3   It does not assume that one must always go back to the initial step to recycle the programme development process. Instead, recycling can start at any point depending on the problems envisaged during the implementation stage.

The use of a non-linear model is usually more difficult and requires greater resources, especially human resources. This is particularly true when several programme development steps are being completed at the same time. For this reason, non-linear models are not used as frequently as linear models.

⊞ ACTIVITY

1   What are the differences between linear and non-linear models? Discuss their relative strengths and weaknesses.
2   What is your understanding of the statement that linear models can be used in an integrated and non-integrated fashion?

WESTERN MODELS OF PROGRAMME DEVELOPMENT

A programme grows out of the identified problems or needs of people. Adult educators are normally interested in the needs of adult learners in their immediate environments. To address such specific needs, programmes are therefore logically developed. Programme development can thus be defined as, 'a conscious effort to look objectively at the situation and come up with an estimate of what needs to be done, eliminating the less important and focusing on the more important problems and needs' (Pesson, 1972: 142-143). This process is complex. It involves continuous decision-making, flexibility in design and action, information sharing and an openness to different perspectives.

The literature of adult education presents a number of theories on developing programmes. Many of these theories have been conceived and developed in environments outside of Africa. The non-African nature of these programme development theories means that caution should be exercised when using them in an African context. Furthermore, several commentators have identified flaws in these theories (Cervero, 1988; Cervero and Wilson, 1994). The purpose of this section is to look at these models' shortcomings, with the intention of helping programme developers make informed decisions when developing programmes for learners in the African context.

Disregard of contextual factors

Theoretically, the task of developing programmes has been conceived of as a pre-set exercise with some steps to be followed. In the recent past, concerned adult educators such as Semali (1999) drew attention to the critical influence of the contextual factors in developing adult education programmes.

Today, practitioners agree that developing programmes is more complicated than any model can reflect (Cervero and Wilson, 1994; Dominick, 1990). To address problems, programme developers need to consider the situation as it presents itself and work out strategies that complement the existing situation. Sometimes it may be difficult to discover the predetermined steps. Prescribed, predetermined steps can be used only to the extent that human actions are static. Where there are continuous changes in values and goals, and where actions are spontaneous, predetermined sets of steps may not work well. Cervero and Wilson (1994), for example, advise practitioners not to base their decisions on prescriptive planning frameworks, known as espoused theories. Rather, they should rely on theories-in-use. Theories-in-use are guidelines or principles that emanate from the actual process of developing programmes.

Kowalski (1988) contends that developing programmes for adults is more complicated than current models of programme planning reflect. Today, the practitioner must be able to identify and address the values and needs of both the learner and the sponsoring organisation. The prevailing models of programme development describe the role of the practitioner as one that is concerned with prioritising the needs of the adult learner exclusively. Most of Tyler's literature, for example, focuses on prioritising the learner's needs, which although necessary, does not deal with the other variables of the programme development process,

such as the sponsoring institution, programmer, stakeholders, and resources.

The models approach programme development from a curriculum perspective and attempt to structure the learning process, but they do not address the contextual setting in which programme development occurs. This perspective, according to Kowalski (1988), has persisted for several decades because adult education has not been effectively mainstreamed into the mission, philosophy and operations of educational institutions.

Difficulties in theory application

Another contention with programme models is the difficulty involved in applying models to real-life situations. A number of reasons have been identified for practitioners not applying current programming models in practice, including (i) the models' prescriptive nature; (ii) the sheer number of models, and (iii) the absence of information concerning the institutional impact on practitioner's behaviour (Cervero, 1988; Kowalski, 1988).

From the many programme models developed by various authors, we can observe substantial differences in complexity and in the degree to which certain values are expressed. Early models tended to be rather simplistic in nature. Gradually, adult education scholars began recognising the problems caused by this emphasis on simplicity. Houle (1972), for example, devised a seven-step model, which included numerous sub-categories in the critical areas of format design and fitting this format into larger patterns of life.

The social context issue has become a focal point of efforts in programme development for the past 30 years. Many adult educators have accepted the notion that the failure to address the social, psychological and technical variables affecting programme development was a serious defect in earlier models (Long, 1983). Emphasis, therefore, has shifted towards interactive designs.

In summary, we can say that the environmental and organisational contexts in which adult education occurs must be analysed in the process of programme development.

Problems with prescriptive procedures

Concerned practitioners complain that programme development theories merely prescribe steps for programmers to follow. In reality, developing programmes is a task that cannot be reduced to predetermined, rigid steps. Among the familiar steps are: (i) assessing needs, (ii) setting goals, (iii) designing a learning activity, and (iv) carrying out evaluation (Cervero, 1988; Dominick, 1990; Kowalski, 1988). The main concern is that this simple step-by-step methodology to developing programmes may give the incorrect impression that there is a standard pattern for developing relevant and meaningful programmes. The listing of steps may mislead some people. For example, novice developers may be tempted to believe in and follow the steps in a rigid manner. Rigidity implies a lack of critical analysis and decisional process. Also, the step-by-step approach may signify a lack of spontaneous action. Spontaneity is an integral part of developing adult education programmes – it is a sign of real and active engagement in the development process.

In short, there is no single, simple recipe or standardised way of developing programmes. Everything depends on who makes the team; how team members interact; the philosophies at play; the goal for developing the programme, as well as the clientele group. Negotiation, advocacy and decision-making skills are essential elements of this complex process. Highly prescriptive procedures do not have a place

in the ever-changing and complex process of developing programmes for adult learners in Africa.

Reducing complex processes to simple tasks

As already stated, many of the programme development models are presented in terms of linear steps. These steps reflect tasks that programme developers should undertake. In other words, the literature presumes that there are predetermined patterns of communicating and acting. In practice, however, this is not the case. Practically, programme developers do more than just perform a series of inflexible tasks; they talk with each other, debate on some issues, agree or disagree and act accordingly when addressing a current situation of needs, challenges and problems.

The task of developing programmes is not just a question of taking actions but a critical reflection and analysis of the what, why, and how of developing programmes. Furthermore, we can also note that programmers attend to the question of 'where?' For example, most of the models in the literature state that the learners' needs must be assessed and prioritised. The concepts of needs-assessment and prioritisation are discussed in depth in Chapter 5. At this point, we will merely observe that there is no or little indication of what it takes to assess and prioritise in real-life situations. The inference here is that the literature provides insufficient information to help novice programme developers anticipate the type of challenges and problems they may encounter during the programme development process. The literature does not present programme developers as they truly are – critical thinkers and decision-makers (Cervero and Wilson, 1994).

Critical thinking is a skill and a process. It assumes that programme developers are capable of assessing the situation, judging the worth of decisions they take, and giving reasons for what they do and how they act. Deprived of the opportunity for critical self-analysis, the programming process is likely to become meaningless and irrelevant. How often have we heard a person say, 'I only followed what was prescribed but I don't think I would have done it in this manner.' This attitude should not be allowed when developing adult education programmes. Adult educators should not be coerced into using prescribed models that, according to their professional judgment, are not the best for a particular situation. No-one should follow the prescribed steps blindly. And those that do follow the models without critically analysing them, are likely to become confused and fail.

It should be noted that the above discussion does not negate the fact that some models, or at least a number of their elements, can be applied to the African context. The concern is that when any model is used, it has to be critically scrutinised to see if it is applicable to the circumstances of a specific situation.

DEVELOPMENT FROM AN AFRICAN PERSPECTIVE

The question addressed here is, 'Why conduct a programme development process from an African perspective?' There are two rationales that form the basis for developing an adult education programme from an African perspective: the philosophical and the educational. We will consider only the educational aspect of the development process since the significance of African philosophies has already been addressed at some length in Chapter 1.

For further reading on these issues, readers are referred to the *Foundations of*

Adult Education in Africa book in the series by Nafukho, Amutabi and Otunga (2005).

Education, learning and training are not recent inventions for the many ethnic groups of Africa but a long-standing and integral part of life. In traditional African societies, education, learning and training had and still have their own specific principles, methods and institutional arrangements. These were different to the type of schooling that was later introduced by missionary societies and the colonial administration. African educationalists and policy makers generally neglected these values of African traditional pedagogy, preferring to borrow theories and models from the modern developed countries of the West. Because these theories and models are not rooted in African culture, they cannot be successfully implemented in the African context.

One principle of African pedagogy is that of learning-through-doing, which trains the intellect, imparts technical skills and instils moral values. Current practices in adult education are acting strongly against this very important principle and thus acting against African culture. Learning through practical experience is not encouraged (Hinzen, 1994).

African education is also informal in nature. Informal education implies spontaneous learning by individuals as they interact with their social and physical environment in their process of day-to day-living (Ocitti, 1994). The same author also points out:

Since indigenous education is not bound by time and place and it is open to all members of the society (i.e. children, youth and adults) and it presents a truly lifelong process of learning, it may be reasonable to say that it resembles informal education to a very large extent (Ocitti, 1994: 19–20).

Indigenous education, as well as being informal, can also be conscious or unconscious. For example, indigenous education is conscious:

when individuals want to learn something from the life situation of the family, lineage, clan or the age group organization and its environment, purely on their own initiatives or through the process of stimulated learning and directed practices (Ocitti, 1994: 19).

On the other hand, unconscious and incidental learning occurs when individuals come into contact with the day-to-day life of societal institutions.

Though informality is a key feature of African teaching and learning, certain elements of indigenous education are formal. Both short and prolonged formal aspects of indigenous education are reflected in:

formal learning, which took place in organized learning groups, in secluded fixed places, and under the guidance of recognized and acceptable instructors. Examples of formal learning situations included, among others, the bush schools or secret societies (i.e. bondo, poro, gbangbani, wonde) of Sierra Leone, the Chisungu of the Benda of North East Zambia, the age group organization among the Kikuyu, Maasai, Nandi of Kenya, the Wenyekongo of the Ubena of Southern Tanzania, the Thondo of the Bowenda of Western Transvaal (Ocitti, 1994: 20).

These kinds of institutionalised learning resemble modern schooling in their provision of opportunities for full-time learning lasting for a few weeks up to many months, even years. Education for the Thondo of the Bavenda of South Africa lasts for five to seven years, while the Wenyekongo of the Ubena of Tanzania receives up to ten years of formal boarding education. In many of the above situations, formal learning addressed issues such as raising a family, making farm tools, medication, agriculture, warfare, and leadership.

One of the crucial aspects of indigenous education is that is intrinsically related to a community's physical and human landscapes. As Ocitti comments:

Indigenous education is deeply rooted in the society's natural and human environment. For example, its subject matter springs directly from the culture of the society. Its purpose therefore represents the totality of people's approved experiences in their culture or society. Pedagogically, indigenous education encompassed both instructional and non-instructional models of learning, which may be termed formal, informal and unconscious (Ocitti, 1994: 21).

Indigenous education does not rely so heavily on formal instruction because it was and is still concerned with the acquisition of practical skills. Its ultimate goal is to integrate the individual into his or her society.

There are many forms of indigenous education in Africa. Although the differences in content and methods of delivery may not be significant, they can still be observed as you move from one region of the continent to another (Callaway, 1977; Hake, 1972). Irrespective of the region, however, indigenous forms of education in Africa tend to reflect the values, wisdom and expectations of the community or wider society as a whole. This is contrary to Western forms of education, which tend to stress the intellectual development of the individual and pay less attention to the needs, goals and expectations of the wider society (Bray, Clarke and Stephens, 1986).

The polarisation of the African and Western forms of education does not imply that the two must be treated as opposites, or that one form of education should be abandoned for the other. Rather, the two forms can be regarded as complementing each other. A formal education system can play an important role in Africa. Such a system, if it is to meet the cultural, social, moral and intellectual, as well as political and economic needs of Africa, needs to be adapted and integrated into the indigenous form of education.

An education development model from an African perspective

The presentation of an alternative model of programme development from an African perspectives centres on the clients. The authors believe that this approach represents an important missing link, or at least a previously marginalised feature, of the traditional models of programme development. In building a programme development model from an African perspective, the authors have drawn from the literature on participation, Afrocentrism, Africanism and indigenous education in Africa (Higgs, Vakalisa, Mda and Assie-Lumumba, 2000). Participation, co-operation, respect for members, and community involvement are central themes in the African developmental model.

The steps involved in developing a programme range from as few as four to as many as twelve in the Interactive Model (Caffarella, 2002). However, our intention here is not to reinvent the wheel! The models developed by earlier programme developers are sound and are embraced by the authors of this book. Our focus is on how to apply these models to meet the cultural, social, moral, intellectual, economic and political needs of Africa. These indicators have been given minimal attention in the development of educational programmes affecting the lives of African adult learners.

Programme development from an African perspective remains flexible and open to the choice of model selected. We suggest that professionals in the educational development arena should adhere to a set of critical practices, which are listed below. We consider these practices the ten pillars of the African perspective:

1 African knowledge and experience must take centre stage in the programme development process and the process must be steered by Africans.
2 Programme developers must have an appreciation and understanding of African indigenous knowledge and experiences and have capacity to integrate the two into programme development.
3 The goal of programme content must be geared to integrating the individuals into their communities and the wider African society.
4 Professionals must have faith in the African continent and her people.
5 Programme development must emphasise the needs, goals and expectations of communities or wider African society.
6 Programme developers must adhere to the principle of indigenous African pedagogy, which stresses learning-by-doing for training the intellect, imparting technical skills and instilling moral values.
7 Programme content must be the outcome of the African society's natural and human environment.
8 Programme developers must use both instructional and non-instructional methods of teaching and learning.
9 There must be stakeholder commitment to ensure African solutions to meeting the needs of adult learners.
10 The programme development process must embrace non-African formal

education but this must be domesticated to meet the cultural, social, moral, intellectual, economic and political needs of Africa and Africans.

Assumptions

An attempt to implement radical programme development reforms in African adult education is based on a number of assumptions. These are:

1 A belief by programme developers that an adult education system can play an important role in Africa, and that such a system must meet the cultural, social, moral and intellectual, as well as the political and economic needs, of Africans.
2 An understanding and appreciation of African indigenous knowledge systems. Aspects of African life such as customary law, inheritance rights, beliefs about witchcraft, taboos and rituals, could form the wisdom of how things can be done in the villages.
3 Availability of local staff to lead the programme development process.
4 Avoiding foreign assistance that may dictate programme content.
5 Reliance on holistic programme development, which in turn addresses local conditions, population growth, basic needs, indigenous knowledge, and disparities between regional, urban, rural and remote areas.
6 African governments to fund and support research into indigenous education.
7 Use of appropriate research methodologies, which could lead to the development of African teaching methodology for use in delivering adult education programmes.

ACTIVITY

1 What is the basis for having a programme development model from an African perspective?
2 Discuss the critical practices one must adhere to in developing a programme from an African perspective.

SUMMARY

In this chapter, the authors have tried to familiarise you with some of the approaches and models commonly used in adult education programme development. The chapter began with a description of the types of programmes available for a range of adult learners. We also investigated the educational rationale behind developing adult education programmes from an African perspective. We presented a number of approaches and models that educators could use as a guide in developing their own programmes. The approaches and models were critiqued, which we hope helped you to identify their inadequacies, especially when it comes to application. The models were accompanied with a review of the literature to help you in your selection of a suitable model or model combination. An African perspective on programme development offered an examination of how African cultural, educational and moral values represent an integral part of the programme development process.

KEY POINTS

■ Western models of programme development are generally prescriptive and non-contextualised in nature. These characteristics do not suit African educational systems and practices and can create problems in application.

- The gap between model theory and practice is a major constraint upon programme development in Africa.
- Traditional African teaching and learning is informal, co-operative and practical in nature. These qualities have been largely ignored under conventional models of programme development.
- The model for programme development from an African perspective places the adult learners at the centre of the process. The model also places great emphasis on the importance of African knowledge and experience to the development process.
- Adult programme development must meet the cultural, social, moral, intellectual, as well as the political and economic needs of Africans.

✦ ACTIVITY

Discuss the ten critical practices a programmer should adhere to in developing an adult education programme from an African perspective.

FURTHER QUESTIONS

1 What factors will you consider in choosing a programme development model?
2 What are the differences between linear and non-linear programming models?

SUGGESTED READING

Higgs, P., Vakalisa, N. C. G., Mda, T. V. and Assie-Lumumba, N. T. 2000. *African voices in education.* Cape Town: Juta.

Chapter 4

The pre-planning/programme proposal phase

OVERVIEW

The process of developing adult education programmes involves several different phases. This chapter explores the first phase: pre-planning. Other phases are addressed in different chapters of this book. The discussion in this chapter is organised around the following sub-headings: (i) the concept of pre-planning; (ii) pre-planning in an African context; (iii) how ideas originate; (iv) building support and commitment; (v) understanding the concept of planning; and (vi) basic principles of planning.

LEARNING OBJECTIVES

At the end of the chapter, you should be able to:

1   Define the concept of pre-planning/programme proposal.
2   State basic principles of developing programmes for learners in an African context.
3   Sketch a preliminary plan for building support and commitment for a new idea.

bese saka

KEY TERMS

pre-planning   A concept that refers to an initial programme proposal, in which the initiator of the idea consults and negotiates, solicits support and builds commitment to see the new idea grow and develop into a programme.

planning   A skill of arranging or organising activities, resources and facilities for running a specific programme of educational activities.

needs assessment   A problem-driven process of finding out the most pressing challenges facing potential adult learners in order to establish genuine teaching and learning activities that address these challenges.

⬚ BEFORE YOU START

Suppose you come up with an idea that is so exciting that you want to share it with other people. Would you share your idea with anyone, or would you only consider talking to certain people about it? Would you share your idea with someone who is likely to discourage you from putting the idea into practice?

THE CONCEPT OF PRE-PLANNING

There is a time when a person or group of people may come up with an idea of doing something. When this happens, one individual may want to introduce the idea to the others. At this time, the idea is still in its initial stage – it is still the property of the originator(s). We may even say that at this stage that the idea is still passive, meaning that it has not been actualised. The idea still has to progress some distance before it can be implemented for the benefit of the target group(s).

For the originators to establish support of and commitment to the idea, they have to consult relevant people. The consultation is done in order to check if the idea constitutes a legitimate concern that can be addressed through educational programmes. It is during this consultation period that the idea moves from the passive stage to being active. We use the word *active* to imply that relevant people get to know about it and start acting on it. The steps that are described here constitute what is referred to as the pre-planning or programme-proposal stage. This is an important stage despite the fact that it is rarely addressed in the literature of adult education.

For many people, the pre-planning stage is primarily informal in the sense that the idea can be aborted if the originator feels that it is not supported by people whose support is needed most. This stage marks the beginning of the search for and acquisition of relevant information. Almost all programmes start with pre-planning.

PRE-PLANNING IN AN AFRICAN CONTEXT

The pre-planning stage is ideally suited to the work of programme developers in contemporary Africa. When a person understands the origin of an idea, it becomes easier for that person to understand the philosophy behind its implementation. For Africans per se, as well as for programme developers in the region, pre-planning is compatible with the notion of communal activity.

It is important here to explain further the compatibility of the pre-planning phase concept with African cultural practices.

A fairly widespread traditional practice in Africa is that of marriage. This is a time when relatives are introduced or awakened to communal living. When a young man meets a girl whom he intends to marry, the first thing is to make his intention known (soliciting support and building commitment). In African culture, the first person to be told is the father. This does not mean the biological father only, but may also include a respected older male relative – a 'father figure'. The father therefore symbolises the leader of an organisation whose commitment to the idea (in this example, the idea of marriage) must be secured. Without the initial consultation stage, the marriage may never materialise.

Once consultations have begun and commitment to the idea has been established, follow-ups are made. For example, 'to enquire if the suggestion for such a marriage is favorable, the parents of the boy send an intermediary to the girl's parents' (Mbiti, 1988: 136). This marks the beginning of serious consultations, negotiations and amicable working relationships between the two families. These types of consultations reflect the African belief that, '[an] individual exists only because the corporate group exists, thus in marriage, the most important contract of life, other members of the corporate community must get involved' (Mbiti, 1988: 136). This brings out the principles of consultation and participation.

It may happen that an elderly relative strongly rejects the prospective marriage partner. If the reasons behind this rejection are legitimate (shared by others), negotiations with the other family are broken down (Mbiti, 1988). Should consent to the marriage proposal be given, however, then the ceremony follows.

The wedding celebrations, dancing, singing and rejoicing strengthen community solidarity. They vividly reflect the African belief in participatory or communal undertakings. Although African marriage ceremonies may differ in detail, the basic significance of principles such as community solidarity and participatory action are common to all.

From the preceding discussion, you should now be aware that programmes grow out of the ideas of an individual or several people. We will now go on to look at the various stages of this pre-planning phase and what, ideally, should happen when an idea (to embark on a programme) comes to mind.

HOW IDEAS ORIGINATE

Someone or some people must come up with a new idea of developing programmes to address certain concerns. The idea is triggered by a number of things, for example, observation of some practices, experiences or problems. Such observation may relate to the following factors:

■ Unsatisfactory living conditions. For example, the problems caused by the HIV/AIDS pandemic are many and affect individuals in different ways. People may consider different ideas for approaching and solving their situation-specific problems. That is, strategies or ideas may be initiated by particular individuals. The initiators will then promote their ideas to relevant people. For example, there may

be a need to equip the public with prevention and survival skills; an idea that will have to be 'sold' to the target group; that is, to the members of the public.

■ A programme in process. Ideas for developing new programmes can be triggered by what happens in an on-going programme. When adult learners attend any programme they do so because they expect to gain something. Thus, during the programme process there is a natural instinct to assess/evaluate the worth of the programme being attended – 'Are my expectations being met?'; 'What is missing from this programme?' If a person feels their current programme is lacking in some respect (that it is not meeting their expectations), this may lead them to think about an alternative programme that is capable of meeting their expectations.

As an example, let us imagine a married couple attending a programme designed to equip them with the skills needed to engage in home-based education. One of the participants, the woman, observes that while the programme equips them with good information on some issues, such as the values of good courtship and marriage, it does not adequately address other family matters. It does not, for example, address the issue of having children.

In traditional African culture, to be unable to bear children is the, 'worst misfortune and punishment that any person can suffer. Traditionally, it is believed that to die without getting married and without children is to be completely cut off from the human society' (Mbiti, 1988: 134). Thus, any programme that separates marriage and procreation is bound to be considered lacking, as the woman in our example recognised.

The idea that then came to the woman's mind was to develop a programme that addressed this important issue, bearing in mind that in African culture, marriage and procreation cannot be separated. For her new programme idea to bear fruit, she, as the originator, must begin by soliciting support and building commitment to it.

■ Challenging events such as technological conditions. New innovations often bring challenges that may demand a new programme to be put in place to deal with these challenges. Take, for example, the introduction of computers. If an organisation has relied for many years on typewriters, the advent of computers may cause management to think of replacing the old technology (typewriters) with the new (computers).

Before introducing the computers, management may think of introducing an educational programme to equip employees with the appropriate computer skills. For this idea to become a reality, management, in its role as originator, has to sell the idea to the intended programme beneficiaries – the organisation's employees. The ideas that are finally implemented are those that are considered worthwhile by all participants in the development process; that is, by both management and employees.

BUILDING SUPPORT AND COMMITMENT

Although there is no single method for building support and commitment to the idea, a few general guidelines are applicable.

The main task for the initiator is to consult the relevant people. Consultation is an important factor in getting people to work and learn together and therefore requires careful consideration. The initiator must approach the task of consultation with enthusiasm and an analytical frame of

mind. He or she must also establish clear and realistic goals that indicate why the new idea is worth pursuing. Critical questions at this point include:

■ What problem is being addressed?
■ Does everyone recognise the problem?
■ What is the new idea all about?
■ Is the new idea achievable?
■ Who will benefit and how?

These questions can help the initiator assess the worth of the idea he or she has originated. When the initiator is certain that the new idea is worth exploring, she or he may work out procedural details, guided by the question: 'How do I go about soliciting support and input and building commitment to the new idea?' Below, we present some suggestions.

Developing action plans

The initiator(s) will note down whom to consult, and why and how to carry out the consultation. The initiator(s) can be either, (i) the target group itself, as is the case when, for example, a women's group requests a workshop on property rights; (ii) policy makers testing, for example, their newly developed policies on self-help; (iii) employers or administrators thinking of a workplace literacy scheme for their non-literate employees; and (iv) community leaders proposing a social service project, or something of a similar nature. Initiators should include potential participants, sponsors and the programme housing institution when they consider the individuals and organisations to consult.

When soliciting input and commitment, the following factors deserve consideration:

1 Intellectual resources. This refers to people who are knowledgeable about the proposed issue and are in a position to

offer valuable inputs or help broaden or refine the new idea as necessary. The initiator can judge the validity of his or her programme proposal from the responses of people approached for their input, for example, from their apparent enthusiasm for the idea or the quality and comprehensiveness of their suggestions.

2 Resource capability. For the idea to be put into practice, the necessary resources should be available. Examples of resources include money, materials, equipment and personnel. When soliciting financial aid, the originator must ensure that the original idea is one that will appeal to potential funders and is therefore a realistic, economically viable proposal.

3 Field receptivity. People will support the idea if they believe it addresses real-life problems. The initiators cannot expect commitment to or support of an idea that does not directly impact on the lives of the intended recipients. Foregrounding the practical elements of the programme proposal is advisable.

4 Institutional intervention. The initiator must identify and consult institutions that might be interested in the new idea. If the programme has to be housed within specific institutions, for example, it is essential that these institutions are listed for consultation. The idea being proposed should promise to promote the mission and goals of the 'mother' institution. In organisations with relatively few people, soliciting support and participation from the members should not be as complex as that for larger organisations.

5 The preferential mode of participation. For people to become involved in the programme, it is necessary to think of relevant and realistic means of getting them to participate at the right time. If, for example, a programme is arranged for villagers who are predominantly

farmers, and organisers decide to run this programme during the farming season, participation may be poor. Ensuring people's participation for the entire development process is also essential.

❖ ACTIVITY

Explain in your own words what you understand by the meaning and importance of the pre-planning stage.

UNDERSTANDING THE CONCEPT OF PLANNING

To understand this pre-planning phase properly, planning as a concept must be defined. Planning is an idea that has long been used in the field of adult education. However, how this concept is understood remains a subject of debate. Generally speaking, most people would agree that planning may be viewed as a process of decision-making and acting upon such decisions. Refining this definition slightly, we can say that planning is as a conscious effort of deciding what needs to be done, then eliminating the less important and focusing on the more important problems and needs. From this initial understanding we can observe that planning can be presented as a systematic process.

Planning as a process

A process is defined as, 'a systematic series of actions directed to some end' (*The Random House College Dictionary*, 1988: 1055). When the initiators of an idea solicit support for their new idea, they direct their actions towards some desired results. Establishing support and building commitment to the idea is not a single isolated action, but a series of actions performed over a period of time. These actions combine to form a coherent and convincing approach to addressing the new idea. Specifically, planning in the pre-planning phase mainly involves, (i) coming up with an idea to embark on a new programme, and (ii) soliciting support and building commitment through consultations and negotiations. These two steps comprise what is referred to here as the pre-planning phase.

At a more comprehensive level, planning can be viewed as a multi-faceted process. It is multi-faceted because it can present itself in different forms, as indicated in the discussion that follows.

Planning as a controlled process

When planning is described as controlled process, it denotes one group or person having power over another. The phrase 'top-down' is commonly used to describe this type of relationship. The 'top' usually refers to the professionals, adult educators and senior management figures; while 'down' refers to the community, target group(s), learners, as well as junior staff, such as line managers and auxiliary staff. Thus, the top-down approach to planning implies that the 'down' follow directions issued from the 'top'. These concepts are used to define the relationship that exists between the two parties.

If concepts of 'top' and 'bottom' are applied to an African setting, they would carry a different meaning from the one expressed above. In African culture, social relationships are predominantly defined by the concept of kinship. Kinship, as one commentator states, 'largely governs the behavior, thinking and the whole life of the individual in the society of which he is a member' (Mbiti, 1988: 104). Kinship terms such as sister, brother, uncle, aunt, niece, nephew, and so on, are used to define the relationships that exist between or among people.

For example, when two strangers meet in a village, one of their first duties is to sort out how they may be related to each other. Having discovered how the kingship system applies to them, they relate to each other according to the accepted behaviour patterns of their community. If they discover, for example, that they are 'brothers' then they will treat each other as equals, or as an older or younger brother; if they are uncle and nephew, then the nephew may be expected to give much respect to the uncle because this type of relationship is required by the society (Mbiti, 1988: 104).

Mbiti's comment suggests that the top-down relationship is not one concerning the controller and the controlled, but one that relates to the degree of respect one person shows towards another. This notion of respect is useful in our consideration of programme development from an African perspective. Developing education programmes involves the contributions of various people offering a range of competencies. Some of these people will be more experienced than others, making the contributing unit of people one that consists of, broadly speaking, experts and novices. These differences should be appreciated and not used to promote the practice of 'the controller and the controlled'. Instead, the situation can be regarded as beneficial because the less experienced can learn from the more experienced – as the African saying goes, 'From the word of an elder is derived a bone.'

Individual differences such as positional power, professional expertise and assigned power should be acknowledged not as a weapon of control but as a foundation for sharing knowledge and learning together. To make use of these different contributions, 'it is important to clearly define the strengths of each partner in ways that speak to why the partners are working together and this draws our attention to differences in competencies and capacities, but it also highlights differences in interests which serve important purposes in collaboration' (Donaldson and Kozoll, 1999: 102). Pre-planning thus becomes the first stage of establishing and encouraging the working together of different people in the immediate environment.

Planning as an expression of culture

Approaches to developing programmes for learners in Africa should address the cultural expectations of the target group. Culture here refers to practices informed by the values, beliefs, norms and behaviours of the local people. These practices are influenced by factors such as, (i) existing technology (locally used skills, knowledge and other tools); (ii) economic climate (local ways and means of survival/production); (iii) political climate (local/common ways and means of making decision); and (iv) conceptual belief(s) (such as the rationale and justification residents cite for supporting and engaging in specific programmes).

Technological, economic, and political and conceptual belief factors cannot be treated as minor or incidental issues when programme development for learners in Africa is discussed. When a new programme is conceptualised, these aspects should form an integral part of the thought process.

For example, it would be unreasonable to think of offering a programme that demands the use of linked audio-visual materials in remote rural areas (*teng-nyana-teng*, as commonly known in Botswana) when educators know that such materials cannot be found there. Indeed, these materials are completely unknown in many parts of Africa, where sand, for example, would provide a simple and highly effective writing medium. We believe that programme

developers are knowledgeable and experienced people who are aware of the status of technology in many African countries. They should therefore be realistic in their choices of content, media and materials.

▒ ACTIVITY

1 What advantages and disadvantages are there to following the top-down (controller and the controlled) approach when undertaking the pre-planning stage of developing adult education programmes?
2 Indicate your understanding of the following phrase: 'Planning is an expression of culture.'

BASIC PRINCIPLES OF PLANNING

Adult education programmes address realistic problems/needs. Thus, when a proposal is made for a new programme, the initiators must ensure that their idea addresses problems experienced by a specific group of people. Therefore, when an idea of developing a new programme arises, certain principles should be considered. These principles are: (i) functionalism and immediacy of application; (ii) problem-based and relevant; (ii) participation and collaboration; and (iv) continuous assessment and decision-making. Before we go on to discuss some of these principles, it is worth reminding ourselves that a principle can be defined as, 'a guiding sense', or 'an accepted rule of action' (*Random House College Dictionary*, 1988: 1053).

The principle of functionalism
Programmes that address realistic problems tend to promote the principle of

functionalism or immediacy of application. Functionalism is a concept that indicates the need to focus programmes on skills, competencies, attitudes and values that can have an immediate application to the learners' life situations (home-life, work-life, religious life and community life). Most adult learners would not like to sit in a programme and learn information that lacks relevance to their lives (Birkenholz, 1999). This principle of functionalism will eliminate negative attitudes or answers to the questions, 'What does this information have to do with me' (Birkenholz, 1999: 34), or 'What is in here for me?' For example, those that live in fishing areas should learn the skills needed to catch, preserve, market and sell their fish.

Programmes that give learners skills that they can apply to their living environment are of high quality. The principle of functionalism thus speaks to the importance of offering programmes that address immediate challenges existing in an African context.

The problem-based principle

Programmes in adult education are developed because there is a problem to be addressed. The word 'problem' here can be used synonymously with anything that presents itself as a challenge, concern or a gap. A programme is thus seen as way of addressing some of the problems of adult learners in an African context. The changing nature of African societies, due to the influences of the outside world, has distracted our attention from the ongoing problems of our traditional societies. There are, for example:

Problems of women with children out of wed-lock, and others who only go to the city for a few days or weeks to stay with their husband and get fertilized. There are poor people who sit about in the street beg-

ging for money and food, some of whom are crippled and others are too lazy to work. There are problems of unwanted children, orphans, criminals, delinquents and prisoners, all of whom need special social care to be brought up or integrated into the communities. Increasingly, there is a gap in the wealth between the few relatively rich men in top positions of government and commercial employment and the poor masses who barely earn enough on which to live. This great imbalance in wealth can only breed discontent, jealousy, greed, theft and even open uprising (Mbiti, 1988: 224).

The litany of problems cited in the above quotation is not exhaustive, but it does point to the fact that adult education programmes emerge from the hardships and lived realities of a continent that faces enormous challenges. Therefore, any and all ideas connected to adult education programme development must speak to the problems (and others) that Mbiti identifies. If an idea does not engage with these problems, it should be considered void. Thus, the principle of relevance should be borne in mind from the time the programme is being proposed to the time it is implemented and evaluated.

The principle of participation and collaboration

Participation and collaboration is necessary with a wide range of interested parties. These people may include lay people, target clientele, programme planners, sponsors, administrators, advisory staff, evaluators and community members (Donaldson and Kozoll, 1999).

The pre-planning stage actually serves as a 'checkpoint' for who can/should be included in the team of developing a proposed programme. The team has to be carefully constituted. For example, members are selected bearing in mind the critical tasks or functions to be performed. The team has to assess needs, set priorities, make some critical decisions, market the programme and recruit facilitators. Members of the planning team should be able to share these tasks, professionally.

Below is a case study that will help you to consolidate what you have learned in this chapter.

CASE STUDY: UNDERSTANDING TEAM DYNAMICS

Mr Ike is a 60-year-old worker who is well established in planning adult education programmes. Ike and two junior colleagues, Mr Lolo and Ms Lobopo, are asked at short notice to initiate an adult education programme. As the financial year is nearly over, they have two weeks to come up with a suitable proposal, either through consultation with potential participants or as a team, otherwise the allocated funds will be returned to the central resource.

Ike proposes the excellent idea of holding a workshop on 'How to write a research proposal', for personnel in the research and publication unit of their department. Ike explains that he once held a similar workshop and thus has all the necessary materials. His two colleagues are also excited about the idea and they all decide to see their supervisor the following morning at 8.30 a.m.

The following morning Mr Lolo and Ms Lobopo arrive on time but Ike is absent. The supervisor sends someone to call Ike and is informed that he is experiencing difficulties in getting to work. The two junior colleagues decide to present Ike's proposal as if it were their on, aware that their supervisor would guess it was Ike's idea if they insist on

waiting for him. Ike eventually appears at 10.00 a.m. and discovers that the meeting is over and that the supervisor has appointed two additional people to help with the preparations. Feeling hurt and resentful, Ike decides to withdraw his participation and also refuses to share his prior knowledge and experience with the others.

On the day of the workshop, very few people turn up as the workshop organisers forgot to send notices on time. Some officers who received invitations refuse to come, saying they were not consulted prior to running the programme.

⌘ ACTIVITY

Study the above case study then answer the following questions:

1 What do you think went wrong in the planning of this programme?
2 Were Lolo and Lobopo justified in pretending that Ike's idea was their own? Explain your answer.
3 What would you have done that Lolo and Lobopo did not do?
4 Was it wise for Ike to withdraw his participation in the planning of the programme?

SUMMARY

This chapter raised critical points regarding the process of developing programmes in general and the pre-planning phase in particular. The chapter has stressed the importance of programme development being directly related to the specific, real-life needs, problems and challenges of African communities, which include the prevailing issues of poverty, unemployment, illiteracy, passive attitudes towards self-help activities, and the weakening or disappearance of the strong institution of marriage and of indigenous beliefs. We have also suggested that when the idea to develop a programme is born, a number of important principles should be considered, such as the principles of problem-based programmes, participatory and collaborative undertakings, and functionalism and immediacy of application. An explanation of these principles led us to conclude that they should form the basis for the construction of all adult education programmes developed in an African context.

KEY POINTS

- Pre-planning refers to the stage in the programme development process where a person or a group of people solicit input for and support of a new idea – to run a new programme.
- All programme proposals should address real-life problems.
- A systematic plan of how to go about soliciting input and support and building commitment should be developed.
- Pre-planning is best regarded as an exercise of collaborative endeavour, where all interested parties are encouraged to offer inputs to the development process.
- Pre-planning is a 'take-off' stage.

ACTIVITY

A number of principles that can guide the process of developing programmes for learners in Africa have been discussed in this chapter. Describe two principles that you consider particularly important.

FURTHER QUESTIONS

1 What do you understand as the main purpose of the pre-planning phase?
2 Is it possible that some programmes can take off without having gone through the pre-planning phase?

SUGGESTED READING

Birkenholz, R. 1999. *Adult learning.* Danville: Interstate.

Donaldson, J. and Kozoll, C. 1999. *Collaborative program planning: Principles, practices and strategies.* Malabar, Fl: Krieger.

Dakenwald, G. and Merriam, S. 1982. *Adult education: Foundations of practice.* New York: HarperCollins.

Mbiti, J. 1988. *African religions and philosophies.* London: Heinemann.

Chapter 5

Identifying and assessing learning needs

OVERVIEW

The aim of this chapter is to familiarise you with the process of identifying and assessing the learning needs of adults for adult education programmes. To achieve this, we will begin by examining the concept of need and the importance of conducting a needs assessment. The chapter then addresses the process of identifying adult learning needs for adult education programmes. In the next section, several needs-assessment approaches are discussed, with special emphasis on the survey and participatory approaches. The final section of the chapter deals with how to prioritise learning needs for an adult education programme.

LEARNING OBJECTIVES

After reading this chapter, you should be able to:

1 Describe the nature of adult learners' needs in an African context.
2 Discuss the complexities of identifying and analysing learning needs of adult learners in an African context.
3 Explain the various types of approaches commonly used by adult educators for assessing the needs of learners.
4 Discuss the importance of conducting a needs assessment for an adult education programme.
5 Anticipate times when needs may arise in an adult education programme and conduct a needs assessment.
6 List identified needs in order of priority using relevant criteria.

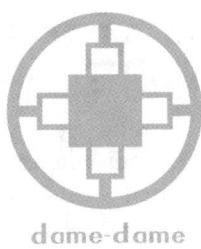

dame-dame

KEY TERMS

andragogy   This is a term whose popularity in adult education can be attributed
to Knowles (1978), who described it as,
'the art and science of helping adults
learn'. The term presents adult learners as
self-directed, independent and problem-
centred people who are curious to apply
what they learn immediately.

felt needs   These are derived from individual beliefs that something in the
community is a necessity. They may not
be real or representative of learning needs
in the community. This phenomenon
is referred to as 'false consciousness'
under Freirean analysis. While a felt
need may be a real learning need, there
is a tendency to circumscribe the actual
community needs when programmes are
based on meeting felt needs.

learning need   A learning need is the
measurable difference between what the
learners already know and what they
want to know.

needs assessment   A problem-driven
process of finding out the most pressing
challenges facing potential adult learners
in order to establish a genuine need for
the teaching and learning activities that
address these challenges.

pedagogy   Pedagogy is the theory of
teaching people via different methods
of educational instruction. Learners
are assumed to have no powers of
self-direction, to be dependent on the
teacher-instructor, and to be uncon-
cerned about the application of
knowledge because the learning experience is not a problem-solving exercise.
Pedagogy is the antithesis of andragogy.

BEFORE YOU START

1   What is your understanding of a
    learning need?
2   Identify and discuss some needs of adult
    learners in a particular community in
    your country.
3   Who assesses the learning needs of adult
    learners for non-formal and formal
    adult education programmes in your
    community?

WHAT IS A LEARNING NEED?

A learning need may be understood as a measurable discrepancy between 'where we are now' and 'where we should be' in terms of results and outcomes. Baker (1984) defined a need as a state that exists when there is a gap between the present situation (what is) and the required situation (what should be). If an individual adult learner, for example, has a certain level of knowledge but requires a higher level of knowledge in order to improve performance, then a knowledge gap or need exists. All things being equal, the individual adult learner will, in this case, strive to close the gap by gaining additional knowledge.

Though superficially straightforward, the concept of need is actually more complex than it appears. A number of environmental factors may impact upon the process of needs assessment and needs satisfaction. For example, an individual in a rural village might see an obvious need for adult literacy classes. However, the rest of the villagers do not regard illiteracy as a priority problem. For these villagers, gaining political recognition as a township is a priority need. For a programme developer, understanding the factors involved in needs identification is therefore an important factor in determining how to prioritise needs.

The concept of a learning need has a strong link to the theory of motivation. Human motives, according to Weihrich and Koontz (1994), are based on needs, whether consciously or subconsciously felt. Weihrich and Koontz believe that needs vary in intensity and over time among different individuals. One of the common explanations for human motivation is the hierarchy of needs theory proposed by Maslow (1970). Maslow proposed that within every human being there is a hierarchy of five needs. These needs are:

1　Physiological needs – including hunger, thirst, shelter, sex, and other bodily needs;
2　Safety needs – including security and protection from physical and emotional harm;
3　Love – including affection, belongingness, acceptance, and friendship;
4　Esteem needs – including internal esteem factors such as self-respect, autonomy and achievement; and external esteem factors such as status, recognition and attention; and
5　Self-actualisation – referring to the drive to become what one is capable of becoming, which includes growth, achieving one's potential, and self-fulfillment.

Maslow categorised the five needs into higher and lower levels. Physiological and safety needs were described as lower-order, while love, esteem and self-actualisation were considered higher-order needs. Maslow concluded that human needs at the higher level serve as motivators only when those in the lower level are satisfied. Unfortunately, Maslow's theory was not founded on any research evidence, while several studies that sought to prove Maslow's theory (for example, Robbins (1989)), gained no support.

From an African perspective, Maslow's theory is flawed for a number of reasons. Firstly, in many African societies needs are not regarded in hierarchical terms, with some achievable only after others have been satisfied. In many poverty-stricken communities of Africa, the desire to satisfy physiological and safety needs fully is impossible. Consequently, people do not necessarily satisfy lower-level needs before moving on to higher-levels needs. For example, a village chief or a person belonging to the Village Development Committee (VDC) may feel the same intensity for lower needs such as hunger, shelter and clothing, despite their elevated status within the community. Secondly, it is impossible for programme developers to know the precise need level of individuals or communities in order to tailor programmes based on that knowledge. In fact, most individuals will not express their needs based on this hierarchical conception. Thirdly, it is not clear where to place the learning need of an African adult in Maslow's hierarchy. Does it belong to the safety, self-esteem or self-actualisation category?

We can also note that a hierarchical approach to the learning experience assumes that adult learners are essentially alike. This is clearly not the case. It is important to recognise that adult learners are unique in the different aspirations, values, needs, knowledge, skills, experiences and problems they have. As a result of these differences, adults' learning needs may differ greatly from one individual to another. For example, one woman's need to learn about small-scale entrepreneurship to improve her family business is different to another woman's need to learn about dairy cattle for the purposes of farming.

The assumption of learner similarity would only be appropriate for organised efforts addressing an identified national need, such as, for example, an HIV/AIDS education programme to be rolled out across the country. At local and community levels, this may also apply if there is a common community education need, such as the need to know how to purify water from unsafe water sources, for example.

For a detailed exploration of the concept of need, we recommend the *Foundations* and *Psychology* books in this series by Nafukho, Amutabi and Otunga (2004) and Fasokun, Katahoire and Oduaran (2004), respectively.

THE IMPORTANCE OF CONDUCTING NEEDS ASSESSMENT

Needs assessment is an important step in the development process of adult education programmes. The programme developer must realise that his or her credibility, and that of the proposed programme, depends on meeting the real needs of the adult learners. While adult education programmes cannot represent all of the needs of adult learners, an outright rejection of learners' needs may destroy the kind of personal relationships underlying much effective adult education work. Consequently, adult education personnel must be prepared and willing to deal with the totality of the concerns of adult learners. From the work of Baker (1984), the following are reasons for identifying needs of adult learners in programme development:

1 Needs assessments of potential adult learners gives programming staff the opportunity to assess learner needs and priorities impartially, free from the personal preferences and biases of the target group.
2 By conducting needs assessment, potential conflict and resistance can be avoided, especially if the needs-identification process involves the learners.
3 Need assessment, if participatory in nature, can have a positive effect on motivation and improve levels of participation and commitment on the part of potential learners. In addition, the needs-assessment exercise can help identify reasons for any apparent lack of enthusiasm among adult learners for a proposed programme.
4 Needs assessment helps determine people's skills, attitudes and knowledge. This in turn ensures that programmes remain relevant in terms of approach and

content to the needs, skills, attitudes and knowledge of learners.

5 Specific efforts at needs identification are more likely to result in determining what the real needs are, and will help avoid basing programmes on symptoms or assumptions only.

6 Needs assessment is a form of programme evaluation that addresses accountability through the provision of input and guidance into the programme development process, which will form the basis for the formulation of appropriate programme goals and objectives.

7 Participants' diverse views and experiences are sought and recognised, with more powerful stakeholders encouraged to support the participation of the less powerful.

8 A needs-assessment process is a learning experience for participants. The emphasis is on identifying lessons learned that will help participants improve programme implementation, and on committing resources to ensure that targets are met.

9 Need assessment ensures early ownership of the programme by a range of stakeholders who come with a variety of roles to play.

10 If participants' inputs are welcomed, agreement on needs-assessment findings, addressing problems and formulating improvement plans is more likely.

An important consideration for the programme developer of adult education programmes is the fact that needs vary in type as well and in the way they are perceived by people. Different conceptions of needs include learning needs, expressed needs, felt needs, and normative needs. The adult learners will have needs that they will classify as basic or felt needs, or as wants and interests, which are not always expressed or real needs. The subtle distinctions of meanings in these concepts are critical for the programme developer. Compton (1984) suggests the necessity of dealing with people's interests (or aspirations) before they will willingly state their wants, which must then be analysed to provide an identification of real needs.

Based on the interaction occurring between a programme developer and adult learners in needs identification, four different scenarios may be anticipated:

Scenario 1. There is a consensus or common understanding of the needs between the learners and the programme developer.

This means that the programme developer correctly recognises the needs felt by the people. This is a rare situation but one that the programme developer can strive for by working closely with the participants. For example, a group of potential adult learners feel that their failure with government credit schemes in the community is because they lack the reading and writing skills needed to keep simple records of their activities. Instead of being tempted to concentrate efforts on redressing illiteracy, the programme developer decides to involve the participants in identifying and prioritising needs. Together, the participants and the programme developer soon agree that developing appropriate entrepreneurial skills to manage projects under the credit schemes is more of a priority need than learning to read and write.

Scenario 2. The programme developer fails to recognise the needs felt by the people.

This happens when the people fail to express their felt needs or fail to discuss their needs with the programme developer, even if they consider these needs to be high priority. For example, a village community is worried because the youth are dying of HIV/AIDS at an alarming rate. The village is in need of an intervention strategy that can reduce both mortality and the infection rate.

A team of experts is in the village to develop a programme in response to the villagers' plight and they start with a needs assessment. Due to the stigma associated with HIV/AIDS, the people do not express HIV/AIDS as a priority need. This suggests that the programme developer needs to understand the factors preventing the expression of needs, so that he or she can then develop strategies to encourage people to be more open. The extent to which people are willing to express their needs to a programme developer, whom they inevitably view as an outsider, is greatly influenced by a number of factors, including:

- Lack of knowledge and/or skills on the part of the programme developer. If this is the case, potential participants may not feel sufficient trust or confidence in the programme developer to express their real needs.
- Fear of being judged or regarded as going against the community norm may prevent some individuals or groups from expressing a need. Many African cultural norms are not easily made known to outsiders. For example, although a belief in black magic and charms for learning attainment is common to many African communities, programme participants may consider it inappropriate to reveal this kind of information and fear that disclosure may even result in punishment.
- Negative past experiences that have left the community feeling less confident about their ability to carry out a project successfully. When this kind of feeling exists, learners become cautious about tackling projects, even though they consider these projects to be important. The fear of failure de-motivates the community in this scenario. For example, a community that has failed in implementing a conservation project may lack

the courage and confidence to accept a community health education programme on sanitation.

Scenario 3. The programme developer knows about needs that are not known by the people.

This scenario is more likely to occur in circumstances where specialised knowledge may be required to discover certain needs. For example, a community health worker or programme developer may discover that the village water source is poor and, unless this knowledge is shared with the community members, they will not be aware of the need to act. The programme developer will have to demonstrate the need to act on this urgent problem before starting a literacy programme that the community considers a felt need.

Scenario 4. A programme developer incorrectly identifies a need that is not actually present in the community.

This can happen when the programme developer's value system is different to the community's. For example, a programme developer may interpret the shortage of food in a community as lack of production skills or laziness. This is likely to prompt a negative reaction from the programme participants. In this scenario, the programme developer must remain aware of his or her own value system and be careful not to impose it on the community.

⬚ ACTIVITY

1 List four adult learning needs of a non-formal and formal adult education programme.
2 Why is it important to identify the learning needs of adult learners?

IDENTIFYING LEARNING NEEDS

While the assessment of individual needs dominates the literature on programme development in adult education, the influences of sponsoring organisations and the larger society remain important for the programme developer. Ultimately, the needs for developing a programme are expressed by society, organisations and the individual learner.

In Chapter 1 we argued in favour of developing adult education programmes from an African perspective. This argument involves integrating the thinking of African philosophies such as Pan-Africanism, African humanism, Afrocentrism, *Ujamaa* and Black Consciousness. To this list we can add the philosophy of 'authentic existence', which is particularly relevant to the assessment of needs for adult education programmes. Authentic existence, according to Teffo (2000), is a mode of human existence in which a person affirms his or her individual freedom. However, the same author suggests that this definition does not make the identification of learning needs any simpler because:

> *human beings are not truly themselves. Throughout life, individuals in society simply play a part, acting out assigned roles, following customary patterns of behaviour taken over unquestioned from the society surrounding them* (Teffo 2000: 104).

The concept of authentic existence is, as Teffo observes, affected by the cultural, economic, social and political factors influencing an individual's perception of his or her needs. A need is therefore not determined by isolated circumstances, but rather by the combined action of multiple forces. From the adult education perspective, the critical element in the assessment of a need is the learner's perception of the discrepancy or the gap between where they are and where they want to be. Needs assessment is thus, according to Knowles (1978), essentially a self-assessment exercise; though one augmented by the programme developer's provision of tools and procedures designed to help learners obtain data about their level of development and competencies.

It should be noted that gaps do not only reflect problems; they also represent positive opportunities to develop potential and build on strengths. The positive as well as the problematic nature of gaps must be addressed if people are to manage change successfully. Thomas and Mellon (1995) suggest four main ways of identifying existing or potential gaps for training and development programmes, which are described below.

Observing performance within the programme environment

Observing problems regarding the contributions of individuals in the achievement of their personal and group goals may help in identifying gaps. We can use the example of the literacy programme of an adult education organisation to illustrate this point. The community and individual participants on the literacy programme appear satisfied and the literacy group leaders are hard-working and well motivated. However, in the documentation department the project co-ordinator observes a lack of progress: reports are frequently late and lack essential information, statistics are not up to date, and the work is not systematically documented. By identifying the lack of progress in the documentation department, the literacy project coordinator has identified a performance gap that will call for needs assessment to determine the reasons for lack of progress.

Alternatively, needs may be identified as problems via complaints from other colleagues or participants, or in the form of frustrations experienced by those carrying out the work. For example, an adult learner group complains that it is not achieving the expected results given the amount of time and materials invested in their home-based care project for HIV/AIDS patients. A constructive analysis of the problem will often uncover educational, training, or development needs.

The impact of a specific incident or activity

Incidents or activities sometimes occur in an educational organisation that reveal a need not immediately apparent. Often the crisis is dealt with but the underlying causes are not addressed, leaving the possibility for the incident to reoccur in the future. For example, a mysterious health problem affecting the lives of children in the community could form a need for health education, environmental education and mandatory sanitation practices.

Ongoing monitoring of performance

Many organisations, especially non-government organisations (NGOs), use methods such as surveys, data collection and analysis and regular meetings with individual workers to monitor programme progression. Information gained in this way can be used to identify needs in the organisation. An example would be a project aimed at training traditional birth attendants in practices designed to reduce mother-to-child transmission of the AIDS virus during birth. Although specific training has been given to the attendants, infection and mortality rates are still increasing. Monitoring of project performance in this case may lead to the identification of a need.

Forward-planning processes

The aim of a programme developer in working with communities is to bring about change for the better. As both external and internal changes are experienced in the programme environment, the opportunity arises for doing new things and/or doing the same things differently. Good programme developers will capitalise on these opportunities to improve the participants' abilities and maximise their potentials. The following situations, for example, present opportunities for the programme developer to take advantage of in needs identification:

- Learners are now expected to type their assignments using new computer software.
- Learners are now required to read the daily papers for government information, which they previously accessed via the radio.
- Learners are now required to withdraw money using the Automatic Teller Machine (ATM) rather than over the counter.
- Some learners feel they should be performing a specific task to a standard but they are not yet able to do so, meaning their effort to progress is falling behind the standard.

Being able to identify a gap should prompt the programme developer into taking the decision to conduct a needs assessment. Actions taken on limited information about needs and without systematic assessment of them could lead to actions that are flawed. In the next section, some of the approaches used for systematic needs assessment are looked at.

ACTIVITY

Imagine yourself to be a Literacy Group Leader in your community. List five examples of learning gaps that are likely to occur in the community where changes are occurring, problems are being experienced, and the adults' potential is not being realised.

CASE STUDY: BAYAMA'S EMPTY HOUSES

At the end of ten years of rebel war in Sierra Leone, the national government and the international community saw the need for rural reconstruction and rehabilitation. One aspect of this included building houses for those who had suffered, with the aim of providing them with a new start in life. In the village of Bayama in the Kailahun District, about 14 houses were built for the community during 2005. One year after construction was completed none of the houses were occupied.

When Matthew Gboku (the co-author of this book) visited the village in September of 2006, he talked with the Section Chief Mr Sewa, who is an influential political figure in the community. When Gboku asked Mr Sewa to explain why the people in the village were unwilling to occupy the houses, the following reasons were given: (i) The people did not experience individual ownership over the houses and strongly felt that it was an embarrassment to live in houses that they had not themselves put up. (ii) Since the local leadership was the custodian of the houses, community members felt a sense of insecurity knowing that, for political reasons, they could be ejected from the houses at any time. (iii) Before the war started in 1991, the village community was divided into sections. Each section belonged to an extended family, where every member of that family had access and control of land.

The reconstruction and rehabilitation project did not take this aspect of people's lives into consideration. Consequently, people did not believe that they should abandon their ancestral lands in order to live with rival families in a part of the village where they would not normally choose to reside. (iv) The people are proud and are hardworking. Competing to build their own homes earned villagers the respect of their community, which would not apply if they decided to live like a refugee in a government-sponsored house.

ACTIVITY

Study the case study presented above then answer the following questions:

1 Do you think members of the Bayama village were involved in the needs-identification stage of the housing project?
2 Which of the African ways of thinking or philosophy could best explain the behaviour of the villagers in not occupying the houses?
3 What would you do differently to ensure the success of the housing project, that is, to get villagers to live in the houses?

NEEDS ASSESSMENT APPROACHES AND MODELS

One aspect of education practice that most sharply differentiates the adult learner from the child learner is the role of the learner in planning and executing the learning process. In children, the responsibility for planning is assigned almost exclusively to an authority figure such as a teacher, or programme developer. This practice, according to Knowles (1978), is in conflict with the adult learner's need to be self-directing, which is a cardinal principle of andragogy (the art or science of teaching adults). In adult education programme development, ways must be provided for involving all the stakeholders in developing and planning learning content, methods and assessment procedures. This is in accordance with the basic discoveries of applied behavioural science research, which suggests that people feel committed to a decision or activity in direct proportion to their participation in or influence on its planning and decision-making. For further reading on the concept of adult learning, you are referred to the *Psychology of Adult Learning in Africa* by Fasokun, Katahoire and Oduaran (2004).

Adult learning is concerned with changes in information, knowledge, skills, appreciation and attitudes, which adults require to solve personal and community problems. To the developer of adult education programmes, therefore, these competencies that adults strive for are important in developing an educational programme for them. Consequently, the starting point for adult learning is what the individual adult learner wants to be able to achieve, the level at which the learner wants to perform, the learner's perception of what he or she wants to ultimately become, and how all of these relate to the community where the learner lives.

The programme developer cannot and should not avoid involving the learner in the diagnosis of learning needs. By involving the adult learners in determining their own learning needs, the programme developer will be able to know about the abilities and skills desired by the learners. Involving the learner does not, however, suggest that the professional responsibility of the programme developer as a facilitator is dismissed. Because the desired skills and abilities may sometimes be unknown to the learners, especially in a new learning situation, the programme developer still

has a vital role to perform. Therefore, the programme developer is responsible for integrating the learner's understanding of skills with the desired skills as understood by the organisation sponsoring the programme.

Using the data from the three sources of learner, programme developer, and sponsoring organisation provides a solid base for identifying and prioritising the learning needs of adult learners. Below are some of the approaches commonly used for assessing learning needs in adult education programmes. Detailed discussions are limited to these approaches because the authors view them as the most appropriate in an African context. The approaches include:

- the survey;
- the participatory;
- the key informant;
- the critical incident;
- the community forum;
- social indicators; and
- informal conversations.

The survey approach

A survey is a popular method of determining the needs of adult learners. Survey methodology investigates populations by selecting samples to analyse and discovers the percentage distribution of subjects on particular characteristics such as education, income, family size and age. It is also used to collect facts and to assess knowledge, beliefs, interests, opinions, attitudes, practices, performance, aspirations and resource availability in order to resolve problems or to meet needs.

The two main techniques commonly used for collecting survey data are the questionnaire and an interview schedule. The difference between these two data-collection techniques is that with the questionnaire, a set of questions posed by the needs assessor is answered without questioner-and-respondent interaction. Interviews, on the other hand, involve face-to-face interaction or telephone interviews. Many of the steps taken in conducting an interview are essentially the same as those for conducting a questionnaire survey. The number of steps for an interview survey can vary from one research situation to another. Borg and Gull (1989) have developed seven steps; Steward and Cash (1982) suggest ten steps, while the Central Statistics Office of Botswana recommends eight steps (CSO, 1982).

For an effective interview survey, an adapted and consolidated list of steps from these three sources should include: (i) defining the purpose and objectives of the survey; (ii) reviewing the relevant literature; (iii) selecting a sample; (iv) structuring the interview; (v) developing and writing interview questions; (vi) selecting and training interviewers; (vii) conducting a pre-testing of the interview guide; (viii) conducting the interview; (ix) coding and tabulating responses; and (x) analysing and interpreting results.

Interview and questionnaire surveys both have their strengths and weaknesses. We suggest you read *Research Methods for Adult Educators in Africa* by Chilisa and Preece (2005) in this series to learn more about the techniques of data collection.

In general, the use of a survey for needs assessment is recommended, because: (i) a considerable amount of information can be obtained from a large population or across numerous sub-populations; (ii) it is well suited to extensive needs assessment because, if properly resourced, larger samples can be surveyed; (iii) cross-sectional surveys provide data quickly. The major weakness of the survey approach to needs assessment is that it may be superficial and might not permit an in-depth analysis of phenomena or the relationships involved between them.

It is possible that survey designers either pay too much attention to selected components and lose sight of the overall system, or execute the survey using an undesirable sequence of operations. While some of the steps can be interchanged, others can only be performed following the completion of a particular task. For example, formulating the purpose and objectives can come before or after literature review, while conducting a pre-test and administration of the interview can only come after sample selection and training of interviewers.

The participatory approach

The participatory approach is essential in both problematic and non-problematic situations. However, it is easier to apply in the latter situation where there is relative normalcy and cordial working relationships among families and communities. Conducting a needs-assessment exercise where conflict is recurrent as a result of tribal, ethnic or religious factions can cause difficulties. This is because during conflicts, traditional systems of support such as the family are disrupted and livelihood systems lost. In such a situation, it is important to start programmes with strategies that encourage the participants to identify, by themselves, appropriate resources and skills to rebuild their lives.

Because trust is lost during conflicts, it is essential for the programme developer to conduct needs assessment in an open and equitable fashion between the groups, in order to avoid aggravating the conflict. The participatory needs-assessment approach relies heavily on the participation of all those associated with the educational programme (including the programme development staff, representatives of the sponsoring organisation(s) and the participants) in providing relevant inputs or suggestions throughout the needs-assessment process.

The general rule for participatory needs assessment is that all parties involved in the programme development process should be consulted. Potential programme implementers, such as adult educators, trainers, mentors and community leaders should also be involved in the needs assessment. By seeking inputs from all stakeholders, the needs-assessment activities are more likely to address relevant problems and issues and to provide practical solutions based on the needs of potential learners. An open assessment of needs with the learners allows the programme developer, the learners and other stakeholders to obtain and share information about and with each other within the programme environment or community. This enables the stakeholders to reach consensus on what action should be taken and which group's needs require prioritising.

In building the participatory needs-assessment approach introduced in this chapter, many ideas were drawn from the UNHCR's Framework for People Oriented Planning in Refugee Situations (International Institute for Environment and Development, 1998). The unique feature of the UNHCR's work here is that a use of the participatory approach in a refugee situation proved invaluable. Another source of ideas for developing the participatory needs assessment approach was taken from the *Strategic Extension Campaign: A participatory method of agricultural extension* (Adhikarya, 1994).

The participatory needs-assessment approach appears similar to other highly structured needs-assessment approaches, such as the already discussed survey approach and Caffarella's (2000) revised 11-step model. However, the participatory needs-assessment approach differs from these in several ways, including:

1 It emphasises the importance of involving programme participants in the design and implementation of the needs-assessment process, as well as consulting with them. It does not assume participants to be objects of the development process but views them as subjects who possess intrinsically important indigenous knowledge, values and belief systems that are essential to the development process.

2 It considers an individual's well-being at the household level as an integral part of broader community needs, rather than allowing individual needs to be subsumed by community concerns.

3 It uses a broad definition of resources, including those dealing with social protection and organisation of special groups, such as refugees and displaced persons. For example, topics discussed during interviews can include land, recent harvests, livestock, off-farm incomes, education, employment, local groups and social networks, water and sanitation, and illness and health care.

4 It is gender sensitive in its emphasis on differentiated access and control over resources and benefits for both men and women.

5 It empowers individuals and communities through training in participatory processes and activities.

6 It applies bottom-up and participatory procedures, which afford a high priority to meeting the interests and needs of the programme participants.

Elements of the participatory needs-assessment approach

The elements of the participatory needs assessment approach are partly derived from the Participatory Rural Appraisal (PRA). The PRA is a multi-faceted, community-based data gathering and resource

mobilisation technique, which evolved out of the concern of development workers to surmount two major obstacles common to many underdeveloped countries. The obstacles were:
(a) an insufficiency in the kind of data deemed necessary for conventional planning purposes; and (b) insufficient government resources, including human and material, to meet the services and need requirements of many communities. These two obstacles demand that if change is to take place, then communities need to take a significant part in their own development.

PRA is preferred to other methods of needs assessment among the methods described in this chapter because it is participant-centred, which is a principle of central importance to the authors of this book. For a more detailed explanation of the PRA methodology, we recommend you read the *Research Methods for Adult Educators in Africa* book in this series, by Chilisa and Preece (2005). The main elements of the participatory needs assessment are:

1 initiating and planning the needs-assessment process;
2 designing the purpose and outcomes of the needs assessment;
3 identifying targets for the needs assessment;
4 identifying resources for the needs assessment;
5 training target groups in participatory data gathering, analysis and interpretation;
6 selecting participatory data-collection techniques;
7 collecting and analysing data;
8 sorting out and prioritising needs;
9 reporting findings of needs assessment; and
10 planning the use of findings.

As a result of the numerous techniques used in participatory data collection, an elaboration of this element is considered necessary at this point.

Selecting participatory data-collection techniques

Data-collection tools that have proved useful in PRA include semi-structured interviews, diagrams, maps, transects, historical profiles, calendars, ranking techniques, use of photographs, and gathering of data from secondary sources. While a brief explanation of each of the tools follows, not all of them may have equal relevance for all situations of data gathering and resource mobilisation. The programme developer must carefully select those tools that are most useful for the specific objectives of the needs assessment.

Semi-structured interviews
Instead of formal, pre-prepared questions, semi-structured interviews use a checklist to guide the interviewers through the topics under consideration. The interviewer formulates questions as the interview unfolds. Since this requires fast-thinking on the part of the interviewer, this technique may prove difficult, especially for first-time users. In any given interview, the interviewer may not be able to cover all the topics and items on the checklist. Consequently, the programme developer must decide which topics and issues to focus on, depending on their relative importance to the interviewee.

Once an interview begins on a certain topic, the interviewer can develop the issue by asking further incisive questions in an effort to deepen his or her understanding. This requires the interviewer to remain alert, listen carefully, and to formulate successive questions rapidly. For example, if your checklist says: 'Find out about previous adult education programmes in the community', you can probe further by asking questions about:

1 the threat of rivalry from other community projects;
2 the impact of the programme on the lives of community residents;
3 any major problems encountered during implementation;
4 what skills or resources people possess in community; and
5 the level of community involvement in determining programme content.

To the interviewee, the semi-structured interview should seem like an informal conversation, with one topic leading naturally into another. To the interviewer, there are unlimited sub-topics that could be pursued, with each probing question linked to dozens of sub-questions. It is up to the needs-assessment team to focus on the issues that are relevant to their study.

Diagrams and maps
Diagrams include a variety of pictorial representations used to generate and analyse information. Diagrams are used to clarify abstract discussions and often provoke discussion and increase learner participation. A Venn diagram (that is, a diagram that uses circles to represent data sets and their relationships), for example, is a way of exploring organisational issues and a village community's linkages with outside organisations.

Maps introduce participants to the general spatial layout of an area and can enhance their perception and understanding of their surroundings. For example, a map may attempt to answer questions related to territory and land-holding issues. Questions to ask during this map-drawing exercise include:

1 Where are the land boundaries of the community being studied?
2 Are there any areas that are shared with other villages? What villages have

adjacent territories? What is the relationship with those villages?
3 Within the territory, what are the different important landmarks (for example, hospital, church, school)?
4 Who is the holder of the land? Who actually uses the land? What is the relationship between ownership and use of land?
5 What activities take place on the different parcels of land? Does this change by season or year?

Transects
A transect is a cross-section of an area of land showing patterns of use and various geographic features. Maps and transects provide complementary information. While the map gives a birds-eye view of the land or region, the transect offers a ground-level observation of the same area. Depending on the size of the area to be covered and the nature of the terrain, a transect can be done on foot, animal or cart, or in a motor vehicle. Slower forms of transportation are recommended because they allow for greater observation. A route is chosen that will travel across a variety of micro-ecological zones. As the participants walk along the chosen route, they must make a sketch of their observations and attempt to answer the following questions:

1 Where does the group cross into different micro-ecological zones?
2 Are there different land uses in different micro-ecological zones?
3 What is the significance of any fences or boundaries that are observed? Are there more fences in some areas than others? Why?
4 Do people plant trees; protect trees; participate in adult education programmes?
5 Where do people go for adult education? Do both men and women participate? Does the level of participation in adult

education programmes vary at different times of the year?

Historical profiles

These are timelines that show not just what happens over one year, but what the important events in the life of the village or area have been. Figure 5.1 provides an example of such a profile.

1500	The village founded and first water point identified
Early 1600s	Reign of terror by chief Dudu II
Mid 1600s	Islam introduced
1903–1904	Drought and hunger period
1932	Mosque built in the village
1937–1943	Locust invasion resulting in period of great hunger
1952	Fire disaster burned the whole village
1962	Market place established
1963	The first extension officer posted to the village
1967	Community hall built in the village
1972	Literacy classes began with ten participants
1980	HIV/AIDS campaign started by the District Health Officer
1985	First adult education trade fair held in the District

Figure 5.1 An historical profile of a village.

Calendars

Just as maps give clues to the geographic characteristics of an area, calendars help to understand changes that take place over the course of a year. Anything that has a temporal dimension can be represented on a calendar. Calendars can be either seasonal or labour-oriented, or a combination of seasonal and labour. Questions to ask while drawing a calendar include:

1   What adult education programmes exist in the community? What is the yearly schedule of learning activities in each programme?
2   Apart from adult educational activities, what economic, social and cultural activities are performed? When are the different crops grown?
3   What is the importance of crop products to household consumption or for resale purposes?
4   What is the relationship between economic activities and participation in adult education programmes?

Answers to these questions must be provided by the participants, who note down the various activities occurring each month.

Ranking techniques

These include preference ranking, wealth ranking, problem ranking, and well-being ranking. The importance of ranking lies in the fact that there is no need to have absolute figures for certain items of information. For many purposes, relative rankings are just as useful. Thus, wealth ranking enables you to get a wealth profile of the village by indicating who the richer or poorer people are, without necessarily stating in absolute terms how much anybody has. Ranking is useful in adult education programme development because it makes it easy to identify the priority needs of the community that require immediate solutions.

Photographs

Photographs are very effective in provoking discussions or people's reactions to a certain situation. Aerial photographs, for example, can be used with local people to assess various environmental and geographic features in their surroundings. Snapshots, on the other hand, can be used to record and compare different situations over time and can help in stimulating discussions on possible options open to the community.

Secondary sources

Secondary source materials include any publications written by someone who was not a direct observer of or participant in the events described. Examples of secondary sources include textbooks and encyclopedias. Secondary sources are useful because they often combine knowledge from many primary sources within a single publication. Reading secondary sources helps the programme developer to develop a thorough understanding and insight into previous work and the trends that have emerged.

The key informant approach

The key informant approach uses information from selected community members and experts in the field of adult education to provide social, economic, cultural and political data in response to questions raised by the programme developer. The key informants help to identify problems and needs and the resources required for developing and implementing an adult education programme.

The key informants should be stakeholders in the adult education programme but may not necessarily be potential beneficiaries of the programme. The use of the key informant approach is based on two conditions. Firstly, the informants used to provide the needs-assessment data are considered to be knowledgeable about the needs of the potential adult learners. Secondly, the needs identified by the key informants must match the felt needs of the potential adult learners.

The discrepancy between the needs identified by the key informants and the felt needs of the programme participants forms the basis for selecting content and developing teaching and learning materials. If key informants identify needs that do not match the perceived needs of the participants, this may lead to a lower rate of participation in the proposed programme. For example, a

key informant may identify skills training in reading and writing as a need for the participants of an adult education programme. However, from the participants' perspective knowledge about water and environmental pollution is considered a more pressing need than acquiring literacy skills.

The critical incident approach

This approach is used for developing educational programmes for adult learners undertaking specific jobs or professions. Although the approach is usually used to identify the competencies of a profession or for quality assurance purposes, it can also be used on an individual basis to identify learning needs.

The approach involves individuals identifying and recording, for example, one incident each week where they feel they should have performed better. The individual analyses the incident in its setting, noting down exactly what occurred, the outcome, and why the incident proved ineffective. For example, a bookkeeper of a community co-operative store is unable to inform the shareholders on whether the business is making profit or a loss. The critical incident here is that the bookkeeper does not know how to save typed information on the computer.

Rather than depending on opinions and guesses, the critical incident approach relies on the recording of specific behaviours by those in the best position to make the necessary observations and evaluations. Analysis and tabulation of observations may help in determining the critical requirements of an activity. These critical requirements or behaviours will then provide the basis for making reasonable conclusions regarding aptitudes, training content and other requirements for a programme based on the data collected.

The community forum approach

The community forum approach involves the process of gathering the perceptions of targeted individuals or groups in a community or organisation. The forum should be structured to allow each of the participants to provide input regarding their perceptions of needs relating to a particular programme, problem or issue. For example, some members of a community may regard the problem of a high infant mortality rate in their community as a need for medical facilities, while others may see it as a need for food and nutrition. Yet other people may see it as a need for education of parents in pre-natal and ante-natal childcare.

The community forum approach is particularly useful in promoting a free-flowing discussion that has the potential to produce the most accurate picture of the felt needs of the target audience. However, without an effective moderator, the forum structure may also result in a chaotic discussion that does not produce the information needed to guide the planning process effectively.

Another point worth noting concerns the logistical difficulties involved in getting people together to discuss and debate their shared needs and concerns. However, every effort must be made to overcome such barriers by carefully considering the following factors:

1 determining when and where to hold the meeting;
2 ensuring accessibility of the venue to all members of the target audience;
3 having multiple meetings at various times during the day and week;
4 providing childcare;
5 notifying programme participants of the community forum date, time, location and purpose;
6 providing transportation for people who want to attend but don't have or can't access transport;

7 selecting appropriate, accessible media for notifying people (for example, by using posted flyers in communities without television or radio);
8 assessing the receptivity of the potential participants. Acknowledging and respecting a community's cultural composition (language, beliefs, values, taboos, and so on) will help build trust between the programme developer and the community; and
9 ensuring that all participants can freely express their views without fear of retaliation or intimidation from people holding opposing views.

Social indicators approach

The social indicators model utilises secondary data sources in planning adult education programmes. Increasing access to information databases increases the opportunity to use secondary information sources in the needs-assessment process. The rapid growth of the Internet has also placed extraordinary volumes of information at our disposal. While the use of secondary data is recommended for needs assessment, users of this approach must exercise great caution. Without knowing the purpose, methods, audience and method of collection used to compile the database, it may be easy to misinterpret or misapply the information.

Using frequently collected statistics from government agencies such as the Ministries of Agriculture, Health or Education, may be helpful in explaining situational characteristics in a broader context. However, this should not be viewed as an adequate replacement for information collected directly from a more focused target audience.

Newspapers, magazines and newsletters may also offer sources of secondary information that can be used in the needs-assessment process. Again, you should recognise that the information presented in such documents could be biased or invalid in a specific situation. Secondary source information, though often factual in nature, is not generally considered as reliable as first-hand research data, which is guided by experience, observation or experiment.

Informal conversations

Informal conversations between the programme developer and programme participants occur regularly as the two parties go about their daily tasks. During informal conversations, ideas, problems and needs may emerge that are relevant to the programme development process. The programme developer must take the relevant ideas, problems and needs to other community members for verification, such as to the village head, head teacher, family health educator, members of the village development committee and local community business people. Common places for informal conversations are the church, village community hall during a meeting, school premises during a Parent Teacher Association (PTA) meeting, and around a water source where people come to collect water or do their laundry.

⊞ ACTIVITY

The table below lists the various needs assessment approaches we have considered in this chapter. Use the information gained in the preceding discussions to complete the table.

DETERMINING PROGRAMME PRIORITIES

Priority refers to the arrangement of learning needs in order of importance. Importance in this context will depend on a number of factors, including the resources required to satisfy the need, the magnitude of gap created by the need, the number of people affected by the need and how well the need fits into the organisational mission.

Adult education programmes in many African countries are faced with too many problems to work on, too much content to teach, and too many groups of learners to reach within the limited time and resources available. For example, in a single country there may be the need for adult education to provide the following programmes:

- adult education for adult beginners with no previous formal education;
- functional literacy courses, specifically designed to improve the specialised skills of a specific learner group (for example, poultry or dairy farmers);
- adult education for people with disabilities;
- adult education for people in employment; and
- adult education for out-of-school youth who may require Standard Five or Seven equivalence, or Junior Certificate (Form three) or Senior Secondary School Certificate (Form five) equivalence.

Approach	Description	Strengths	Weaknesses
Survey			
Participatory			
Key informant			
Critical incident			
Community forum			
Social indicator			

Given the financial constraints placed upon African governments, priority setting must be an important component of the programme development process if the efficient use of limited resources is to be maximised.

Determining priority must also be a continuous process, present during all phases of programme development, including needs identification, goals specification, adult learners identification, resource availability assessment, and action planning. Once needs identification has been carried out, there may be more needs identified that can be acted upon. Prioritising needs permits them to be tackled systematically; it also lets people know when their specific concerns will be addressed. As noted by Compton (1984), the problems of any human group are usually numerous, and it is impossible to concentrate on solving all of them at the same time. This implies concentrating on more important needs first and dealing with relatively less important or ill-defined needs at a later time.

A common mistake for a programme developer to make is to assume that resources will be available to address all needs and problems. Sork (1998) cautions that such an assumption is not only naïve but also dangerous, because resource allocation is always constrained and people's expectations differ regarding the choice of programme and the anticipated outcomes.

Prioritising needs is important because it helps the programme developer address those that are important to both the potential adult learners and the sponsoring organisation. From an economic perspective, needs are unlimited while the means to satisfy them are limited. The needs, according to Sork, present competing claims on limited education resources.

Approaches to priority setting

There are several ways of determining programme priorities. Caffarella (1994) proposes a four-step process of determining priorities that consists of: (i) identifying the people who should be involved in setting priorities; (ii) selecting or developing appropriate criteria; (iii) recording the ideas, along with criteria, on a priority rating chart and assigning weighting factors to each criterion; and (iv) applying each criterion to each idea using the priority rating chart.

Nobody should be prevented from participating in priority setting, as all stakeholders have the potential to make a contribution. People commonly considered central to the priority setting process include content experts, past and current participants, paid or volunteer staff members, supervisors of potential participants, key management personnel, colleagues from different divisions of the organisations, education committee and board members, representatives of sponsoring organisations, community leaders, consultants, and legislative leaders (Caffarella, 2000). From an African perspective, people can be selected from subgroups within a community that have various needs, resources and priorities. For example, individuals may come from subgroups such as the elderly, low-income families, business people, a youth group, the village development committee, and a farmers' association.

The critical step or task in priority setting is establishing the criteria on which decisions are made (Sork, 1998). The two main criteria to consider are the importance of the need and the feasibility of meeting the need. What follows is an appraisal of these criteria.

Importance of the need

The importance criterion focuses on answering the question, 'How important is the need?' The factors involved in answering this question are, according to Baker (1984) and Sork (1998):

The relationship of the need to the organisational mission
Do the mission and objectives of the adult education organisation relate to the needs identified? If the answer to this question is yes, then the need is important and should be placed on the priority list. This criterion is relevant because, among the numerous needs articulated, there will be those that do not fit the organisational mission. Programme needs that do not correspond to the organisational mandate may not receive funding priority. For example, due to a high illiteracy rate in many African countries, the mission statements of adult education organisations emphasise the provision of reading, writing and computational skills to adult learners. Developers of adult education programmes must acknowledge the importance of the mission statement when identifying needs and formulating programme objectives.

Urgency of the need
It is evident that among the needs identified, some will need immediate attention while action on others can be delayed. The decision the programme developer needs to take is to identify those needs that require immediate action. This is important because delaying certain needs may result in more harm or new problems. For example, the need to learn about using a cell phone is not as urgent as the need to learn how to read and write. Delaying action on the provision of reading and writing skills will prolong the hardship of adults seeking these essential skills.

Magnitude of the gap created by a need
Earlier in this chapter, we defined a need as a gap or discrepancy between 'what is' and 'what should be'. The programme developer needs to use his or her judgment to determine whether the gap or discrepancy is large or small. Using these criteria, needs representing a large gap should be accorded higher priority than those presenting smaller gaps. For example: Miss Keletso needs to learn about communication skills to improve her present relationship with people in her job as a secretary and receptionist. Because Miss Keletso received no pre-service training for her job, the gap between what she is doing and what she ought to do is so wide that the need to train her is imperative.

Number of people affected by the need
The more people a need affects, the higher priority that need must be given. Acting to address a higher priority need means that many more people are likely to benefit from such action. The easiest way to know how many people are affected by a need is to calculate the proportion of people who have identified the need in a survey.

Sequence of the need relative to other needs
Many of the needs identified for a programme are interrelated, and dealing with one need may have a positive or negative effect on the size and relevance of the others. If responding to one particular need will increase the potential of addressing other needs, then such a need could be classified as high priority.

Feasibility of meeting the need

Determining feasibility criteria also depends on addressing a number of key factors, including:

Acceptance of change from 'what is' to 'what should be'

To ensure acceptance of change and commitment to it by the participants, the programme developer must involve them in identifying the needs. Resistance to change is a common human characteristic, but it can be overcome if people feel that their concerns will be listened to, discussed and acted upon.

Resource requirement and availability

The requirement for and availability of human and material resources are important criteria in prioritising a need. Sork (1998) suggests that where resource capability can potentially meet demand, or where few or no resources are required, the needs here would be given higher priority than needs for which the resource requirement is unlikely to be met.

The potential of change occurring in the planned direction

Not all needs are met by providing an education programme. Using this criterion, needs that are considered to have a greater potential of being met by a proposed educational programme are given higher priority. This possibility for change can be determined by assessing the perceptions of stakeholders. Where a community offers support to an identified need because it senses the possibility of success, it may be advisable to deal with this need without further delay.

▓ ACTIVITY

Below is a simplified example of how to use a Priority Rating Chart (PRC). Ask your classmates to act as different members of a village and for each person to rank their needs based on the following importance criteria scale.

Calculate the total for each need by multiplying the scale rank by the number of respondents (r) and dividing the sum by the number of people in the class (n).

Example: $(1 \times r) + (2 \times r) + (3 \times r) + (4 \times r) + (5 \times r)/n$.

Rank the needs based on the outcome of your scores, with the highest score ranked first and the smallest score ranked last.

Need	1	2	3	4	5	Total	Rank	Priority
1. Reading and writing								
2. Family planning								
3. Environmental health								
4. PMTCT education								
5. Water sanitation								
6. Food processing								
7. Food preservation								
8. Rain water harvest								
9. Driver education								
10. AIDS awareness								

Scale rank: 1 = Lowest importance; 2 = Low importance; 3 = Medium importance; 4 = High importance; 5 = Very high importance.

SUMMARY

Needs assessment is an important step in programme development. The process is a way of checking the perceptions of programme staff regarding needs and priorities; avoiding potential conflict and resistance; enhancing more participation and commitment from learners; determining people's skills, attitudes and knowledge; basing programmes on real needs rather than on symptoms or assumptions; seeking and recognising diversity of views and experiences; ensuring early ownership of programmes; and reaching agreement on needs-assessment findings. There are four main ways of identifying needs: (a) through a growing concern about performance of potential learners within the programme environment; (b) as a result of an activity or incident that attracts attention because of its impact; (c) through ongoing monitoring of performance; and (d) during forward planning processes.

There are a number of approaches and models used for conducting needs assessment. The approaches commonly used are the survey, participatory, key informant, critical incident, community forum, social indicators and informal conversations.

Prioritising identified needs helps the programme meet these needs in a systematic manner. The two main criteria commonly used in prioritising programme needs and objectives are the importance and feasibility criteria.

KEY POINTS

- Adult learners differ in their aspirations, attitudes, needs, levels of knowledge and skills, abilities and experiences. Therefore, the way to tackle problems differs greatly from one adult to another.
- While adult education programmes cannot address all of the needs of adult learners, needs assessment is an important first step in the development of adult education programmes.
- Adult educators must remain alert and anticipate when and where needs are likely to arise in a programme environment, so that all relevant stakeholders can be involved at an early stage in taking action to redress the situation.
- The critical element in the assessment of a need is the learner's perception of the gap the need creates between 'what is' and 'what should be'.
- Perceived gaps do not only reflect problems; they sometimes also represent positive opportunities to develop potential and build on strength. Both the problematic and positive nature of gaps must be addressed in the assessment of programme needs.

⊞ ACTIVITY

1 Consider the factors discussed under the importance and feasibility criteria and provide a practical example of each factor as it would apply to developing an adult education programme in your community.
2 Describe an approach that you would use in your community for prioritising programme needs and objectives.

FURTHER QUESTIONS

1 Why is needs assessment an important component of programme development?
2 Discuss three situations in which needs are likely to arise in an adult education programme environment.

3   Compare and contrast the survey and
    participatory approaches to assessing
    programme needs.

SUGGESTED READING

Adhikarya, R. 1994. *Strategic Extension
    Campaign: A participatory-oriented
    method of agricultural extension.* Rome:
    FAO of the United Nations.

Caffarella, R. S. 2000. *Planning programmes
    for adult learners: A practical guide for
    educators, trainers, and staff developers
    (2nd edition).* San Francisco: Jossey-Bass.

Central Statistics Office. 1982. *Guidelines for
    designing and executing small scale surveys
    in Botswana.* Gaborone: Ministry of
    Finance and Development Planning.

Hamilton, C., Kaudia, A. and Gibbon, D.
    1998. Participatory basic needs assess-
    ment with the internally displaced
    using well being ranking. In PLA Notes.
    Participation, Literacy and Empowerment.
    London: IIED.

Higgs, P., Vakalisa, N. C. G., Mda, T. V.
    and Assie-Lumumba, N. T. 2000. *African
    voices in education.* Ndabeni: The Rustica
    Press.

Chapter 6

Determining programme goals, objectives and content

OVERVIEW

A number of fundamental principles guide the content of this chapter. These principles argue for: (i) a relationship between programme development and African ways of thinking and doing; (ii) a relationship between programme goals, objectives and content on the one hand, and the practical realities of the African situation on the other; and (iii) involvement of the participants in the programme development process. The aim of this chapter is therefore to establish the practical application of these principles in the determination of programme goals, objectives and content in an African context. In order to achieve this aim, the learner-centred approach is used as the framework for discussing the process of determining goals, objectives and programme content.

In our discussions, programme participants adopt a central position in the decision-making process, which reflects our belief in ensuring programme relevance for adult learners. Due to the importance attached to the adult learner's role in determining programme goals, objectives and content, the chapter begins with an assessment of the learner-centred approach and examples of its application in Africa.

LEARNING OBJECTIVES

After reading this chapter, you should be able to:

1 Differentiate between programme goals and programme objectives.
2 Formulate programme goals and objectives based on the needs of participants.
3 Determine programme content using strategies that embrace African perspectives.
4 Identify the factors that are necessary in determining programme content.

dwennimmen

KEY TERMS

learner-centred approach   This refers to any approach to training or education that shifts the focus of learning responsibility from the trainer to the learner. The trainer in the learner-centred approach acts as a facilitator of the learning process, and not as an authority figure that transfers knowledge to the learners by way of instruction.

programme goals   These are statements concerning what should happen during the programme and what should result from it. They are guides for choosing resources, and techniques, and are essential to programme evaluation and improvement.

programme objectives   These are the intended learning outcomes. Unlike goals, objectives are specific, measurable, achievable, realistic and time-bound.

programme content   This refers to the specific tasks and activities that must be performed in order to achieve the outcomes specified in the objectives.

⊞ BEFORE YOU START

Think of a learning activity (for example, training course, workshop, conference) in your school, workplace, or community where you were a participant. Were you involved in programme development for this activity? What did the organisers of the learning activity intend to achieve? What were your own objectives? Did you achieve your objectives?

WHAT IS LEARNER-CENTRED ADULT EDUCATION?

The concept of learner-centred education emerged as an alternative to the traditional teacher-centred approach to adult education, which many practitioners considered authoritarian. Traditional teacher-centred approaches to adult education are based on the notion of transmitting a predetermined body of knowledge to a learner who is regarded as an object. Dissatisfaction with teacher-centred approaches resulted in adult education practitioners exploring ways of making teaching responsive to adult learners' needs and interests, as well as allowing learners to play a fuller, more active and participatory role in the day-to-day processes of teaching and learning.

The shift to a learner-centred approach to adult education is not the outcome of a single structured school of thought. Instead, the approach draws upon and has evolved out of a diversity of theories and grassroots experiences (including the work of Paulo Freire) participatory approaches, popular education, and empowerment-based approaches to development. All of these approaches condemn the traditional teacher-centred approach and see learning as a coming together of the learners and the teacher, which can be classified as 'partnership education'. This partnership involves a mutual relationship between the teacher and the learners, and the knowledge and experiences of the learners are considered invaluable.

The learner-centred approach draws heavily upon the theory of constructivism, with the assumption that effective learning occurs when learners are actively engaged in the construction of knowledge for themselves. Fardouly (1998), for example, views learners as both individuals and a social process. Learners are individuals because

they decide what they need to learn by setting personal learning goals and objectives for themselves. Learners are a social process because they set goals and objectives as a result of their own activities and interaction with others in society.

Constructivism focuses on the development of learners' understanding through exposure to the same materials for different purposes at different times, which facilitates the knowledge transfer process (Jonassen et al., 1995). Unless new knowledge becomes integrated with the learners' prior knowledge and understanding, the new knowledge remains isolated and cannot transfer readily to the new situations, and hence, cannot be used effectively in new tasks.

The teacher can assist learners in acquiring and integrating knowledge by using a number of strategies that have proved to be effective with learners of varying abilities. These strategies include library research, problem and case-based learning, assignments and projects, group works, discussions and fieldwork. From the perspective of constructivism, Wagner (1994) suggests that the goal of learner-centred education is to produce lifelong learners who have problem-solving abilities, and who can understand and be informed about their culture and society. In this situation, the learners are responsible for participating actively, positively and ethically within the learning and teaching environment. Adult educators would be responsible for providing the supportive structure for learner-centred learning. Educators would also be active in providing clear statements of curricula, assignment and assessment requirements, materials to support learning, and effective and timely feedback on learner progress and performance.

The humanistic theory also emphasises the personal and subjective feelings of learners and what each learner as a 'whole person' goes through during the learning process. Confidence building, creating an anxiety-free atmosphere for learning, and emphasising what learners know, rather than what they do not know, are the characteristics of the humanistic approach to adult education. The humanistic approach, therefore, highlights the importance of the learners' affective involvement in the learning process. Under this perspective, learner-centred education assumes that people learn and develop through experiences that involve the exercise of their autonomy, and develop their abilities to become autonomous learners through the very experiences of professing their autonomy.

Learner-centred education offers learners a learning context where they can select an area of interest and then select the available resources to satisfy their own particular learning needs and interests. The learner-centred approach is, therefore, an active and dynamic process where learners develop an understanding of taking responsibility for their own learning. As Muller (1998) points out, the learner-centred approach empowers the learner to take control of their learning as they take control of their destiny. Gibbs (1992) reiterates the importance of the learner in the learning process by defining learner-centred education as, 'an approach that gives greater autonomy and control to learners over choice of subject matter, learning methods and pace of study'.

Learner-centred education is a rationale that focuses on an individual learner's heredity, experiences, perspectives, background, talents, interests, capabilities and needs. It also focuses on the best available knowledge about learning and how it occurs, as well as the teaching processes that are most effective in promoting learner motivation.

The use of the learner-centred approach in Africa

The learner-centred approach is used for both the training and education of adults in Africa. Learner-centred training is described as a process that switches the focus of learning responsibility from the trainer to the learner. The trainer in the learner-centred approach acts as a facilitator of the learning process or a resource provider in the learning system (Ronan, 1994). The philosophy of involving adults in developing their educational programmes (the learner-centred approach) can be predicated on a number of assumptions, including the following (Imhabekhai, 1998; Ronan, 1994):

1 Adult learners are eager to take responsibility for their own learning.
2 Adult learners can, with minimal assistance, determine their own learning needs.
3 Adult learners will participate in learning events when they can see the relevance of it to their own development needs.
4 Adults have various useful experiences, which can help in developing realistic programmes for them.
5 Adults will have opportunities to express their needs and interests, which must be included in the programmes.
6 Adults and non-formal education programmes transcend teaching and learning activities. They include mobilisation and sensitisation of participants in programmes such as social welfare, community development, and environmental education.
7 Adults participate more in educational programmes if they are involved in the programme development process.

Based on the above characteristics of adult learners, the prospective learners in learner-centred education must themselves be represented in decision-making. Their representation helps to ensure that programmes are relevant to the intended beneficiaries. Including the participants in decision-making also encourages a sense of mutual responsibility and ownership, which is an essential requirement for programme sustainability. Experience with adult education programmes in a number of African countries indicates that the learner-centred approach works in Africa and does, in fact, provide several long-term benefits. The use of the learner-centred approach at the Malawi College of Accountancy in training financial managers at the certificate level produced the following results (Ronan, 1994):

1 The participants learned some valuable lessons about themselves and petitioned the college authorities to have the learner-centred methodology applied to all their courses.
2 The approach generated enormous enthusiasm for learning.
3 The participants took control of their learning and appreciated the freedom they were given to decide how learning should take place.
4 The confidence of the participants continued to increase as the sessions progressed.
5 There was a 'buzz' of excitement in the classroom.
6 Once participants realised that their own knowledge and experience were valuable learning resources, shared learning began.
7 The participants appreciated being treated as adults.

Several small-scale literacy programmes in West Africa illustrate the success of the learner-centred approach at the local level. In Cameroon, committees in each community took responsibility for mobilising support for their adult literacy programme and identifying the community's needs that would be served by it (Robinson, 1990). In Côte d'Ivoire, a bilingual literacy programme began with numeracy rather than reading and writing because that was the need identified by the learners (Burmeister, 1987). And in mother-tongue literacy projects in Ghana, people in each community took responsibility for all aspects of their programmes, from selecting teachers to preparing and distributing literature (Hampton, 1994).

In all of the above examples, projects were more likely to succeed when their objectives corresponded to the priorities of the poor, and where the intended programme participants were regularly consulted and involved in decision-making at all stages of the programme cycle. Although there was some evidence of success in programmes lacking this participation, the benefits derived in the target groups were unlikely to be sustained over the longer term without more direct involvement of the participants (Robinson, 1992).

Although the learner-centred approach can work in Africa, Ronan (1994) cautions that the approach does require a radical change in how the role of the teacher is perceived. In the past, highly structured, teacher-centered materials were needed to cater for the needs of adult learners because they depended to a great extent on teacher direction. However, if learners are capable of taking control of the learning process into their own hands, the focus should be shifted from teacher-centred to learner-centred and they (the learners) should be helped in this endeavour by the teacher acting as a facilitator (Hoven, 1999). The learner-centred approach involves change in teachers as well as learners for the learning experience to prove fully beneficial. Teachers have to commit themselves to a learning process that is interactive, creative and learner-centred and be convinced of the importance of their own continuing professional growth (Riel, 1992).

In a constructivist learner-centred environment, the teacher can no longer assume the traditional role of knowledge transmitter. Instead, he or she now has to act as a knowledge facilitator. The teacher has to be sensitive towards the process of learning and be willing to provide encouragement and help whenever this is needed by the learner. This new environment also requires extra input and programme development on the part of a teacher and he or she would be better served by thinking of teaching as the design of learning environments. The teacher has to consider carefully her or his part in each and every teaching-learning process in order to help the learners realise their learning objectives.

In designing learning experiences that emphasise learner-centredness, the teacher-facilitator will be expected to perform a range of important tasks, including:

- stimulating proactive, self-directed learning;
- making resource-based learning more flexible;
- enhancing learner motivation;
- providing opportunities for learning founded on collaboration, group or social approaches;
- providing individual enrichment;
- capitalising on situated and workplace learning opportunities;
- promoting learning situations that support constructivist orientation to knowledge acquisition; and
- stimulating self-awareness of learning processes and encouraging meta-cognitive activities.

▧ ACTIVITY

Consider the constructivist and humanistic theories outlined above. Then, in a small group discussion with some of your classmates, try to answer the following questions:

1 What are the main arguments of each of the two theories?
2 How do the theories support or relate to the learner-centred approach to adult education?
3 What aspects do the theories have in common?
4 What are the differences, if any, between the two theories?

DEVELOPING PROGRAMME GOALS

A programme's goals describe in general terms what the stakeholders hope will happen in the future as a result of the adult education programme. The goals are usually expressed in broad terms that include all issues of interest to the programme participants. These are the programme's intended long-term consequences for the learners, the community, the education system, and for the nation as a whole.

The goals describe an ideal future but should also be realistic, so that stakeholders will be encouraged as they see themselves making progress. Goals for learner-centred adult education programmes should be compatible with national policies and plans and also with the educational goals of the prospective learners (their reasons for wanting to join the adult education programme). In a community adult education programme for out-of-school or unemployed youth, for example, a goal formulated by the learners might be that they can acquire the knowledge, skills and motivation to find and keep gainful employment. An additional goal of the programme formulated by the programme's sponsors might be that the crime rate among the community's youth will be reduced.

The process of setting goals begins by seeking agreement among stakeholders at each level of implementation about why the programme is needed (the problems it is meant to solve) and achieving a consensus regarding the overall purpose it will serve. At national and sub-national levels, goal-setting might be the focus of early programme development sessions involving representatives of the different groups who will implement, manage and support the programme at that level, together with representatives of the prospective learners. At local level, a community's goals for an adult education programme might be formulated through formal meetings and informal discussions with the prospective learners, community leaders, and with local government agencies and NGOs. The different ideas of stakeholders at the national, sub-national and local levels are important in guiding the needs-assessment process. In the final analysis, the programme goals and objectives derived must be a true reflection of the needs and problems identified in the needs assessment.

During the needs-assessment phase of programme development, potential adult learners must be involved in problem identification and invited to list the most important challenges they face in their homes, workplace, extended family setting, and community. Since most African communities, homes, families and workplaces are plagued with problems, participants will generate a long list of problems, which will be classified into generic themes such as decision-making, community conflict, unemployment, labour disputes, illiteracy, environmental degradation, and disease. The learning goals must be designed around these themes. The focus of each learning goal will be on developing the relevant knowledge, skills and attitudes that could be applied in the participants' varied situations, which will lead to self-reliance, effectiveness, and an improved standard of living. Figure 6.1 provides examples of goal statements in several teaching-learning environments.

Goal Statements

I Provide preparation for the vocation of home economics for male and female adults.

II Help adult learners become competent in the fundamental skills of reading, writing and arithmetic.

III Prepare youth and adult learners to become qualified for further education and/or development.

IV Contribute to vegetable production abilities and the employability of urban adults in their dual role as homemaker and wage earner.

V Encourage interest in agriculture-related occupations.

Figure 6.1 Examples of goal statements.

If we study Figure 6.1 we can see that, unlike objectives, goal statements are not measurable and cannot provide a basis for evaluation, even if they do provide direction for an adult education programme. Although the development of knowledge, skills and attitudes is central to the formulation of goals, goals do not specify how the relevant knowledge, skills, and attitudes will be achieved or measured. Consequently, it is difficult to determine from goals when and how the learners have fulfilled the intended learning outcomes of an adult education programme. In the next section, we will discuss the formulation of objectives, which describe the specific actions needed to attain the programme goals.

DETERMINING PROGRAMME OBJECTIVES

Once the goals have been established, the immediate objectives of the programme will be formulated, based on the priority problems and needs of participants. Unlike the goals, which state the general purposes of the programme, the objectives refer to more narrowly focused targets of action. Objectives describe the specific targets that are to be reached within the period of time covered in the programme plan. They are the explicit statements on which the programme will be periodically assessed during the process of achieving the programme's long-term goals.

Objectives are flexible so that they can be adjusted if assessment reveals that they are unrealistic or that they are not serving their intended purpose(s). An objective for a community adult education programme for out-of-school youth might be, for example, to complete a reading programme that is equivalent to Standard Five in a regular school system, within the first two years. At sub-national level, an objective might state the number of adult men and women that will be trained in environmental sanitation practices within a specific time period. A national level objective might list several districts in which a certain number of adults will be trained in poultry production as a component of an income-generating project.

Whether programme development takes place at a national, sub-national, or local level, the process of formulating objectives requires knowledge of the resources and activities needed for programme sustainability, as well as an awareness of currently available resources and the activities that are already taking place. To achieve this, programme participants should become involved, as they have better knowledge of the resources and ongoing activities in their own communities, as well as their current preferences and needs.

Importance of programme objectives

The statement of programme objectives in an explicit manner is important for a number of reasons, as identified by various authors (Mager, 1984; Boyle, 1981; Newcomb, McCracken and Warmbrod, 1993). By stating your programme objectives in clear and specific terms:

1 They provide a sound basis for the selection or designing of learning materials, content, and methods of delivering content.
2 They provide a basis for evaluating or assessing the success of the learners.
3 They provide a basis for organising the learners' own efforts and activities for the accomplishment of learning activities.
4 They permit the learners to know precisely what performance is expected of them and to what degree it must be demonstrated.
5 They contribute to the achievement of programme goals.
6 The programme developer and stakeholders will know exactly what they are trying to achieve and the reasons for doing so.
7 The programme developers will be able to estimate the scope of the programme and the required resources in a more accurate manner.
8 The goals can become measurable in terms of time, cost and quality.
9 It is possible to judge whether the goals are realistic and achievable.
10 It enables those involved in the programme development to estimate when the programme goals should be accomplished.

11 There is better understanding of the learners' roles and how they contribute to the accomplishment of programme objectives.

▩ ACTIVITY

1 **Why is it important to formulate objectives in programme development?**
2 **How would you differentiate programme goals from programme objectives?**

Characteristics of programme objectives

For an adult education programme to produce the desired results, the objectives must conform to certain characteristics, including:

Alignment with organisational goals and objectives

Developers of adult education programmes do not operate in isolation, but rather develop the programme within the context of a providing or sponsoring organisation. Programme development is done on behalf of these organisations and it is the responsibility of the programme developer to align the programme objectives with the philosophy and goals of the providing and/or sponsoring organisation.

Objectives should be flexible

Flexibility means programme objectives can be reviewed and modified to suit prevailing conditions, especially if the conditions specified in some objectives have changed. For example, an objective could be to train 20 adult learners how to use the Internet, using 20 computers to be purchased by the Department of Non-Formal Education. In this example, the objective can simply be reformulated if the condition of purchasing computers could not be met. The flexibility specification is important for programme objectives influenced by external factors, such as the availability of materials from a donor agency, and natural factors such as rainfall levels, where in both cases the programme developer has little or no control.

Objectives should be specific

The objective must focus on a specific area and be clear and precise. General statements should be replaced with specific targets for performance. Specific objectives must specify what is to be accomplished, how much, over what period of time, for which group of people, and the expected results. The difficulty of setting specific objectives appears to be a fairly common problem when programme developers fail to specify these indicators. It is only when these indicators or benchmarks are established that the programme can be adequately planned, implemented and evaluated.

Objectives should be measurable

Measurability means that the objectives can be objectively evaluated in terms of quality, quantity, cost, time, and a defined end product. The objective must be measurable so the learners know when they have achieved it. Secondly, measurability of objectives facilitates control of standards for outcomes. Some measuring standards may be quantitative, while others may be qualitative. Both quantitative and qualitative measures can be used to address the same objective. In fact, multiple measures are often necessary to provide adequate indicators of a successful outcome.

Objectives should be attainable

Based on the current situation, challenges, and available resources, the objectives must be do-able and provide a meaningful level of engagement and challenge for the learners, as well as the programme developer.

Objectives should be realistic

Failure to be realistic about what is to be achieved is another common problem in programme development. Unrealistic objectives, which set out to achieve a high level of change over too short a time period, can result in a programme being deemed a failure when the objectives are not met. For example, an adult education programme that sets an objective of having a 100% literacy rate in a two-year period is unrealistic. An objective of reducing illiteracy by 20% or of increasing literacy by 40% over a five-year period would be far more realistic.

Objectives should be consistent

In Chapter 2 we talked about the beliefs and values of the programme developer as well as those of the learners as important elements in programme development. An adult educator is more likely to pursue programme goals that are consistent with his or her beliefs and values. Similarly, when the programme developer takes the needs, values and beliefs of learners into consideration, the learners will give approval to the programme and remain committed to the attainment of goals. To ensure acceptability of progammes, therefore, the objectives must be consistent with the needs, beliefs and values of all stakeholders, especially the adult learners.

Objectives should relevant

Relevance has two components: (i) linkage to the organisation's current strategic and operational priorities; and (ii) overall value of the contribution to programme or entire organisational goals.

Objectives should be congruent

If objectives are congruent this means that they co-exist without conflict or friction and are essentially compatible with one another. It also means that the attainment of one objective does not prevent the attainment of the other(s). For example, suppose that the objective of the Adult Basic Education Department is to increase enrolment to 5 000 adult literacy participants in 2007. However, the objective of the Department of Human Resources Management is to reduce the number of literacy group leaders by 25% in 2007. In this scenario it is likely that the attainment of the second objective will prevent the attainment of the first objective. Effective programme developers will avoid the formulation of incongruent goals such as these.

Objectives should be time-bound

An objective must have a beginning and a proposed end. The end can be adjusted as situations within the organisation change. Making an objective time-bound allows the stakeholders to report on the progress that is being made in achieving the objectives.

⊞ ACTIVITY

1 Discuss the characteristics of programme objectives with some members of your class.
2 Write down examples of programme objectives and determine whether the

characteristics you have discussed are included in the objectives.

FORMULATING PROGRAMME GOALS AND OBJECTIVES

In formulating programme goals and objectives, it is important to understand the ideological context of programme development within which the adult education organisation operates. There are three possible options for formulating programme goals and objectives, depending on the socio-political orientation of a particular group.

The first option relates to the situation where the programme developers wish to expand services on behalf of government but do not wish to give new powers and status to the participants. For example, in an immunisation health programme the ideas are developed in the best interests of the public, and then delivered. People's participation in goals and objectives formulation in this scenario is largely irrelevant. The second option relates to programme development performed on behalf of the government with the programme developers seeking to effect gradual socio-economic change. For example, a consultant acting on behalf of government may or may not involve local participation and interest. The third option calls for the programme developer to be an outsider, and not someone working within government structures.

The process of preparing programme goals and objectives requires the programme developer and the participants to think through what is to be taught or done by participants, the resources required to achieve programme objectives, and the end product expected. Representing the interests of learners in programme goals and objectives can take several forms, including the following:

1 representation in goal setting;
2 consultation;
3 community tours and meetings; and
4 opinion surveys.

Representation in goal setting

This method involves the selection of a number of people who represent the interests and aspirations of various segments of the community. Examples of groups to be considered for representation are: youth, men, women, farmers, teachers, members of the clergy, the elderly, people with disabilities, and community leaders. All these groups have varying interests and aspirations, which are significant for inclusion in the adult education programme.

Consultation

Consultations for developing programme content can be formal or informal. In either case, the purposes of consultation are:

1 to check with the programme participants on the desirability of what is happening in the community regarding programme implementation. The feedback from participants can provide input into the preparation of ongoing and subsequent programmes;
2 to allow participants in the consultation process to disseminate important information on community affairs to other residents;
3 to increase initiative at a community level, encouraging people to demand action on urgent needs and concerns; and
4 to serve as a monitoring tool for activity implementation. Consultation can be used to answer questions such as, 'Are

the projects that were planned for the community progressing or are they behind schedule?'; 'What are the reasons behind the delay?', and so on.

Whether formal or informal, the main elements of the consultation process are:

1   assessing priorities and resources for developing programme goals and objectives;
2   providing information to people on what has been planned for implementation during the coming year;
3   monitoring and reassessing programme goals and objectives for possible modification and/or change based on new information emerging from the consultation process; and
4   increasing people's self-reliance so that they can take part in their own development rather than depending on government to do everything.

The timing of consultation is important. For the consultation to have an impact on the preparation of an adult education programme, it must be held before the programme is developed. This will give the programme developers and the programme participants time to analyse the data emerging from the consultation. Several methods of consultation have proved effective at various times and there is no single method that can be recommended for all situations. This is because every situation presents its own particular problems, needs and challenges relating to issues such as participant numbers, population density, remoteness of programme location, availability of staff, and access to material resources.

The main method of consultation is the consultation conference. This has been the traditional method of consulting people in Botswana, for instance, and has been used

by adult educators in many communities at one time or another. At a consultation conference, the selected representatives of programme participants are called together to discuss local problems and priority needs, and to make their input into the formulation of goals and objectives. At the conference one or more learning themes or topics (for example, HIV/AIDS and attitude/behaviour change; skills training in team work) can be discussed. The length of discussion, however, depends on how much time has been allocated for the conference. The results of the consultation exercise must be used immediately. People will very quickly grow disillusioned if they perceive that their efforts have no impact upon the development process. The information gathered in the consultation exercise should be relevant for use in plan evaluation and monitoring, and in terms of providing inputs into future programme development.

A major disadvantage with the conference method is that only a small number of people can be directly consulted. This shortcoming led to the development of the consultation conference plus follow-up method. The consultation conference plus follow-up method is basically the same as the method described above, except that a structured follow-up has been added. The steps involved are as follows:

1   Participants are supplied with materials at the conference. These materials become their reference documents once they have returned home.
2   Using the materials handed out at the conference, participants discuss these materials and complete a programme-development questionnaire on a village-by-village basis.
3   After completion of the questionnaire and a discussion session at the conference on the issues raised, participants and programme developers agree on dates to

hold village meetings. They also agree on when the completed questionnaire will be returned to programme developers.

4 Meetings are called in the village. This is where the rest of the village will be told about what happened at the conference and the programme development questionnaire is discussed.

5 The completed questionnaire is sent to programme developers in time for the data to be incorporated into the plan.

With this method, it is very important to set specific deadlines and to secure the participants' agreement on the action they will take. This is necessary because once the participants have dispersed it becomes more difficult to make sure that all the required steps are followed. To support this method of consultation, it is extremely important that the community members are well briefed on what they need to do. Their involvement is crucial.

Community tours and meetings

This method is only practicable in localities with a relatively small number of villages. It consists of programme developers and several community leaders touring the community and explaining the proposed programme plan, as well as listening to participants' reactions and recording their responses. This can be a time-consuming process, especially when there are many villages and there are lengthy travelling distances involved. A major advantage is that key community stakeholders get the opportunity to hear directly from the programme developers and the participants. Secondly, this method gives programme participants the opportunity to hear immediate, first-hand responses from the community stakeholders.

Opinion surveys

Surveys have already been discussed in Chapter 5 as a method for assessing learning needs. The same method can be used for canvassing participants' views on the development of programme goals, objectives and content. The guiding principle for the programme developer is to ask pertinent questions on the specific aspect of the programme (goals, objectives, content) that is being considered. As we mentioned in the previous chapter, *Research Methods for Adult Educators in Africa* by Chilisa and Preece (2005) is a recommended text on this subject.

CASE STUDY: PARTICIPATION IN ACTION

Although much work has been done in recent Agricultural Development Plans to integrate a concern for the specific problems of women farmers, the problem remains that agricultural sector planners and extension personnel rarely take rural women's needs into consideration. This means that agricultural training and services do not reach women, with serious repercussions for food security and agricultural development. In many cases, planners lack information about the important role that women play in agricultural production and household food security. But more often than not, they neither know how to learn from women farmers about their activities nor how to respond to their needs. To address this problem, the Women Farmer Development Division designed the project 'Improving Information on Women's Contribution to Agricultural Production for Gender Sensitive Planning' and launched it in the three pilot communities of Mamuto, Bubengu and Kebawana, in Botswana.

The aim of the project was to improve information on the situation of rural women and men and to involve them in local processes of planning in the agricultural sector. Participation was a key component of these projects and included involving rural people in information collection and planning processes. However, it was also necessary to train those people responsible for the planning and delivery of agricultural services in how to work in a participatory manner with women as well as men farmers.

The main thrust of the project was to involve men and women farmers in the three selected communities together with district level planners and agricultural outreach staff in a gender-sensitive planning exercise. To begin with, district level staff were trained in the use of gender analysis and participatory rural appraisal techniques to help them identify both women and men farmers' needs. The trainees then gained practical experience by performing gender-sensitive PRAs in designated villages, with the purpose of working together with the villagers to develop community action plans. Following the PRAs, community-level planning workshops provided an opportunity for the participants to present their findings and discuss their community action plans with district level planners. Based on the experience of these planning exercises in the three pilot communities, the Women Farmer Development Division developed guidelines for gender-sensitive planning at the district level. The project ended with a national level workshop to discuss these guidelines with policy makers and Ministry staff and to encourage their adoption into the overall planning process of the Ministry.

 **ACTIVITY**

Read the previous case study. Discuss how you would use it for representing the interests of community members in the formulation of goals and objectives of a similar project that you are in charge of planning.

SEQUENCING PROGRAMME OBJECTIVES

The sequencing of objectives within a programme contributes directly to participants' understanding of the organisation and structures the subject matter to be dealt with. How the educator goes about ordering the problem areas that have been identified and selected for implementation is important. It is also a process that is influenced by several factors, including the following:

1   Seasonality. Where there are distinct seasons (such as in West Africa, which has rainy and dry seasons) learning activities may have to be scheduled to coincide with a particular season, since the weather in the other season(s) would be unsuitable.
2   Logistics. Sequencing of objectives must be examined in light of logistical considerations within a particular educational organisation. Since sequencing often depends upon what may be available and when, the logistics of providing learning experiences becomes very important. Logistical considerations include availability of facilities, teaching staff and teaching equipment, travel arrangements, and seasonal variability.
3   Schedule of national events. The schedule of important national events, such as trade fairs, judging contests, skills contests, and annual adult education

conventions, should encourage the educator to integrate these events into the teaching calendar. Basing a teaching calendar on national events facilitates the learning experience by incorporating related, relevant activities that provide the opportunity for motivation and application.

4 Relationship of concepts. The purpose of sequencing objectives is to ensure that programme activities take place with each objective placed in logical relationship to the others. Determining the relationships between the objectives involves asking questions such as: 'Does the achievement of one objective depend on the completion of another objective?', and 'Which objectives are unrelated and independent?'

5 Practical experiences of the educator. The programme developer's practical experience is useful in sequencing, for example, simple to complex; theory to application; known to unknown; part to whole; concrete to abstract; familiar to remote; and closest to farthest tasks, as reflected in the objectives.

⊞ ACTIVITY

1 What are the differences between programme goals and programme objectives? Use examples to illustrate your answer.
2 Why is it important for a programme developer to develop a clear statement of objectives?
3 List any six features of good programme objectives.
4 What do you understand by sequencing of programme objectives?
5 Discuss any five factors that influence the sequencing of programme objectives.

DETERMINING PROGRAMME CONTENT

Once the programme objectives have been formulated, the next step is to break the programme down into the tasks that must be carried out to meet the objectives. A prerequisite of the learner-centred approach is that the learners should be given the opportunity to process information, solve problems and make decisions on their own. The knowledge in this process is not imparted to the learners but acquired by them through an open enquiry process (Blumenteld et al, 1991). In this regard, the content determination must be guided by a number of principles including, but not limited to, the following:

1 The programme content must be based on the needs of the learner rather than the needs of the teacher or the institution. Programme content must be flexible and also give the learner control over what, where, when and how to learn. In this way, the teacher is not a source of knowledge but a facilitator or manager of learning situations.
2 The programme content should encourage independent and critical thinking and provide the capacity to enquire, reason, weigh evidence in order to form judgments, and achieve understanding.
3 The focus of programme content should be on what the learner experiences in learning and not on the factors that comprise good content delivery on the part of the facilitator.
4 Subject matter included in the programme content must have relevance and meaning for the learner.
5 Programme content must allow for learner participation in order to effect educational change.

6 There must be a mutual relationship between the learner and the facilitator, where both parties share power over decision-making relating to the teaching-learning process.

7 Learners see themselves differently as a result of their learning experiences, in terms of their behaviour, attitudes, skills and knowledge.

8 Learners need to be aware of the concept of adult education and the specific educational issues the programme developer wishes to convey to them.

9 Learners' awareness of the environment and their relationship to it is also important, as well as the need for them to become more actively involved in seeking solutions to their own problems.

10 Because adults are different to children, the content for adult education programmes must conform to the following requirements:

- The selection and sequencing of content and materials must be determined by placing subject matter knowledge within the context of the learner's life, family, community, and society.
- The adult learning activities built into the programme content must be geared towards the achievement of programme goals.
- The anticipated results of the programme must be made clear to the learners in terms of expectations that participants would develop or acquire after the programme has been implemented.

Choosing the programme content

Choosing the educational content for most adult education programmes involves selecting content in the following areas:

Knowledge

Participants cannot take action without a basic understanding of natural processes as well as social, economic, and ecological realities. These will be an important component of any adult education programme. There is no point in teaching people about Prevention of Mother-to-Child Transmission (PMCT), for example, if they do not know the basics of HIV/AIDS. Basic infection and prevention information would be an important component of PMCT educational programmes. It will also be important for the programme developer to consider any existing indigenous knowledge systems (IKS) of participants in relation to the content negotiated.

Attitudes, values and beliefs

Programme development is not only concerned with visible learning content, it also pays attention to invisible learning content, such as the ways in which adults regard and value education and learning and the reasons why they learn something. Since culture determines what counts as educational knowledge, programme content must reflect the attitudes, alternative knowledge systems, beliefs and values regarded as important by potential participants.

Participants engaging in a learning programme about their environment will probably develop new attitudes towards their world and their place in it. This may be an attitude about leadership or responsibility or a political attitude. Whatever fits best in the local situation of participants will be discovered during the needs analysis and content determination stages.

Skills

There are many skills that are relevant to an adult education programme. In

Namibia, for instance, the learning needs of adults were anticipated in the Adult Basic Education (ABE) Curriculum Guidelines of June 1994. These guideline were translated by the Ministry of Education and Culture into programme goals with specific objectives, including: language and communication skills; numeracy and mathematics skills for application to everyday life; creative intellect, problem-solving, and rational analysis of issues; empowerment from personal development, self-esteem, self-reliance, and learning through life; positive attitudes, physical and mental health; social, cultural, and political development through application of democratic principles and practices including tolerance and gender equality; understanding Namibia's Constitution, promoting national unity, and international understanding; gaining vocational skills for income generation and employment; and developing environmental awareness (Namibia, 1996a, 1996b).

Factors to consider in determining programme content

Content determination is a way of controlling what and how people will learn and think. For example, the choice of what and how people will learn reinforces or promotes certain cultural beliefs, values and qualities. Because of this, all programme stakeholders must play a full part in the development of programme content, in order to avoid biases that may marginalise certain groups. For example, when left in the hands of professionals or providers alone, content determination can become politicised. This in turn can result in unwanted social inequalities, based on class, gender, race or culture being created or maintained.

Determining programme content therefore poses serious challenges. Two important challenges that the programme developer faces here are: (i) developing final programme content that participants can actually use in the programme environment to achieve specified goals and objectives; and (ii) identifying programme activities that are truly relevant to the adult education settings of participants.

The following paragraphs focus on these concerns by discussing the real-life factors that influence content determination.

Beneficiaries of programme content

The most important factor in determining relevant programme content for adult learners is the learners themselves. For adult education programmes, the programme developer must demonstrate great flexibility when deciding on content. Since adults come to the learning situation with different needs, integrating their needs into the teaching-learning process can be enhanced through participatory content development.

For example, many ethnic groups on the African continent, such as the Kissi of Sierra Leone, Liberia and Guinea, believe that if a pregnant woman eats eggs, her baby will develop a speech difficulty. Within the same tribe there are also ethnic groups that dictate people's behaviour. For instance, each family has an animal totem that they must not eat; if they do, it is believed that they will develop skin rashes. Violating this cultural taboo carries serious consequences.

While scientists and medical doctors have disproved some traditional beliefs of this nature, there is still the need for a programme developer to respect all taboos and beliefs. For example, in a nutrition programme for Kissi women, pregnant learners could be advised to substitute eggs with non-taboo food products of a similar nutritional value. The best approach for the programme developer of an adult education programme is to cater for all types of participants, including youths, mothers, fathers, fat and thin people, the elderly, pregnant women, and the sick; remembering to respect the cultural values of each group.

Educational philosophy

A philosophy reflects the beliefs, values and principles that govern the ways people behave. Though not in written form, many adult educators have a philosophy about adult learning and learners, adult teaching, and programme development in adult education. A properly developed philosophy guides the direction of local programmes. The educational philosophy of a programme developer, or that of the organisation he or she works for, will have a major influence on the determination of programme objectives and content selection. It is good practice to disclose this philosophy to the participants so that they can reconcile the programme developer's beliefs, values and aspirations with their own. You can refer to Chapter 1 for a more detailed discussion of philosophy within the context of adult education.

Expertise of the programme developer

Developers of adult education programmes must be knowledgeable in the theory and practice of adult education and must have previous experience in developing adult education programmes. Without these attributes, it is unlikely that they could successfully identify and select content that is relevant to programme participants of varying economic, social and educational needs. A programme developer with insufficient theoretical or practical knowledge will be less effective in providing leadership and direction to a team when determining programme content. Of course, a programme developer is entitled to fill gaps in his or her knowledge by consulting or utilising other sources, but only in areas where he or she could not reasonably be expected to have this knowledge.

Educational facilities and equipment

Adult skills and knowledge must be taught irrespective of the adequacy of facilities and equipment. When inadequate facilities and equipment do exist, the adult educator should still facilitate learning by using community resources, field trips, simulations and other methods that do not need sophisticated equipment. This is why it is essential for content developers to find out about the existing resources and constraints by involving participants in content determination.

Time, money and human resources

The entire process of programme development requires a significant number of resources. These resources include time, personnel to do the work, and money to pay for personnel, office space, stationery, secretarial services, postage, printing, and travel. Whether the programme developer is an outsider or an employee of the organisation sponsoring the programme development process, the common practice is that the process must be completed within specified time limits. In this context, the time available for developing content is only a portion of the total time required for overall programme development. And, because there are several activities competing for time during programme development, the effective use of this relatively scarce resource is an issue that the programme developer must address very carefully.

The amount of money put aside for the complete programme development process must also be divided amongst the different programme activities. The cost of determining programme content competes for funds with the other activities and against the budget constraints imposed by the funding organisation(s). Because money is arguably the scarcest of all resources, the programme developer must monitor development costs carefully and, where possible, try to secure resources that the community can provide for free.

Internal and external forces

During the course of content determination, the programme developer may encounter pressure from both within and outside the organisation sponsoring the programme development effort. Internal pressure comes from administrators, professional adult educators, literacy teachers, and learners. External pressure comes from employing organisations, professional business or trade associations, trade unions, advisory committees and politicians.

Individuals, groups and organisations with vested interests in the community may use their influence to try and contribute content to the programme that is not in the best interests of the intended beneficiaries. While it is difficult for the programme developer to determine whether contributions in this scenario are genuine or flawed, it remains his or her responsibility to assess the various information sources to establish the true worth of the proposed contributions. The programme developer's overriding concern is that all programme content is meaningful and relevant to his or her adult learners. With this in mind, the programme developer should adopt a careful approach, assessing contributions on their real merits and avoiding those that are poorly motivated.

Government and organisational requirements

Programme developers seldom determine instructional content alone. In numerous occupational areas specified content requirements serve as a basic framework for curricula. These requirements, possibly already established at a national level, tend to limit the extent to which a programme developer can become involved in the content determination process (Finch and Crunkilton, 1993). For example, in many adult-learning situations content has been established through national surveys of professionals working in the occupational field. Deviating from this established content or replacing it with new material will only be acceptable if legitimate reasons for doing so are supplied. Changes that cannot be justified, on the other hand, will be rejected.

There are many types of organisations that sponsor adult education programmes. In Africa, the most commonplace include government ministries, universities, parastatals, non-government organisations (NGOs) and community based organisations (CBOs). In addition to formal organisations such as these, a number of more informal groups, such as hobby clubs, support groups, book clubs, and community action committees, also provide educational programmes for their members (Caffarella, 2002). As with programme goals, the determination of instructional content is closely linked to the purpose and mission of the sponsoring organisation.

Skills needed by employing organisations

As already established in Chapter 2, the training and education offered in adult education institutions prepares adults for full personal development and participation in balanced and independent social, economic, and cultural life. In the determination of programme content, therefore, consideration must be given to future as well as current employer needs. This task is made easier through the use of the content determination strategies discussed in the next section. What is important here is that the determination of what employers need must form part of the content of the adult education programme.

⊞ ACTIVITY

1 Discuss the principles that guide content determination in adult education programmes.
2 Why is content determination an important phase of the programme development process?
3 What five factors would you take into consideration in the process of determining programme content for an adult education programme?

CONTENT DETERMINATION STRATEGIES

Professionals in adult education use a number of content determination strategies. Many of the strategies have proved useful in the situations where they were used and possess the potential to be used in other contexts. However, the commonly used strategies that have been successful are Eurocentric in nature and most have no relevance to the African context. Among the Eurocentric strategies are the Philosophical, Introspection, DACUM, Task Analysis, Critical Incident, and the Delphi techniques. Many of these strategies have in one way or the other proven to be useful in different educational situations. However, we cannot recommend them for adult education practice in adult education programmes in Africa for the following reasons:

1 The application of these strategies has been effective in vocational and technical education that focuses on specific aspects of an occupation. In applying the strategies to these fields, consideration was given to the three content areas of awareness of work, exploration of work, and preparation for work. The strategies may not necessarily be as useful for adult education programmes in Africa, particularly when the programme's purpose does not relate to occupational or career development, which is very often the case.
2 The strategies were developed to address problems within the context of modern, Western societies. The application of these strategies in Africa may not necessarily produce results similar to those achieved in a North American or European setting.
3 The strategies emphasise curriculum content for classroom instruction and the use of methods and materials that are not typical of adult learning in an African context.
4 The strategies rely heavily on expert knowledge. As a result, the strategies often preclude the poor and marginalised from participating in decision-making regarding programme goals, objectives and content.

In response to the above observations, we propose participatory strategies to content determination as a solution to the problems associated with existing techniques. This proposal forms the basis of the discussion that follows.

Alternative strategies for content determination

Alternative approaches to programme content determination, which are more participatory and learner-centred in nature, have been applied to teaching and learning in an African context. Two of these alternative strategies are now considered.

Workshop for content development

A workshop for content development should be participative and must follow the principle of 'learning by doing', where the participants learn about the theory and practice of content development before engaging in developing their own content. Although a workshop is a broadly democratic, non-doctrinaire environment, a considerable amount of expert work may have to be done before the arrival of the workshop participants on site (Bhola, 1999; UNESCO, 1993). The model of learner-centred content development will be explained to participants at both the theoretical and the practical level. This is preferably done on the first day of the workshop when introductions, team-building, and approval of objectives occur, and when processes and the products expected by the end of the workshop are explained. After this, the total workshop time remaining must be allocated to the practical work of developing learning content (Bhola, 1999).

The Freirean approach

The Freirean approach to content development is based on the doctrines and teachings of Paulo Freire. In Freire's view of education, learning to take control and achieve power is a group objective. For the poor and dispossessed, social change is accomplished through unity. Freire suggests that shared power in learning is exercised via control over the learning content, methods of delivery, and the manner in which the learning activities are coordinated. Education for liberation provides a forum open to the imaginations and free exercise of control by learners, teachers, and the community, while it also provides the skills and competencies development needed to make the exercise of power possible.

Empowerment is both the means and outcome of Freire's view of adult education.

This learner-centred approach to programme development encourages learners to develop a sense of responsibility towards their learning experience as early as possible. It means enhancing the participation of adult learners in formulating programme goals and objectives and in determining programme content. The programme developer acts as a facilitator, providing guidance and support to participants as they seek to meet specific learning goals. The varying educational backgrounds of learners, their work experiences, learning styles and present life situations all contribute towards the effective development of programme goals, objectives and content.

ACTIVITY

Discuss with several of your classmates the limitations of using a traditional Eurocentric approach towards content determination in an African teaching and learning situation.

SUMMARY

Adult education programme development requires defining the three important elements of goals, objectives, and content. Goals reflect the philosophy or mission of an organisation and provide a basis for developing the more detailed objectives. All stakeholders must agree on the goals and objectives to be achieved.

Once objectives are formulated, they are sequenced. The sequencing process is affected by a number of influential factors. Content determination is also influenced by several factors, including philosophy, expertise of programme developer, educational facilities and equipment, resources (time, money, human), internal and external forces, government and organisational requirements, skills needed by employing organisations, and beneficiaries of programme content.

A number of traditional approaches are used in determining programme content. A critical analysis of these approaches suggests a number of weaknesses regarding their application to adult education programmes in Africa. As a result, alternative approaches to content determination, based on the principle of full learner participation, are suggested for the African teaching and learning environment.

KEY POINTS

- Programme goals are general statements regarding the overall purpose and aims of an adult education programme. Programme objectives are more detailed descriptions of the specific action or actions needed to achieve agreed targets.
- Formulating goals and objectives is a process that involves all programme participants. The participants consider the aims of the teaching and learning process and the resources needed to achieve these aims.
- Determining programme content also involves all the stakeholders in the development process. In the learner-centred approach to adult education, programme content is based on the real-life needs of the learners.
- Many factors influence content determination, including the needs of the intended beneficiaries, the expertise of the programme developer, the prevailing

educational philosophy, the availability of resources, educational facilities, internal and external forces, government and organisational requirements, and the skills required by employers.

- Traditional content determination strategies focus strongly on the concept of 'teacher as expert' and pay little attention to the involvement of other programme participants.
- The learner-centred approach to content determination aims to share power among programme participants and promotes the ideal of learner empowerment.

⌗ ACTIVITY

1 Arrange a visit to two ongoing adult education programmes. During your visit, interview several programme participants about the role they played in determining and developing goals, objectives and content. Make a note of your own independent observations while you are on site.
2 Using your own knowledge, experiences, and the information obtained during the site visits, what content determination strategy would you say was used by the programme developers?

FURTHER QUESTIONS

1 What factors influence the sequencing of programme objectives?
2 What benefits are there for the adult learner who attends an education programme based on the Freirean approach to teaching and learning?

SUGGESTED READING

Bhola, H. S. 1999. Equivalent Curriculum Construction as Situated Discourse: A case in the context of adult education in Namibia. *Curriculum Inquiry, Vol. 29, No. 4.*

Centre for Adult and Continuing Education (CACE). 1988. What is People's Education?: An Approach to Running Workshops. *People's education research project working document No. 3.* Cape Town: University of the Western Cape.

Namibia. 1996a. Brief Report on ABE (Post Literacy) Workshop held at Sundown Lodge, 15 – 17 April 1996. Windhoek, Namibia: Directorate of Adult Basic Education, Ministry of Basic Education and Culture.

Namibia. 1996b. Pilot Curriculum for Formal Basic Education. Windhoek, Namibia: Directorate of Adult Basic Education, Ministry of Basic Education and Culture.

Chapter 7

Identifying and selecting teaching and learning materials

OVERVIEW

This chapter offers practical guidelines on how to identify and select materials for use in the teaching and learning activities of adult learners in Africa. The purpose of this chapter is to familiarise readers with the different types of teaching and learning materials available, as well as their purpose. The chapter also discusses the rationale for choosing certain teaching and learning materials over others, as well as offering some selection criteria for use, especially in an African context. What you should keep in mind when reading this chapter is that well-selected teaching and learning materials can enhance the effectiveness of the teaching-learning process.

LEARNING OBJECTIVES

At the end of the chapter, you should be able to:

1 Explain what teaching and learning materials are.
2 List the types of teaching and learning materials available for adult learners.
3 Select teaching and learning materials that are most suitable for adult learners in an African context.

KEY TERMS

teaching and learning materials This refers to the print and non-print resources needed to drive and enhance the teaching and learning experiences of adult learners.

print materials All textual or printed teaching and learning resources, such as books, reports, journals, newspapers and magazines.

non-print materials All teaching and learning resources that do not come in textual or printed form, including chalkboards, overhead projectors, audio or visual materials, audio-visual materials, radio and television.

locally produced materials Materials developed in a local environment that are made using local experiences, knowledge and skills.

indigenous knowledge A term used to refer to knowledge gained in everyday life challenges, problems and situations. It is about what the local people believe in, value, know and do or have known and done for generations (Semali, 1999: 307).

BEFORE YOU START

What comes to mind when you think of the term, 'materials' or when you hear someone else using this term? In the classroom environment, what items do you think could be classified as materials?

THE PURPOSE OF TEACHING AND LEARNING MATERIALS

Teaching and learning materials are resources that drive and enhance the effectiveness of the teaching-learning environment of the adult learner. They provide the essence of the programme's subject matter and guide the teaching-learning experience.

Adult education settings in Africa vary greatly, ranging from the traditional to the high-tech. Traditional, in this chapter, refers to educational environments where the chalkboard and books are the main teaching and learning materials used. Although many modern learning environments no longer use the chalkboard, it remains a convenient and economical resource for the teacher to incorporate into his or her classroom activities. The chalkboard (or 'blackboard' as it is still commonly known in some parts of Africa) is a good example of a non-print material used in an educational environment. The marker board is similar to the chalkboard, except the teacher uses felt-tip pens, not chalk, to write upon a clear, non-porous surface. Both the chalkboard and marker board are examples of non-projected or still projected materials.

In traditional educational settings, books probably represent the resource most commonly used by teachers and learners. For the teacher, books are a convenient and informative knowledge source that they can extract curricula subject matter from. Case studies, factual information, literary works, dramatic texts, and cultural and environmental knowledge can be accessed from books and then applied or adapted for use in the teaching and learning environment. Knowledge of the printed word, especially in the book form, is equally important to learners. Learners are required to study written texts and to perform a number of written exercises and examinations to demonstrate their understanding of what they have read.

The educator or teacher must try to incorporate the most appropriate and effective materials, whether print or non-print, to drive and enhance the teaching and learning activities.

▦ ACTIVITY

Study the range of teaching and learning materials shown below. Which resources are familiar to you? Which resources could be classified as 'traditional'?

book

radio cassette player

overhead projector

television

newspaper

audio tape

THE USE OF THE BOOK IN AFRICAN EDUCATION

In the twenty-first century, the range of teaching and learning materials available is vast (and possibly bewildering!). However, for many practitioners the cost of many of these items is prohibitive and they still rely on perhaps the most fundamental of all teaching and learning materials – the book. At the primary, secondary and tertiary levels, books represent vital sources of information for teachers and learners in the African education system. The educational book publishing industry in Africa produces material on a wealth of subjects for a wide range of learner groups.

However, although widely used across all teaching and learning environments, the book as a resource is still relatively expensive. One recalls here a situation a few years ago where students in a Botswanan university took strike action over the issue of book costs. The students complained that the government allowance they had been awarded was meagre when measured against the price of the prescribed books. Programme developers and implementers selecting books should bear the cost factor in mind when they plan the resource components needed for their proposed programmes. The element of cost, together with other selection criteria, is discussed in detail later in this chapter.

However, at this point we need to go deeper into why and how books are still largely preferred in many adult education settings in Africa.

The importance of the book as a teaching-learning resource

As mentioned in the introduction, the book is a commonly used print resource in our teaching and learning environments. When facilitators prepare programmes, they usually consult books for more information on the relevant subject matter. Reading books broadens and deepens a facilitator's understanding of his or her area of interest, which can in turn be incorporated into the development of the programme(s) for the ultimate benefit of the adult learners. Reading texts by different authors will also help the facilitator question, refine and modify his or her perspective on a subject or subjects. In a similar way, learners gain a great deal from utilising books during their programme activities. When learners are given an assignment, they are often referred to recommended books to help them in their work. The facilitator should suggest books from a number of sources so learners can gain insight into the thoughts, concepts and approaches of several writers. Reading a number of books enriches the learning experience for programme participants.

We will now look at some of the specific reasons why books are particularly popular in the teaching and learning environment.

- Future use: Books are, generally speaking, a durable teaching and learning material. If properly cared for, a book can last for several generations of learners or potential learners. This is especially useful for books where the content information does not change significantly over time (an obvious example would be mathematics books, where the concepts have remained essentially the same for a considerable period of time).

- Independency: Books are 'stand-alone' resources that do not need electricity, telephone lines, or computer terminals to 'operate'. Of course, the manufacture of books depends on other resources, but, once published, a book is totally unreliant on supporting power sources (http://www.aceproject.org/main/english/ve/ved03d/default.htm). This factor is an important issue in a continent where many Africans do not have access to electricity. In numerous rural communities, for example, a lack of electricity means that the book becomes a vital source of information for learners and teachers.

■ Shared benefits: Books that a learner has contributed to financially usually become his or her property at the end of the development programme. These books are usually taken home, where they can be given, loaned to or exchanged with other family and community members. In this way, the books benefit a number of people in addition to the programme participant and therefore constitute a viable form of informal, lifelong learning.

Books come in different forms, for example: a reference book, a technical handbook, an instruction guidebook, a poetry book, a short story book, an anthology, a biography or autobiography, and a monograph. They are usually classified according to the subject matter they explore.

Other printed teaching and learning materials

As well as books, there are many other printed materials that may feature in a programme of adult education. Many learners will have to make written notes, analyse reports, consult journals, and read newspapers and newsletters during the course of their programme activities. Look at the photographs in Figure 7.1, which represent examples of some printed materials. Think of others that are not included in the list above or in the photographs.

Book

Newspaper

Newsletter

Journal

Figure 7.1 Examples of print materials.

▦ ACTIVITY

Think about the titles of two or three books that you have read. Write down these titles and give a brief description of the subject matter of each book.

A CRITIQUE OF BOOK USE IN AFRICAN EDUCATION

It is a well known and documented fact that most books used in our teaching and learning environments exclude African traditional knowledge and practices. These books are not written from an African perspective and are not intended to address the cultures, beliefs, values and practices of the African continent. In one particular research study, one of the participants, a social worker, complained that, 'we use books from other countries, then we do not make efforts to assess the applicability and relevance of these books to local situations' (Lekoko, 2002: 176).

This concern has been raised by several commentators, who have realised that because African content is not discussed in textbooks, 'the transfer of indigenous knowledge from everyday life to school-work is not always valued or encouraged, and indigenous ways of knowing may not be recognized by teachers' (Semali, 1999: 305). The wealth of valuable teaching and learning resources available in Africa could benefit learners enormously, but because it is not documented in many textbooks it remains unused.

The range of community knowledge that could be put to good use is huge; produced, as one writer observes, 'from local history, information about flora and fauna, and application of local medicine to human and animals to cure diseases endemic to the community' (Semali, 1999: 307). The African belief in mystical powers does not register in conventional textbooks, yet it is a belief that is central to many Africans' way of life. For example, every African villager can relate stories of how supernatural powers intervene in the lives of humans. For example:

A friend whom I have known since he was a school boy told my wife and me that an elderly man with whom he had had a serious quarrel was sending snakes to kill his family. Mr. M. told us that twice within a short time, snakes had entered his home and gone to the children's beds, while the children slept at night. Fortunately, they were killed before they had bitten the children (Mbiti, 1988: 196).

While tales of this nature may sound unusual to outsiders or modernists, for many Africans the story is not illusive, rather, it is what people know and have believed in for years (Semali, 1999). The belief in the supernatural is such that many Africans enact certain rituals or modify their behaviour according to what the mystical forces dictate. In many cases, they will, 'wear charms, eat medicine, or get them rubbed into their bodies. Everyone is directly or indirectly affected' (Mbiti, 1988: 196). Learning in adulthood that does not address some of these traditional beliefs is incomplete, because it fails to address a genuine aspect of African life.

A further concern is the lack of books in Africa's rural communities. Although mobile libraries may operate in these areas, in most cases they do not provide everything the adult learner requires. Adult educators need to consider how to make relevant materials available in all parts of Africa in the most cost-effective manner.

The scarcity of books should not prevent educators from using the knowledge and experiences of local people in developing programmes and programme content. Rather than relying on externally produced materials, such as books, the logical step is to consider what is easily available in an Africa context. African newspapers, stories, songs, poetry and dances are forms of locally produced educational material that could form part of a development programme.

For example, newspapers contain relevant and contemporary local information. They are read widely and they are also cheap to buy. In Botswana, for instance, the *Botswana Daily News* is free and yet it contains valuable information on a variety of subjects, including community affairs, government, business, and local cultural events. A newspaper can also be read by a number of people; an individual rarely refuses to pass his or her newspaper on to another person. Newspapers can be stored and used at a later stage. Although the information may eventually become obsolete, it will always remain useful as an archival information source.

Adult educators can also encourage documentations of some information by adult learners themselves. Learners can do this through story writing, essay writing and producing newsletters and poems. These materials will be rich in local knowledge and culture because they are locally produced. Also, posters and other locally recognised media can be produced to capture the events, problems, challenges and successes of life in Africa.

Women who have experienced domestic violence, for example, may attend a workshop where they produce materials (short stories, poems, letters) addressing their experiences. Posters or pictures that evoke vivid memories of violence can be used to trigger their creativity and to produce interesting and contextual teaching materials.

Once the materials have been produced they become the property of the learners who have produced them. They can be kept in a safe place and accessed when needed. Learners may borrow them, take them home and share stories with their families, or read them during their leisure time to enrich their understanding of the local environment. In sum, when adult learners are used as resources for their own learning, there will be no end to the reservoir of learning available.

Whenever external programme materials are needed, the guiding principle is that of relevance and accessibility. Accessibility here refers not just to the issue of physical availability – can it be located in a bookstore or library? – but also to its financial accessibility. Books, as we have already mentioned, can be expensive resource items and for many learners this will be an important factor. Prescribing books that very few learners can afford to buy makes very little sense and the educator should therefore look for alternatives.

An innovative or creative adult educator knows that learners, too, are rich resources in themselves. Where possible, they can develop their own materials or create their own learning house by bringing materials for their own learning purposes and to share with others. If programme developers and implementers believe that good materials can be produced by learners writing about themselves, their communities and their nations, then local problems can be addressed.

In prisons, for example, inmates' stories about themselves make interesting programme materials. When they are encouraged to write about their personal lives outside prison and the events that led to their imprisonment, the resulting narratives are true programme materials in adult education because they explore real-life problems, as the following story shows.

CASE STUDY: SAME'S STORY

Standing behind some worn-out tiles in a Correctional Institute for Women, Same reads a poem that she wrote about herself three months after she entered prison. Before she began to read, she took a deep breath, fighting back the tears...

Oh, what day, Saturday October 26, 2005 brings such misery? A day that has become the saddest day ever in my life. I sat outside my mother's hut watching the tears fall like a waterfall from my two young sisters. They cried 'We are hungry! Hungry! Hungry!' Inside the hut, there was nothing, around the house, there was nothing too. In the neighborhood too, there was no food.

*See, I am now serving a two-year sentence
in connection with stealing to feed my sisters. What could I have done! What could
I have done Lord! [Fighting to control her
tears]. Why! Why! you cruel disease, why
did you steal our one and only parent from
us? How I wish time could be reversed. I
would do something that will never separate me from my beautiful sisters, Pako 1
year now and Boycy 3 years. I wish I find
them alive to be a good sister.*

One naturally sympathises with Same's situation. Her story is not only about her own
sufferings but it also reflects the sufferings
of poor people in general. This is the kind of
story that many adult learners in Africa can
relate to and appreciate.

Programme planners or implementers
seek material that engages learners in a
meaningful way. Same's story, as most
learners would agree, is certainly meaningful. Her narrative is rooted in the real-life
experiences of countless poor people across
the continent. Her economic plight, for
instance, is a fact of life for many disadvantaged people and it is clear that it is
poverty that has driven her to steal food
for her sisters. The reference to a 'one and
only parent' also reflects the fact that many
families have lost a parent (and often both)
to the AIDS virus, which Same alludes to
when she curses the 'cruel virus'. The complex morality of Same's situation should
also provide a source of lively debate in
a teaching and learning environment.
Although Same was technically guilty of
a criminal act – theft – many learners will
find it difficult to condemn her for her
actions. The educator could prompt learners
by asking them to consider questions like,
'Are there some circumstances where theft
should not be considered a criminal act?', or
'If you had been in Same's position, would
you have let your sisters starve?' Stories such
as Same's give educators and learners the

perfect opportunity to discuss and debate
some of the real-life challenges that face
many Africans in contemporary society.

⊞ ACTIVITY

**Suppose you are an adult educator who
is planning a three-month rehabilitation
workshop for the women inmates of a
prison. You have entitled the programme, 'A
woman's life in prison'. Identify some of the
teaching and learning materials that you
would use in the workshop and explain why
you believe these materials are appropriate.**

TEACHING AND LEARNING MATERIALS IN THE MODERN ERA

While it has been said that books are the
main source of teaching and learning materials in many African contexts, the reality
is that a number of institutions in Africa
are integrating other programme materials.
This is particularly important today, when
Africa is forging links and networks with
other nations who have made it their business to incorporate high-tech materials,
such as audiovisual and computer-mediated
techniques, in their educational activities.

The choice to diversify can be made
easier if practitioners are aware of other
materials that can enhance the effectiveness of the teaching-learning process. Once
aware of the wide variety of materials that
are available, practitioners should, with the
greatest care, select the materials that best
suit their specific situations. Among others
things, all efforts should be made to adapt
materials to local contexts.

What now follows is a discussion of the
types of materials that are available and
accessible to the adult learner and educator
in the modern era.

Categories of materials

The categorisation that follows is informed by Kemp's (1985) and Ellington's (2000) classifications. We will begin by looking at a category we have already introduced: print materials.

Category 1: Print materials

Print materials, commonly used across Africa, come in many different forms. All textual material fits into this category, and the category includes (i) books: a book is defined as a written or printed literary or factual composition bound together in a volume (Random House College Dictionary 1988: 154); (ii) booklets: a small publication dealing with a specific topic; (iii) reports: usually written for the specific purpose of communicating information to a specified group; and (iv) posters: information in an art form. Magazines, newspapers, workbooks, charts and graphs are also classified as printed materials. In the teaching-learning environment, it is common practice that facilitators supply learners with handouts. These are another Category 1 item and they include sets of notes, tables, diagrams, maps and illustrations or extension materials. Further textual material in this classification extends to include assignment sheets, charts, reading lists, lab sheets, briefing sheets for projects and seminars, and worksheets.

Many of the printed materials identified above are used to expand and diversify knowledge bases and resources in teaching and learning environments. Furthermore, different types of print materials can be incorporated in a single programme. Care, however, should be taken in differentiating between the different uses of printed materials. In what situation, for example, is a booklet more relevant than a book?

Category 2: Non-print materials

Non-print is also a broad category. It includes: (i) non-projected display materials; (ii) still projected display materials; (iii) television; (iv) audio materials; and (v) linked audio and still visual materials. Materials in the non-print category are gradually increasing in popularity and are now found in many African institutions and non-institutional settings; for example, in community-based adult education programmes. In almost all instances of use, Category 2 materials are used in conjunction with some form or forms of printed materials – Category 1 items.

We will now look in a little more detail at several of these Category 2 items.

Non-projected display materials
These are usually used by the facilitators and learners in a classroom atmosphere. As we noted earlier in this chapter, the most common examples of non-print display materials are the chalkboard and the marker board. However, this sub-group also includes charts and wall charts, which use large sheets of paper hung on an easel or stand that can be used to present sequential information (by turning the sheets over, one at a time) or to present impromptu information by using a fresh sheet of paper as a blank canvas. Feltboards, hook-and-loop boards, magnetic boards, posters and photographic print also form part of the long list of non-projected display materials. Finally, this sub-group includes what is termed 'realia', which consists of real-life specimens (hence the name) of plants, animals, insects, and other natural phenomena.

Still projected display materials
This sub-group includes all visual display materials that do not incorporate movement and that require an optical projector of some description in order to show them

to a class. Overhead projector transparencies are perhaps the most common example of this type of material. However, the sub-group also encompasses slides, which are single frames of photographic film mounted in cardboard, plastic or metal binders. Filmstrip and microforms such as microfiches and microcards extend the range of items still further.

Audio materials

The radio broadcast is a widely used form of audio material in Africa. In many countries, health and agricultural programmes are transmitted via radio broadcast. The radio is an item found in a great many African homes, which should encourage educators and trainers who wish to broadcast educational content to a large number of learners, or potential learners. The audio tape and the CD (compact disc) can also be used to record and play, on a tape recorder and in a CD player respectively, information and music. Educators may use gramophone records to disseminate information, although this is less common nowadays and records, though relatively cheap, are not as convenient to store, handle or use as tape cassettes.

Linked audio and still visual materials

This sub-group combines audio and visual materials to form integrated instructional systems. The tape-slide programme comes under this category: an audio tape recording synchronised with linked sequences of slides, which can be used in a wide variety of instructional situations, but particularly in individualised circumstances. Tape-photographic programmes are basically the same as tape-slide programmes, except that sequences of photographic prints are used instead of sequences of slides. Film strip with audio support is another example of a linked combination. These are simply film-strips that have an accompanying sound commentary, usually on a compact tape cassette. Other examples include radio-vision programmes (still filmstrips accompanying educational radio programmes), tape text (a combination of printed or duplicated materials with audio recordings) and tape-model.

While the print medium, in the form of books, remains the most powerful and popular way of delivering adult education programme content in Africa, there is still the need for adult education practitioners to think of using other materials to assist, supplement or complement the print format. Each material has its own advantages and disadvantages. Using a combination of materials may reduce or eliminate the weaknesses that are present in any single material (Diamond, 1991). Therefore, an adult educator should consider using a variety of materials in a single programme. The educator's choice can be enhanced by exposure to an expanded range of materials; some of these have been mentioned in the preceding discussion.

The impact of computer technology must also be mentioned. Although a more costly option, many organisations and institutions use computer-generated presentation techniques (such as Microsoft's Powerpoint programme) to transmit information and knowledge to their target groups.

✳ ACTIVITY

Consider the range of print and non-print materials presented above. Which type(s) of material have you used or are you familiar with? What materials would you recommend for an adult education development programme in your area, and why?

SELECTING PROGRAMME MATERIALS

Responsible adult educators exercise caution when thinking of materials to use. Selecting relevant programme materials is a systematic exercise that cannot be rushed and requires a thorough analysis of the different options available.

Two phases of the selection process are explored here: (i) locating relevant materials; and (ii) the selection criteria.

Locating relevant materials

Our starting point here is to consider how the materials can complement the local contexts. This means that a strong attempt should be made to find locally relevant materials. Existing materials may be found in a number of places, including bookstores, libraries, national archives, museums, local schools, churches, homes, and work environments. If there are no existing materials, the facilitators and learners can, as we mentioned earlier, produce them.

At a more informal level, materials present themselves to us each day as we walk the streets, go to the shops, and travel to and from work. During these daily activities, we continually use or encounter different knowledge sources in an unplanned manner. For example, when we read a borrowed newspaper on the train to work, scan a leaflet handed to us at a street corner, or stop to listen to a public speaker addressing an informal crowd in the local park, we are utilising informal information sources. Simply sitting down at home and listening to a local radio programme or watching the local television can turn out to be good way of learning. For adult educators in Africa, these occurrences, and others, provide a rich source of knowledge, and therefore teaching and learning. Locally sourced knowledge is likely to be meaningful and relevant to adult learners, which is something that the programme developer should be aware of when designing programme content

It has been noted already that in many educational institutions in Africa, adult educators rely on published books. However, published books may be suitable for some formal institutional settings but not for others. For example, many textbooks are decontextualised because too often they present data and information that are divorced from the local experiences (Kincheloe, Slattery and Steinberg, 1999). As Africans, we need to talk about what is happening to us. A programme can, therefore, take off with information or media available in the local context.

Local histories can be located in all aspects of community life, and are often concerned with long-established practices concerning a community's religious life, cultural beliefs, value systems, health practices and relationship to the natural world. Indigenous knowledge at a community level should be included, not excluded, from programme content because it approaches adult education from an African perspective and has the values, beliefs and needs of African learners at its centre.

In addition to using local histories, many adult educators use their own or other people's experiences as sources of information. For example, when they teach, educators often pause to tell stories about their students, schools, and themselves (Kincheloe, Slattery and Steinberg, 2000). These stories usually relate the experiences, problems, challenges and concerns experienced in the local environments. In addition, tours or trips to local communities can offer a direct learning experience for programme participants of the lives and livelihoods of African people. Thus, practitioners in an African adult education context should not rely solely on printed materials. They need to explore knowledge in the local environments. Adult educators are critical thinkers, creative beings and responsible professionals, who select and use the most appropriate materials to suit the teaching-learning situation. We encourage adult educators to raise critical questions about the learning materials they encounter.

Selection criteria

Selecting materials for use in programme delivery involves great care and effective decision-making skills. Of course, before the selection process can begin, the educator must know if the programme materials are available. Printed material held in institutions such as libraries, bookstores, and national archives is stored systematically and located using a comprehensive reference system. An educator who decides to select material from the library, for example, is likely to use GATEWAY, the Web, Card Catalogue and OPAC. Professionally trained staff are always available to help those who are not familiar with the organisation's referencing and storage systems.

Once the issue of availability is settled, the selection process begins. Selection is guided by a number of important questions, including:

- Does the material match the programme objectives?
- Can the material be accessed by the largest number of participants?
- Is the material affordable?
- Can the material be made available and purchased on time?
- What setting will the material be used in (formal classroom, home, workshop, and so on)?

A number of other factors also determine material selection. Firstly, it is the duty of an adult educator to ensure that the content of all proposed books meets the programme's stated objectives. It may be that a single book meets all the programme's content requirements. However, it is equally possible that several books contribute one or more content elements. In this situation, the educator could photocopy the relevant pages from each book, bind these together into a single volume, then place this new 'book' in the library for the learners to reference. This option is valid because, as Diamond (1991) notes, it may be uneconomical for learners to buy a book where only part of the content is relevant.

Another option is for the adult educator to duplicate copies of a book for all learners on the programme. This option is only feasible if the number of learners is relatively small – photocopying an entire book for a large programme contingent would be far too costly. Furthermore, duplicating published materials raises copyright questions. As educators, we need to be familiar with these professional norms. If it is necessary to duplicate, it is also necessary to request permission from the publisher to do this. Even if a modest fee is charged, it is better to pay for it than face legal copyright charges (Diamond, 1991).

Cultural sensitivity is another factor that greatly influences the selection of materials to be used by adult learners. Adult educators should select materials that do not conflict with the culture or cultures of the programme participants. Culture here refers mainly to values, beliefs, norms, actions and behaviours influenced by life situations such as existing technologies, and the economic and political climate (Cleaver, 2001).

Time is a factor that affects material selection. Educators must allow sufficient time to assess the properties and value of selected materials; and, as Diamond (1991) observes, this in turn will depend upon the overall time allocation of the programme. In cases where the materials need to be sourced, secured, purchased and made available, this process has to be completed well in advance of the start of the programme. The process often involves calculating a 'rough estimate' of the number of participants expected (Kemp, 1985), as well as the time needed to visit the different locations where the materials are held. At times, an educator needs to schedule the availability of loaned or rental audio-visual resources for use in the programme. This also needs to be planned in conjunction with the overall scope, content, and sequence of the programme (Diamond, 1991).

Other factors impacting upon the selection process are:

(i) considering how materials will be used to complement programme objectives; (ii) considering how participants are going to be used. If learners fulfil a resource function (through providing their own stories, poems, newsletters, artwork, and so on) it is important that they are involved in determining how this is done; (iii) considering how other resources, such as equipment and other teaching aids, are to be used. This will help educators to establish the quantity and quality of the necessary materials; (iv) considering the budget – there may be other things needed to run the programme. An educator must study the programme budget and assess how the costs of the proposed materials affect other necessary resources. If the material costs are too high, changes to the proposed items may be needed; and (v) calculating the approximate number of potential programme participants, to see whether sufficient selected materials have been identified.

▓ ACTIVITY

1 What types of teaching and learning materials, excluding books, would you like to see used more frequently in educational institutions in your area, and why?

2 Discuss the importance and suitability of any two of the selection criteria discussed in this chapter.

SUMMARY

Figure 7.2 on the next page displays the factors that influence the selection of programme materials and is intended to help educators make informed choices about what materials to use.

KEY POINTS

- There are numerous teaching and learning materials and adult educators have to make a wise choice of the ones that are most relevant to adult education within an African context.
- The choice of teaching and learning materials is informed by a number of factors, including, (i) the availability of materials; (ii) the cost of purchasing the materials; (iii) how the materials will be used; and (iv) the relevance of materials in meeting programme objectives and the needs of adult learners.
- Where there is lack or inadequate supply of teaching and learning materials, especially in rural areas, facilitators and learners should produce locally relevant materials rich in local experiences, knowledge and culture.

Do not select		Select	Location
NO	Does material match programme objectives?	YES	Libraries
NO	Is material available in the local environment?	YES	Bookstores
NO	Can material be purchased and delivered on time?	YES	Archives
NO	Is the cost of material affordable?	YES	Workplaces
NO	Is material culturally suitable for use with participants?	YES	Homes
NO	Can material be made available to all or the majority of participants?	YES	Internet

Figure 7.2 Factors influencing material selection.

ACTIVITY

What did you learn from this chapter about (a) how materials are to be selected for use in an African setting; (b) producing locally relevant materials; and (c) using local materials?

FURTHER QUESTIONS

1   What do you understand by programme materials?
2   What advantages can be derived from using a variety of materials in a single programme/course/lesson?

SUGGESTED READING

Diamond. R.M. 1991. *Designing and improving courses and curricula in higher education*. San Francisco: Jossey-Bass.

Ellington, H. 2000. *Producing teaching materials: A handbook for teachers and trainers*. London: Kogan Page.

http://www.aceproject.org/main/english/ve/ved03d/default.htm

Chapter 8

Marketing programmes to adult learners

OVERVIEW

This chapter provides adult educators with information on the tasks associated with social marketing in order to promote positive changes in programme development practice. The chapter begins with a brief overview of the concept of marketing from a commercial perspective. The main body of the chapter looks at the theories, disciplines and practices of social marketing. Because social marketing uses many of the techniques of commercial marketing, our analysis highlights, where appropriate, the similarities between the two disciplines. However, the social marketer is not engaged in the for-profit activities of the commercial sector and we are therefore careful to point out the critical differences that exist between the world of business and the world of adult education. We also consider some of the unique challenges faced by developers of adult education programmes in their efforts to utilise social marketing to instigate behavioural change with respect to adult education programmes.

LEARNING OBJECTIVES

By the end of this chapter, you should be able to:

1 Define the concept of marketing and social marketing as applied to adult education programmes.
2 Differentiate between commercial and social marketing.
3 Explain the objectives and describe the process of social marketing in adult education.
4 Design a marketing programme for an adult education programme following the steps discussed in this chapter.
5 Discuss the factors that influence the effective marketing of adult education programmes.
6 Implement and evaluate a marketing strategy for an adult education programme.

sesa woruban

KEY TERMS

commercial marketing   This refers to the practices used by profit-oriented enterprises to promote their products, services and ideas to a target group or groups of potential consumers.

diffusion   The process by which an innovation is communicated through certain channels over time among the members of a social system.

innovation   Any idea, practice or material artefact perceived to be new by the individual, group or institution adopting it. The 'newness' aspect of an innovation, according to Rogers (1983), may be expressed in terms of knowledge, persuasion, or a decision to adopt.

market segmentation   The process of dividing a potential market into homogeneous subsets or segments of customers. The underlying assumption is that each subset or segment will have similar characteristics and needs and will respond in a similar way to the products, services or ideas targeted for that subset or segment.

social marketing   A process that seeks to influence social behaviours by learning about what customers want and need rather than trying to persuade them to buy what has been produced.

stakeholders/stakeholder groups   Individuals and groups involved in and affected by the programme effort, including programme developers, implementers, managers, donors, supporters, and adult learners.

⊞ BEFORE YOU START

From your knowledge and experiences of the concept and practices of marketing, consider the following questions:

1 How would you define the concept of marketing?
2 What typical activities take place in a marketing situation?
3 Who are the main people involved in developing a marketing strategy?
4 Is marketing important for adult education programmes?

THE MARKETING CONCEPT

Marketing is a term that means many different things to many different people. We shall begin this section by considering some of the definitions in current circulation. Marketing has been defined as: 'the sum of all those business activities that promote the movement of goods and services from producers to consumers or other users, together with the study of consumer circumstances, preferences, and attitudes and the systematic use of this knowledge to create goods and services for consumption' (Bahr and Johnson, 1992: 416). The American Marketing Association, according to Bennet (1995), defines marketing as, 'the process of programme development and executing the conception, pricing, marketing communication and distribution of ideas, products, and services to create exchanges that satisfy individual and organizational goals'. Kotler (2003) defines marketing as a social process by which individuals and groups obtain what they need and want through creating, offering and freely exchanging products and services of value with others. Kotler further believes marketing involves the analysis, programme development, implementation and control of carefully formulated programmes designed to bring about voluntary exchanges of values with target markets for the purpose of achieving organisational objectives. Yet, Simerly (1989) believes that successful marketing is a process for ensuring that an organisation reaches its goals and objectives by exchanging its products, services and knowledge for programme registrations.

What all these different definitions have in common is the concept of an exchange or movement of goods and services between organisations and individuals. In a typical marketing situation, exchange will require two or more individuals or groups; where one side wants goods and/or services and the other side satisfies this want or wants. Each side must desire what it hopes to receive more than what it will have to give up. Both sides must feel that their total satisfaction will be enhanced as a result of the exchange. For exchange to take place, five conditions must be in place. According to Kotler, these conditions are:

- The existence of two or more parties to exchange goods and services;
- Each party to have something that the other party values and wants;
- The ability of each party to communicate with the other party and deliver the goods or services sought by the other party;
- Each party must be free to accept or reject the goods or services offered by the other party; and
- Each party must want to deal with the other party.

However, this conception of commercial marketing is not applicable to the domain of adult education, because in most cases the sponsors of the adult education programmes will determine what is good for the potential adult learners. Similarly, since most adult education programmes are funded by government and non-government organisations (NGOs), with little or no financial contributions from learners, the concept of exchange between the learners and providing organisation is irrelevant.

Exchange in African adult education programmes, in contrast to the commercial marketing situation, does not always involve the use of money. Two parties may enter into exchange of items without necessarily giving up or receiving money. For example, an adult learner participating in literacy classes may not have to pay for his or her studies. What may be required from the learner, however, is his or her effort and time in exchange for the programme classes offered.

 ## ACTIVITY

Refer back to the Before You Start activity at the beginning of the chapter. Having now read more on marketing theory, would you want to change your original definition of the concept of marketing?

SOCIAL MARKETING

We will now consider the concept and nature of social marketing, as well as its relationship to social science theories, disciplines and practices.

The concept of social marketing

The concept of social marketing was first used by Koler and Levy in 1969; then formalised by Kotler and Zaltman in the 1970s when it was realised that the governing principles relating to the sale of products to consumers could also be used to describe the marketing of programmes aimed at promoting social change (Brown, 1984). Since then, the concept has been widely applied to the selling of ideas, attitudes and behaviours, rather than tangible goods and services.

Many non-profit agencies and organisations in both the private and public sector are showing a growing interest in adopting a marketing approach in programme development and implementation. This trend reflects the fact that adult education organisations, which are mostly non-profit seeking, can also adopt the concept of social marketing. In adult and continuing education, marketing must be viewed beyond an economic understanding of what it means to sell, for example, food items, clothing, or petrol. In the same light, consumption of goods in social marketing terms does not refer to the physical gratification of a want or need; for example, the satisfaction gained from eating. Rather, marketing must be interpreted by developers of adult education programmes as a process, which involves determining the needs of clients, developing and implementing a programme to meet those needs, and evaluating the programme's success.

In adult education organisations, the main objective should be programme effectiveness, not profit-making. Programme effectiveness relates to achieving the desired outcomes of a specific programme at the lowest possible cost. For many adult education programmes the desired outcomes will be defined in terms of adult literacy, homemaking, entrepreneurship, and family health. The product here is an idea, knowledge, practice, or attitude change that is identified in meeting sessions between the programme participants and the programme developer. The product is distributed by the branch offices of an adult education organisation such as the Department of Non-Formal Education (DNFE) in different locations across the country. The price, which is not necessarily a monetary value, is paid for by those who use the product and/or services provided by the educational organisation. At this point, you should refer back to the opening pages of Chapter 2 for a reminder of the purposes of adult education. Re-reading those few pages will put into perspective the products and services of adult education programmes referred to in this section.

Each stakeholder in the programme development process should be encouraged to make a contribution to the marketing effort. Since this means that each participant must understand the details of the marketing process, programme developers will have to outline the various steps needed to implement a successful marketing plan.

The purpose of social marketing

Programme marketing deals with mobilising the human, material, and financial resources needed to implement and sustain the programme. Since we have already argued that adult education programmes should be people-centred, intended programme participants must be seen as partners in, rather than targets of, development. The two-fold purpose of social marketing is therefore: i) to encourage the potential learners to think critically about the specific ways that the programme might benefit them and the problems it might help them to solve; and ii) to encourage people's active participation in programme development and maintaining the programme. This approach to programme development is especially important in situations where intended participants have in the past been left out of the decision-making process.

Promoting an adult education programme serves specifically to:

- provide preliminary information about the adult education programme and what will be necessary to establish and maintain it;
- invite representatives from the stakeholder groups – donors, government officials, NGOs, and prospective learners – to work in their respective areas towards overall programme development and to identify and/or develop the infrastructures that will be necessary to sustain it; and
- encourage stakeholders to pinpoint resources that can be used for implementation and maintenance, and also inform them of any external assistance available.

Definition of social marketing

The term 'social marketing' is often wrongly used to describe advertising or mass media campaigns designed to change behaviour. While media can be an important aspect of social marketing, other components such as rigorous programme development and consumer research, channel-specific strategy development, and formative evaluation are equally important. Likewise, other types of interventions, such as training programmes, community activities and materials development are at least as valuable as media campaigns.

After two decades of debate and practice, the confusion regarding the nature and purpose of social marketing continues, even among practitioners. There is still no mutual agreement on what social marketing is. Is it advertising, advocacy, promotion, selling, or education? The following three definitions offer some much-needed clarity on this issue:

1 Definition No. 1. Kotler and Zaltman (1971) define social marketing as the design, implementation, and control of programmes calculated to influence the acceptance of social ideas.
2 Definition No. 2. Bennet (1995) defines social marketing as the process of planning and executing the conception, pricing, promotion, and distribution of ideas, goods, and services to create exchanges that satisfy individual and organisational objectives.
3 Definition No. 3. Smith (1999) defines social marketing as a process for influencing human behaviour on a large scale, using marketing principles for the purpose of societal benefit rather than for commercial profit.

A close look at these definitions reveals that social marketing differs from commercial marketing only with respect to the objectives of the marketer and his or her organisation. Social marketing seeks to influence social behaviours in order to benefit the target audience and general society, not the marketer. The third definition in particular attempts to clarify social marketing's unique purpose and goal. Unlike commercial marketing, social marketing aims to address social problems rather than to produce financial gain for the marketer. The primary focus of social marketing is on learning what people want and need, rather than on trying to persuade them to buy what the organisation produces or offers. Social marketing talks to the consumer, instead of talking about the product.

Social marketers draw upon a number of social science disciplines, theories, and practices to achieve results with their target audience. The most common disciplines and theories cited in the literature are social anthropology, health education, behavioural analysis, mass communication, and commercial marketing.

Social anthropology

Social anthropology is helpful to the marketer of an adult education programme because knowledge of its concepts can help locate the most formidable barriers to behaviour change. It can also help the marketer to determine how to tailor the programme goals, objectives and content to the target audience in a way that will facilitate acceptance and commitment to programme implementation (Kotler and Andreasen, 1996).

Health education

Health education models are useful in social marketing because they explore factors that positively and negatively influence behaviour change in individuals. Two commonly

cited models relating to social marketing are the Precede Model and the Health Belief Model (Bellamy, Salit and Bell, 1997).

The Precede Model examines predisposing, enabling, and reinforcing factors that contribute to behaviour change. The predisposing factors refer to an individual's existing knowledge, behaviour and beliefs, which may affect their willingness to change. Enabling factors include an individual's community or environment, which can impede or facilitate behaviour change. Reinforcing factors are the positive and negative consequences of adopting the behaviour, which will affect whether or not an individual will maintain the behaviour change (NIH, 1992).

The Health Belief Model suggests that behaviour is affected by four beliefs, including: (a) perceived susceptibility to a given health problem; (b) perceived severity of the problem; (c) perceived benefits from acting; and (d) perceived barriers to taking action (Andreasen, 1995).

When developing effective adult education programmes, programme developers have the choice to change potential participants' beliefs, emphasise the benefits of accepting the adult education programme, and/or decrease the perceived barriers to behaviour change.

Behavioural analysis

Needs analysis allows programme developers to understand what motivates and discourages adult learners from participating in programmes designed to bring about desired behaviour change. It is only after preliminary needs assessment that programme developers will determine what behaviour to change by reinforcing the benefits of participating in the programme, or by reducing the barriers to change (Kotler and Andreasen, 1996). Research evidence suggests that individuals progress through stages when contemplating a specific behaviour change. These stages are pre-contemplation, contemplation, preparation, action, and maintenance (Prochaska and DiClemente, 1983; Prochaska, et al., 1994).

The research findings apply directly to the field of adult education, where adult learners at each stage of the programme development process have distinct needs and wants that require different modes of address. The use of this model also helps a programme developer to understand and segment adult learners and to tailor their learning content (Kramish, et al., 1994).

Mass communication

There are many models that explain the process of mass communication in social marketing. William McGuire's model of communication describes 12 steps that a target audience must go through in order to adopt a behaviour (McGuire, 1989).

The first four steps in McGuire's model deal with decision-making and include exposure, attention to, interest in, and comprehension of the message. McGuire believes that people personalise the behaviour by relating it to their lifestyle, before eventually accepting the change. The remaining eight steps of McGuire's model concern maintaining the behaviour, which involves remembering and continuing to agree with the message and making decisions based on the message. In conclusion, McGuire's model suggests that people receive positive reinforcement for the behaviour and accept it as part of their routine. In order for programme participants to pass through these 12 steps, it is recommended that they and the desired behaviour must be carefully chosen, that the source of the message must be seen as credible by the programme participants, and that the message design and delivery channel must be

appropriate for the programme participants (NIH, 1992).

In *Diffusion of Innovations*, Everett Rogers (1983) provides a guide to creating effective messages for marketing adult education programmes, which programmers can utilise. Rogers describes how new products or ideas are introduced or 'diffused' to an audience. Referred to as the 'innovation decision-making process', Rogers' model consists of five sequential stages – knowledge, persuasion, decision, implementation, confirmation – that individuals or organisations pass through when deciding whether or not to incorporate or adopt a new idea or behaviour into their normal routine.

Rogers' research reveals that there are both early and late adopters. Most importantly for social marketers, the research suggests that different communication channels are effective at different stages in the model. For example, mass media channels such as radio, television and newspapers are more appropriate at the knowledge stage where the primary aim is to create awareness. Rogers also believes that these channels are more important for early adopters than for late adopters.

Interpersonal channels involving a face-to-face exchange between two or more individuals are more effective at the persuasion, decision-making and implementation stages and in dealing with resistance or apathy on the part of the audience. Because interpersonal channels provide a two-way exchange of information, individuals can obtain clarification or additional information from their peers or the person delivering the information (Rogers, 1983). The diffusion model has been the basis of traditional agricultural extension approaches in Africa, which is something we will look at in more detail a little later in this chapter.

However, the main failing of the mass communication approach is its inability to recognise or cater for the different needs and preferences of individual adult learners. Learners, in this context, are regarded as an undifferentiated group, exhibiting essentially the same needs, wants and preferences. If different learner requirements are ignored by one programme, therefore, other organisations are likely to enter the market to fill the gap. This in turn may bring about unnecessary competition for limited human and material resources.

Commercial marketing

Social anthropology and behavioural analysis provide the background information for social marketing campaigns, while health education models and mass communication strategies help shape the intended message into a credible, persuasive campaign. Commercial marketing principles provide programme developers with the necessary tools to formulate and implement the most effective adult education programme.

⌗ ACTIVITY

1 What is the purpose of social marketing in the context of developing adult education programmes?
2 What are the differences between social marketing and commercial marketing?

WANTS, DEMAND AND RESOURCE USE

Wants and demand

The discussion of marketing is impossible without reference to the concepts of wants, demand and resources that inform discussions on commercial marketing. It is necessary to understand the economic rationale that supports these terms before we can apply them to our investigation of the phenomenon of social marketing.

Economics is concerned with scarcity. The basic fact of life is that there are simply not enough goods and services to satisfy everyone's wants. Wants are unlimited (plentiful), but the means to satisfy them are limited (scarce). For economic goods and services (for example, food, housing, clothing, consumer durables) this relationship is readily understood. However, a similar analysis can also be applied to adult education programmes, where the demand for programmes generally exceeds the resource capabilities of programme providers and/or the learners themselves.

However, we must differentiate between learning needs and the more basic human needs such as food, water, air, shelter and clothing. These latter needs are survival needs and satisfying them is essential for our survival. Learning needs, as we demonstrated in Chapter 5, refer to the gap between a person's present level of knowledge or skills and his or her desired level of knowledge or skills. Though important, we cannot say that learning needs are essential to survival. But in all other respects, learning needs conform to the characteristics of other needs. For example, learning needs, like other needs, are not absolutely unlimited. An adult's need to participate in a learning programme can be calculated in terms of the resources and services needed to sustain a minimum, and not an unlimited, standard of living while learning.

Learning needs must also be distinguished from wants. Wants are human desires for goods and services and, unlike needs, they are unlimited. Again, however, learning needs and the concept of wants are not completely dissimilar. For instance, although adult education primarily relates to a learning need, adult learners also *want* to choose a programme that best serves their preferences, (learning) needs and abilities. Whether that want can be satisfied again depends upon the distribution of a number of scarce resources, including the availability of funding from the sponsoring organisation.

Demand, unlike wants and needs, is premised on the ability to purchase the goods and services we seek. An adult may want to attend a basic adult education programme, for example. That desire or want may be thought of as a need because reading and writing are considered indispensable skills in today's world. However, this desire and/or need cannot be deemed a demand if the adult has no means of obtaining it. Thus, if the adult has no way of accessing programme funding, the desire to participate will remain a desire (or an unfulfilled need) and not a demand.

The above example exemplifies the plight of many poor and disadvantaged learners who cannot afford to attend adult education programmes. However, understanding the concept is important because it can apply to donor organisations that sponsor adult education programmes on behalf of those who need financial assistance. For example, if UNICEF sees the need to train child-bearing mothers on child health and nutrition and can fund the training course itself, this need can correctly be considered a demand. However, where the government has paid for the services on behalf of potential learners, the concept of demand cannot apply directly to adult learners

Resources

Similar to other human organisations, adult education organisations require many resources in order to implement programmes, including: (i) land to build programme infrastructure; (ii) human resources; (iii) material resources such as machines, furniture and stationery; and (iv) financial resources to purchase equipment and materials and to pay labour costs.

The next section of this chapter will consider the relationship of the economic and marketing concepts just discussed to the social marketing of adult education programmes.

ACTIVITY

What is your understanding of the following concepts: needs, wants, demand?

THE LINK BETWEEN SOCIAL AND COMMERCIAL MARKETING

The modern approach to marketing revolves around 'the four Ps': product, price, place and promotion. Sometimes referred to as 'the marketing mix', the four Ps direct the commercial marketer's efforts to capture a target audience's attention and to sell the product or service to that group of consumers. The commercial marketer must have something he or she believes will sell (the product); it must cost what the consumer is willing to pay (the price); it must be visible and accessible in the correct locations (the place); and creative techniques must be used to sell it to consumers (promotion).

Applying the four Ps of commercial marketing offers the programme developer a basic structure upon which he or she can create a successful social marketing campaign. The description and application of each of the four Ps to social marketing now follows.

The product refers to what is being offered to the adult learners. The range of products offered on adult education programmes is extensive. Products may be physical (condoms provided as an element of a 'safe sex' awareness programme); a service (an HIV screening service); a practice (encouraging personal health and hygiene practices, or nutritional eating habits); or conceptual (an adult basic literacy programme or a course in business administration).

The price associated with an adult education programme may refer to the actual monetary cost of attending the programme. However, price can also refer to the more intangible, qualitative costs an individual may incur in this situation, such as his or her time, effort, embarrassment, inconvenience, or fear. The adult educator should realise that these non-monetary costs can significantly affect an individual's choice of programme. The educator's role here is to persuade participants that the perceived benefits of 'buying' the programme product(s) exceed its perceived costs, which includes the price attached to personal misgivings.

The place describes how the product reaches the target audience. Very often, place simply refers to the building or buildings where the programme activities are conducted and the product delivered. This could include a programme developer's office, community hall, church, educational establishment, and so on. However, place can also mean other locations – on the bus going to work, in the supermarket, in the doctor's waiting room – where learning continues in an informal, unstructured manner. Place also includes communication channels such as radio and television, where information can reach its target audience by way of news, features, music or interviews that relate directly or indirectly to programme content.

Promotion is the means used by the programme developer to communicate messages and images to potential adult learners. The information must appeal to

these learners and persuade them that by changing their behaviour (which is the aim of social marketing) they will benefit from the programme in some meaningful way. Promotion of a product could use many different channels, such as interpersonal (programme developer, other stakeholders, family members, and community or church leaders); group (work events, social or recreational clubs, and classroom activities); organisational or community-based (newsletters, advocacy groups, and community fairs), and mass media (public service announcements, radio spots, direct mail, and newspapers).

However, many social marketing efforts are unfortunately guilty of concentrating on promotion to the detriment of the other essential components of social marketing – product, price and place (Andreasen, 1995). Similarly, many people believe that social marketing relates to advertising only (Andreasen, ibid.).

▩ ACTIVITY

With the use of examples, how would you apply the four Ps of commercial marketing to the development of an adult education programme in your community?

PROCESSES OF PROGRAMME MARKETING

In the most recent edition of their book *Strategic Marketing for Nonprofit Organisations*, Kotler and Andreasen (1996) present several tenets that are central to social marketing. Some of these are relevant to programme developers designing the marketing of their intervention programmes. A discussion of these important principles now follows.

Definition of a recognised problem

Defining a marketing problem is critical because it forms the first impression about the entire marketing programme. The programme developer must correctly identify the need or 'problem' of his or her target audience in order that an appropriate course of action can be initiated. Defining the problem in such a way that it closely corresponds with the need or needs of adult learners will create interest in the target audience. Furthermore, the most significant problem is not judged by the amount of work and money required to solve it, but by the amount of thought that the programme developer applies in the selection and definition of the problem.

Some problems such as 'basic education' are very broad, and need to be divided into sub-problems that are definable and manageable for programme development. In order to achieve this, it is also important for the programme developer to identify the causes of problems rather than simply dealing with the symptoms. For example, the lack of reading and writing skills among a target audience may be identified as the cause of business failure. Although adult literacy programmes designed to overcome this problem may help, the root causes of failure might actually be a lack of learner skills in financial management, record keeping, and entrepreneurial development programmes. Once this is ascertained, the problem can then be stated in marketing terms to read – 'Literacy and entrepreneurial skills development for small businesses'.

Formulation of marketing objectives

The next step in designing a marketing programme is the translation of the problem into objectives by all the stakeholders. Formulation of objectives has already been discussed in Chapter 6. The only difference here is that the objectives are specific to programme marketing. Otherwise, the criteria and characteristics of good objectives apply to the formulation of marketing objectives. This means that the objectives must be specific, measurable, achievable, realistic, time-bound, and congruent with overall agency goals and mandate. Formulation of good objectives is imperative because they form the basis for ultimately evaluating the effectiveness and impact of the marketing programme.

Segmenting the programme participants

The developer of an adult education programme faces the challenge of trying to appeal to a very diverse population. Effective programme development involves breaking down – segmenting – the population into its constituent parts. As Strydom, Jooste and Cant (2000) comment:

> *Market segmentation is the process of dividing a potential market into homogeneous subsets or segments of customers. The assumption underlying market segmentation is that each segment of the market should have similar characteristics and needs, and will likely respond in a similar manner to the market offering and marketing strategy.*

Although the adult learner population in South Africa may be broadly categorised as a low-income group, in all other respects the population is dissimilar. Adult learners adhere to different cultural and ethnic practices and speak different languages; they also possess unique needs, aspirations and problems. The more the programme developer knows about each segment of the audience, the better equipped he or she will be to design appropriate and effective messages that will appeal to the respective audiences.

Following market segmentation, the next decision will focus on which segment or segments to target in order to satisfy their needs. The programme developer may opt to target only one subgroup of the eligible larger population, in order to maximize the use of limited resources. The programme design that follows should be structured upon the specific characteristics displayed by the selected group(s) of adult learners.

Advantages and disadvantages of market segmentation

Market segmentation has both advantages and disadvantages. These have been outlined in the work of, for instance, Strydom, Jooste and Cant (2000). The advantages of market segmentation are:

- It compels the marketer to focus more accurately on customer needs.
- Segmentation leads to the identification of new marketing opportunities if research reveals an unexplored segment.
- Market segmentation provides guidelines for the development of separate market offerings and marketing strategies for the various market segments.
- Segmentation can help guide the proper allocation of marketing resources.

On the other hand, the disadvantages of market segmentation include:

- The development and marketing of separate models and market offerings is very expensive.
- Only limited market coverage is achieved, since marketing strategies would be directed at specific market segments only.

Involvement of all stakeholders

Involving programme stakeholders in the design, development and implementation of an adult education programme campaign is of paramount importance. Working in partnership is fundamental to the successful implementation and institutionalisation of a marketing campaign.

The principle of stakeholder involvement was closely followed during the marketing of an agricultural project for remote area dwellers in the Kgalagadi and Southern Districts of Botswana. Here, the marketing campaign sought the support and assistance of a broad coalition of organisations to partner with the consulting agency – Agro-Business Consulting and Development. The objective was to convince the identified programme beneficiaries to 'buy into' the proposed integrated agricultural project on poultry, vegetables, fish, bee, rabbit and dairy farming. The campaign operated at the national, district, and community levels. The purpose of the marketing campaign was to mobilise and sensitise residents of four remote area settlements (Phuduhu, Inalegolo, Thankane, and Sekhutlane) regarding the intervention (Gboku, Thabang, Keletso and Mphahudi, 2004).

Reflecting on the mobilisation and sensitisation campaign, a number of lessons were learned, including:

- By forming early partnerships with local organisations such as the Village Development Committee, Parent Teacher Association, Extension Teams, Youth Committees, Farmers' Committees, and Home-Based Care Committees, the proposed agricultural project generated support, credibility, and involvement for the campaign. Not only were the campaign messages strengthened by the consensus and co-operation developed through the coalition, but the project benefited from the expertise of its broad membership.

- Early partnership with the community helped to identify a number of key potential threats and opportunities that had a direct bearing on project implementation. For example, the project participants named a number of politicians and business leaders that they thought could hamper the implementation of the project. Participants believed that the proposed agricultural project threatened the interests of the community's political and business elite, which would therefore try to undermine the intentions of Agro-Business Consulting and Development.

Adopting a marketing strategy

After market segmentation, the next logical step in the social marketing process is to adopt a marketing strategy. A marketing strategy involves decisions about the details of the programme to be delivered. Decisions relating to strategy evolve around the issues of what to deliver, how to deliver, where to deliver, when to deliver, whom to deliver to, who should participate, and how to pay for production resources and product. Agro-Business Consulting and Development's marketing campaign in Botswana, for instance, clearly defined the projects and their scope to the communities involved, their expected contributions, the project time frame, and the responsibilities of other stakeholders, such as the District Council, the Agro-Business consultants and local businesses.

Implementation of the marketing programme

Implementing a marketing programme allows the developer to measure the theoretical aims of the programme against what is actually achieved in practice. Where the intended aims of the programme are not being met in practice, remedial action can then be taken to get the programme 'back on track'. Implementation of a marketing programme can be aided by keeping in mind the following factors:

- ensuring that adequate promotion of the programme is carried out;
- ensuring that an official record of the programme implementation activity is kept;
- helping those concerned to change and add to the programme as it develops (if the programme is long-term, a periodic review should be undertaken);
- identifying and giving special attention to critical features of the programme, which may weaken it; and
- involving key people, specialists and advisors in continuously assessing how the implementation is progressing.

Monitoring and evaluating the marketing programme

As the final stage of the marketing programme, the effectiveness and impact of the programme are assessed to establish the degree of its success or failure. The results of evaluation can be used to make important decisions regarding continuity, modification for improving the marketing plan, and/or to provide feedback during implementation. Chapter 10 of this book discusses monitoring and evaluation in more detail.

ACTIVITY

Why is it important for a programme marketer to segment potential target participants of an adult education programme?

FACTORS INFLUENCING MARKETING EFFECTIVENESS

Promoting an adult education idea can present the programme developer with several challenges. The practice of safe sex, planting trees for soil conservation, or attending literacy classes are all ideas that an adult educator may wish to endorse. However, for potential programme participants these ideas are unlikely to bring about remarkable changes in the immediate future. An additional challenge for the programme developer, however, is that the target group may not even be aware of the need to change their sexual habits or their attitudes towards conservation and adult literacy, for example. The issue of marketing effectiveness is further complicated by the fact that an audience may have limited information sources and/or reading skills. The job of a programme developer is to overcome these challenges, using sound research and programme development skills and a talented, creative team.

The purpose of programme marketing is to sell an innovation to potential consumers or users. Realistically, the selling of the innovation is done via simple messages, which potential users can comprehend. The marketer of an adult education programme would want to see his or her messages spread rapidly and be accepted by the largest possible audience within a community. More often that not, however, programme messages received by the intended users do not create the impact they are intended to make. While some messages may be readily accepted, others may need more time and effort spent on them before they are acknowledged by potential users.

The acceptability of an adult education programme depends upon the perceived value of its specific ideas or innovations. In essence, programme marketing involves the promotion of some form of ideas or innovations. There is a need, therefore, for a programme marketer to have knowledge of the diffusion process in order to appreciate how the properties of an innovation influence an individual's decision on whether or not to accept and use the innovation. Such an understanding is of great value to the programme marketer in predicting the reactions of potential beneficiaries to programme ideas, and in modifying these reactions in order to facilitate idea, and therefore programme, acceptance. The fact that some adult education programmes fail while others succeed points to the reality that adult education programmes should be treated as non-identical units, which deserve an unique understanding of the ideas the programme is promoting.

Rogers (1983) provides extensive discussion of the diffusion process and a number of distinct attributes of innovation that are universally relevant. Although the first research on attributes of innovations was conducted with farmers, the research findings suggested that similar attributes may be important in predicting the rate of adoption for educational innovations (Rogers, ibid.). In this section, however, we will discuss a number of common challenges that a marketer of an adult education programme will face, including some of the factors identified by Rogers and by Loudon and Batta. These challenges are:

1 non-existent or negative demand;
2 invisible benefits and intangible products;
3 low-literate audience;
4 limited budgets;
5 relative advantage;
6 compatibility;
7 complexity;
8 observability; and
9 divisibility.

Negative demand for a programme

Commercial marketers promote products or services in an environment where consumers, or potential consumers, readily accept the existence of these products and services. The commercial marketer's job is to convince his or her target group that their current buying habits (of car, clothing, breakfast cereal, and so on) should be modified in favour of his or her brand of car, clothing, or breakfast cereal. The pervasive power of commercial marketing is such that we, as consumers, tend to accept that our behaviour (our buying habits) can be challenged in this way.

However, the social marketer of an adult education programme is often faced with the challenge of influencing the behaviour of programme participants in an area where the participants have not considered changing or do not want to change. Bellamy, Salit and Bell (1997) describe this situation as non-existent or negative demand.

Invisible benefits and intangible products

Social marketers are also faced with the task of promoting behaviours, or promoting behaviour change, where there are no immediate signs of success in the minds of the potential participants. The benefits of a basic adult literacy programme, as we referred to earlier in this chapter, are unlikely to offer spectacular successes in the short term. The 'invisible benefits' of this programme relate to the lifelong skills the adult learner will gain through attending the literacy classes, which will enhance the learner's social, work and personal life immeasurably. Marketing the concept of adult literacy, as opposed to marketing, for example, a new brand of sports shoe, presents a particularly strong test to the social marketer.

Low-literate audience

A high proportion of the populations targeted by adult education programmes have a low literacy rate. Trying to appeal to a low-literate audience may require an emphasis on communication channels that do not rely heavily on print (Bellamy, Salit and Bell (1997). And, if print messages are considered, the style, tone and register of writing must match the ability levels of the target group.

Limited budgets

Financial considerations determine the scope and range of the social marketer's campaign. Unlike commercial operations, adult education programmes cannot generate profit through the sale of products or services to a buying public. Thus, the social marketer's financial 'muscle' is generally limited to the level of funding prescribed by the sponsoring organisation. This in turn means that the social marketer must use his or her creative, as well as financial management skills, to make the best use of limited monetary assistance. When the developers of programme intervention are not financially established, their choice of marketing approaches will be limited to mobilisation and sensitisation only.

Relative advantage

Relative advantage is the degree to which an innovation is perceived as better than the idea it is superseding. The degree of relative advantage, according to Rogers (1983), is expressed in: a) economic feasibility; b) a decrease in discomfort; and c) status giving. In adult education programmes, both the nature of programme content (for example, change of knowledge, attitude, practice) and the characteristics of the potential learners (for example, self-directed, venturesome, respectable, deliberate, sceptical, traditional) determine to a great extent what specific type of relative advantage is important.

Economic feasibility

Economic advantage is measured in terms of how much the learners will pay in order to benefit from programme content. The sub-dimensions of economic advantage are low initial cost, a saving in time and effort, and the immediacy of the reward. There is a positive relationship between these variables and the rate at which adult learners participate in programme implementation. Even though the cost for non-formal adult education programmes is paid by sponsoring organisations (for example, government; non-government organisations), the learners at the community level may be required to contribute resources like land, labour, materials and time. When participants are strongly pressured into providing these resources, the chances of them accepting the programme and adopting its ideas may be reduced. Relative advantage in terms of financial cost may, however, not be important for many African adult learners, since they do not pay directly for their programme participation.

It should be noted that not all adult education programmes are provided for free by governmental and non-governmental organisations. There is a significant private sector in Africa that provides adult education at a cost and engages in commercial marketing and fee charging. A typical example of this situation would be a vocational institute offering a computer course to adults in one of the country's cities or urban environments.

A decrease in discomfort

The more comfort an adult education programme brings to the beneficiaries, the higher the chances of the beneficiaries accepting it. In a technologically revolutionalised world, the use of cell phones, automatic teller machines (ATMs), faxes, cars, on-line banking, and television are making people more comfortable than ever before. The inclusion of these innovations in African adult education programmes is likely to attract more learners. In fact, more adult Africans are learning about these innovations in order to maximise their comfort in the workplace and at home.

Status giving

The desire to gain social status is a motivator for participating in adult education programmes. In Botswana, for example, adult learning covers areas such as agriculture, health and nutrition, HIV/AIDS, consumer education, literacy, and home economics. Government assistance offered through some of these adult learning programmes is perceived as a means of acquiring higher socio-economic status. Many poor businessmen and women in the non-formal sector participated in small-scale Financial Assistance Programmes (FAPs) offering between BWP5 000 to BWP10 000. However, the more prosperous businesspeople may have rejected an innovation of this kind because they perceive it as shameful, believing that if they do accept government assistance their social standing in the community would be threatened.

Compatibility

Compatibility is the degree to which the contents of an adult education programme are consistent with the existing values, past experiences and needs of potential programme participants. Acceptance of a programme will be retarded if programme contents are not compatible with learners' norms. Programme ideas that are more compatible are consequently less uncertain to the potential learners. A programme and its content can be compatible or incompatible with (a) socio-cultural values and beliefs; (b) previously introduced innovations; or (c) participants' needs for a programme.

Compatibility with values

Values need to be shared by everyone in the society so that they are reinforced and become widely accepted. The shared values involve all areas of social activities, such as service, people, production, quality, independence, self-reliance, and profits. Programmes that are not compatible with the held values of a community are more likely to be rejected than accepted. For example, an adult education programme that incorporates teaching and learning on contraception and abortion would probably be resisted by adults whose 'pro-life' religious beliefs are opposed to these methods of birth control.

Compatibility with previous ideas

Old ideas are the benchmark against which new ideas are assessed. This does not mean that the new idea has to be exactly the same as the old one. In fact, when this is the case, the new idea will represent no change and will be rejected. What is required is for the new idea to be compatible with previous positive, successful experiences. If this does not happen, and the new idea then fails, potential programme participants will be conditioned to view all future interventions with apprehension.

Compatibility with participants' needs

This addresses the degree to which change meets the needs felt by the adult learners.

When felt needs are met, programme acceptance occurs more quickly.

Complexity

In the context of adult education, complexity refers to the degree to which programme content is perceived as difficult to understand and use. Complexity of programme ideas as perceived by adult learners is negatively related to acceptance and participation in such programmes.

Observability

Observability refers to the degree to which the results of programme efforts are visible to others. When the results of a programme are conspicuous to the participants, accepting and implementing the programme is more likely to happen. This is why it is advisable to make adult education programmes functional, which means combining learning with some economic activity that has tangible results and therefore makes the learning relevant. When the outcome of learning is latent to the adult learners, convincing them to participate becomes a tough challenge. Many African adult learners, for example, may find it difficult to appreciate the value of participating in adult education programmes occupied with teaching gender, human rights, individual rights and democratic values. Unless learners possess the appropriate intellectual background, it will be difficult for them to visualise the benefits of participating in projects such as these.

CASE STUDY: PARTICIPATION IN ACTION

In Botswana, the Agro-Business Consulting and Development (ABCD) organisation recently took up the challenge of introducing vegetable and poultry farming among remote area dwellers in the Southern and Kgalagadi Districts. The aim of the campaign was to convince the local people that teaching them technical and entrepreneurial skills in vegetable and poultry production would empower them to be self-supporting and less dependent on government food handouts. The behaviours of vegetable and poultry farming, though known by remote area dwellers, were associated in their minds with labour, cost, and other negative implications. Furthermore, the remote area dwellers are provided with food, clothing and shelter as part of the Drought Relief Programme, which made it even more difficult for Agro-Business Consulting and Development to present the project in a positive light. (Gboku, Mokatse, Keletso and Mphahudi, 2003).

The challenging question for ABCD was: 'What will the remote area dwellers lose if they participate in the agricultural intervention?' In light of this challenge, the programme developers resorted to mobilisation and sensitisation of the programme participants, which involved explaining the intervention to the participants in terms of its goals, philosophical operations, components and benefits. Towards the end of the mobilisation and sensitisation campaign, the participants felt that they had been empowered with the confidence to own the idea and to commit their energy, time and material resources to its implementation (Gboku, Keletso and Mphahudi, 2004).

It was difficult to convince programme participants and stakeholders that a vegetable project could succeed in a part of the Kgalagadi desert where the soil is classified as non-productive and where rainfall levels are low, as well as unpredictable. Furthermore, persuading low-income families that they could generate income from vegetable and poultry production, which has never been part of their economic activities,

proved a formidable challenge, especially since no immediate benefits could be predicted. However, ABCD managed to surmount these obstacles by shifting its efforts to focus on the importance of breaking away from government handouts and stressing the reward involved in achieving goals under adverse circumstances.

In the ABCD intervention, there was no basis for print communication because nearly 80% of the programme participants were illiterate, and generally spoke only their own language. The majority of the participants, however, understood the national language of Setswana, which the programme developers used to communicate with the participants and project stakeholders.

Divisibility

Divisibility is the extent to which a programme idea may be tried on a limited basis. Where a programme idea cannot be implemented on a less expensive scale by dividing it into phases, acceptance may consequently be retarded.

⚙ ACTIVITY

1 Consider four new ideas promoted by an adult education programme in your country. How was the spread and acceptance of programme ideas affected by the factors of relative advantage, compatibility, complexity, observability, and divisibility?
2 Discuss an example of an adult education programme that was implemented where there was a negative demand on the part of the intended beneficiaries.

ASSESSMENT OF MARKETING OPPORTUNITIES

The field of adult education has changed rapidly over the past two decades. It has evolved from a one-way reliance on public servants communicating adult education programmes to a more complicated approach, which borrows successful techniques used by commercial marketers. There has also been a sharp move away from the top-down approach to education (where information is dictated by those 'above' to the passive recipients 'below'), to an alternative, participatory approach based on programme developers listening to the needs and desires of the adult learners and building these needs and desires into programme design, development and implementation.

This focus on the adult learners and their needs requires research analysis and a constant re-evaluation of every aspect of the programme. In this section of the chapter, we shall look at how social marketing of adult education programmes is assessed.

SWOT analysis

A SWOT analysis may sound like a form of mission planning for James Bond! However, this is not the case. SWOT simply stands for Strengths, Weaknesses, Opportunities and Threats and it is a business instrument to be found in the toolbox of any commercial marketer. Each element of the analysis forms a box on a grid, which is completed and the information used to help formulate a marketing strategy.

Strengths and Weaknesses are the two elements of the analysis that focus on the internal operations of a business or organisation. Many people find this part of the analysis relatively straightforward, as it asks them to consider issues that they are familiar with already. However, Threats and Opportunities must be analysed with equal rigour because they relate to the practical realities of the external world. This is where a SWOT analysis is helpful: it asks an individual to look outwards, as well as inwards, to see what action is needed.

A SWOT analysis will yield different results for different people or organisations, depending on the subjective assessments of the person or organisation performing the analysis. However, there are a number of benefits that apply in most situations, particularly for the small businessman or woman, and these include:

- insight into where your business should focus in order to achieve growth;
- a better understanding of the industry structure by using a SWOT analysis in your business plan;
- a more focused advertising and marketing campaign in areas that may give you a competitive advantage in the marketplace; and
- the foresight to see imminent threats and to react to these threats proactively.

Although the SWOT analysis is more obviously applicable to commercial activities, the social marketer can still draw upon what it has to offer. For example, a proposed adult education programme can clearly be assessed in terms of its strengths and weaknesses. The programme developer can use the SWOT technique to establish what strengths can be built upon and what weaknesses require remedial action. And, because the programme developer competes for the 'business' of adult learners with other educational providers, a SWOT analysis of the threats and opportunities that exist in the adult education marketplace is also possible.

SUMMARY

In this chapter, we have introduced the concept of programme marketing and its related economic concepts of wants, demand and resources. The interrelationship between these concepts is also explained as far as it applies to adult education programme marketing. Beyond the simple definition of concepts, programme marketing requires an understanding of the principles and processes involved. Programme marketing deals with the mobilisation of human, material and financial resources that are needed to implement and sustain a programme.

In adult and continuing education, marketing must be viewed beyond the commercial understanding of selling a tangible product for physical consumption. Programme marketing in adult education should aim at effectiveness and gaining participation rather than notions of consumption and profit.

The modern approach to marketing revolves around four elements commonly known as 'the four Ps': product, price, place and promotion. These same elements can be applied to the social marketing that occurs during programme development, although their application is interpreted from a social sciences perspective, rather than a market economics one.

Wherever possible in this chapter, we have highlighted the usefulness of drawing upon commercial marketing practices for programme marketing for adult education. The adult educator's work is based in the real world, where competing interests, needs and values exist among potential participants and between different adult education programmes. The programme developer must address these challenges by using sound marketing practices, many of which have their foundation in the commercial arena. The use of the SWOT analysis is one area where we considered the programme developer might achieve success in his or her marketing campaign.

However, programme marketing is crucially different to commercial marketing in several respects. For the social marketer, there is the problem of the invisible benefits and intangible products associated with adult education. Adult learners cannot perceive any immediate or obvious gains arising from a development programme. Often, the benefits of a programme are not realised until a later date, yet the social marketer still has to convince his target audience of the value of participating in the programme. This means that the adult educator must continuously strive to meet the real needs of his or her target group of learners and to design a programme that is fully compatible with these needs. The social marketer is also constrained by limited budgets, a low-literate audience, non-existent or negative demand and several other factors. Together, these factors pose a significant challenge to the social marketer whose intention is to gain acceptance for and use of an adult education programme.

KEY POINTS

- The term social marketing refers to the design, promotion, implementation and control of programmes that seek to increase the acceptability of a social idea or practice in a target group.
- Social marketing is treated as an endeavour that can be engaged in by profit-making as well as non-profit making private and public organisations.
- Social marketing generally encourages people to do something that will be beneficial to others as well as themselves.
- The effectiveness of social marketing is influenced by a number of factors that the social marketer needs to overcome.

ACTIVITY

Consider yourself in the position of District Adult Education Officer.

1 **Prepare a marketing plan for a new course that you are about to implement.**
2 **Discuss some of the problems you are likely to face in selling the plan to potential programme participants.**

FURTHER QUESTIONS

1 How is the concept of demand different to the concepts of needs and wants?
2 Define market segmentation and discuss two criteria that you can use for segmenting potential clients for an adult education programme.
3 Explain how you would apply the commercial concepts of suppliers, consumers and product to the design of a marketing programme for adult learners.
4 Discuss four components of a marketing environment.

SUGGESTED READING

Kotler, P. 2003. Social Marketing: An approach to planned social change. *Journal of Marketing*: 3-12.

Andreasen, A. R. 1995. *Marketing social change: Changing behavior to promote health, social development, and the environment*. San Francisco: Jossey-Bass.

Chapter 9

Participation in programme development

OVERVIEW

This chapter aims to provide you with an understanding of the theory and practice of participation in the African context of adult education programme development. The chapter begins with a conceptual clarification of participation and how the approach can be traced into African cultures. We then move on to discuss the nature of participation and the many interpretations and principles on which it is founded. This section ends with a presentation of commonly documented working interpretations of participation, which is the central theme of this chapter. The next sections address the types and levels of participation in programme development, the rationale for involving people in programme development, and the obstacles that may hamper people's participation in programme development. The last two sections are devoted to the methods and techniques of involving people in programme development.

LEARNING OBJECTIVES

After studying this chapter, you should be able to:

1 Define and describe the nature of participation in programme development.
2 Discuss the rationale for involving people in programme development.
3 Describe the types and levels of people's participation in programme development.
4 Describe the methods and techniques of involving people in programme development.

bese saka

KEY TERMS

involvement   This refers to the activities and actions that an adult educator engages in order to get participation from others.

participation   A process during which individuals, groups and organisations are given the opportunity to become actively involved in programme development.

conscientisation   This is an ongoing process by which a learner moves towards critical consciousness. It means breaking through prevailing mythologies to reach new levels of awareness; in particular, awareness of oppression and of being an 'object' in a world where only 'subjects' have power. The process of conscientisation involves identifying contradictions in experience through dialogue and through becoming part of the process of changing the world.

empowerment   A working style that aims to help people achieve their own purpose by increasing their confidence and capacity. Empowerment is expressed in collective action on behalf of mutually agreed upon goals.

⊞ BEFORE YOU START

Consider a previous learning activity that you have attended (for example, workshop, programme development session, discussion, training exercise) where you believed a participatory approach was used. Based on your experience at that time, answer the following questions:

1   Did the participants have a common and agreed working definition or understanding of 'participation'?
2   What was your understanding of participation in this activity?
3   What were you trying to achieve through participation?
4   Were the right stakeholders involved?
5   What were the constraints placed upon the participation process?

THE CONCEPT OF PARTICIPATION

The concept of participation is not new. Although currently a popular notion in Western countries and international development agencies, the philosophical and theoretical foundations of what is now encompassed by the term 'participation' are rooted in a wide variety of traditions. Participatory approaches can be traced in African cultures. Julius Nyerere, the former president of Tanzania, was concerned with people's ability to act in order to change and control their environment. 'Self-reliance' was the term he used to emphasise that people cannot be developed or educated; they must develop and educate themselves through a process of thinking, problem-solving, and acting. The goal of this process, according to Nyerere, was liberation from constraining forces and increased power over the environment. Nyerere also reiterated the crucial role that adult education played in this process, stimulating the desire for change and encouraging the belief that change can be realised.

Much of the current interest in participation also stems from the concerns of Paulo Freire, the Brazilian educator, who regards people as critical and creative beings capable of knowing and transforming their environments. In Freire's view, education can humanise, liberate and treat people as subjects who control their own lives; or it can domesticate, oppress, and treat them as objects to be manipulated. For education to be humanising, according to Freire, it must involve the learners in a process of problem-posing in which they describe, analyse, and act to redesign their realities. This process can only be done in a context of true communication; one in which learners and facilitators trust and respect one another (Freire, 1990).

A commitment to participation is also reflected in the work of several authors who emphasise group action as a central process in adult education programmes. From this perspective, adult education becomes a process of 'empowerment' that allows individuals, through collective programme development and action, to exercise greater control over the decisions, resources and institutions that affect their lives. When conceived of as an empowering process, adult education programmes assume several distinctive characteristics that relate to participation. These include, among other things:

- small cohesive learning groups;
- a gradual transfer of responsibility from outsiders to the learners themselves; and
- participant leadership.

This perspective implies changes in the relationship between outsiders and learners. The role of the outsider becomes one of raising questions and issues, not prescribing answers or solutions. Acting as a resource person, the outsider seeks to withdraw gradually from leadership in the programme, while still assuming some responsibility for its operation and outcomes. In such an environment, local leaders can become more confident about directing their own programmes.

ACTIVITY

1 Think of an ongoing adult education programme in your community and describe the various roles of local people in the programme.
2 Do you think the various roles played by local people represent participation?
3 How would you define the concept of participation?

TYPES OF PARTICIPATION

Researchers, including Uphoff (1979), have noted that the concept of participation is an ambiguous one, susceptible to many differing interpretations. In simple terms, participation means 'the act of taking part', but the connotations of this in relation to the development of an adult education programme are very complex. For example, an important question to consider is: 'Who is taking part and in what kind of activities?' Hence, using the word 'participation' in any particular context needs careful consideration.

In general, it is possible to identify a spectrum of meaning attached the term 'participation.' At one end of this spectrum, participation is interpreted to mean 'control'. Control in this context refers to an individual's right to be involved in decisions that affect his or her life; thereby asserting control over economic resources and political institutions. At the spectrum's mid-point, participation means 'consultation', whereby those holding economic, political or administrative power ask people for advice, which may be taken or ignored. At the spectrum's other end, participation means 'information', whereby people are told about decisions that have already been made.

The concept of participation also relates to the hierarchical level at which the participative process occurs. We can distinguish decision-making processes taking place at community, district, national and international levels. At each level, the nature of participation changes in terms of the people involved and their relative power relationships, as well as the scope and significance of the decisions to be made.

In this section of the chapter, our discussion will focus on the nature of participation of different groups in adult education programmes. Among the different kinds of participation that have been documented are:

- representational participation;
- information-sharing;
- consultation;
- joint decision-making;
- acting together; and
- building independent community initiatives.

Representational participation

Representational participation is based on the conscious effort of the programme developer to select individuals who represent a broad cross section of needs and interests of the community chosen for an adult education programme.

A Village Development Committee (VDC) in Botswana that is responsible for developing community programmes and projects is an example of representational participation. The VDC consists of the local authorities representation by the village head and ward councilors, the local police, the parent-teacher association, the farmers association, youth groups and religious bodies. Unlike direct participation, representation does not provide the opportunity for every community member to express their views relating to the problems and needs directly affecting them. The question is whether those chosen as representatives do act out of a genuine concern for the needs and wishes of the community.

Information-sharing

Information-sharing is participation that offers the least involvement but underpins all other types of participation. While information-sharing may be appropriate on its own in some circumstances, the programme developer is likely to encounter problems if he or she offers only information to adult learners who anticipate a greater level of involvement. Information-sharing should be seen as an essential, though fairly basic element of the more meaningful participation that occurs at a higher level. Information-sharing is appropriate under the following circumstances: (a) at the start of a consultation process with the promise of more opportunity to participate later; (b) where there is no room for manoeuvre and only one course of action is possible; and (c) in a situation where the course of action does not affect others. If, however, the programme developer wishes to empower programme participants, or there are other alternatives that participants want to pursue, or people want more involvement, then information-sharing becomes inappropriate.

The programme developer, as convener, is responsible for providing the level and quality of information needed for informed participation to occur. This will require efforts to enhance public understanding of programme goals and objectives as well as government policy and resource mobilisation processes. In the interest of creating a climate for public engagement with the process, a detailed initial information brief should spell out to the public what the programme is, what purpose it serves, the preparatory process proposed by the programme developer, and where the entry-points for participant involvement are. The programme participants and their representatives will need to share information in the preparatory stage, which is usually diagnostic or analytical in nature. Ongoing sharing of information is critical to effective monitoring and to end-of-programme evaluation processes.

Consultation

Consultation effectively means giving people a restricted choice and role in solutions. The programme developer may consult on the problems, consider alternative options, allow comments, take account of public opinion and negotiate before proceeding. However, the programme developer is not asking for help in taking action.

Consultation opportunities in programme development will arise throughout needs analysis and programme goal and content development. The boundaries between consultation and joint decision-making may be blurred in some cases. However, an important difference between them is that consultation does not imply any obligation to incorporate the participants' suggestions into the final product. In analytical and diagnostic work such as needs analysis and problem identification, the programme participants can be consulted by the programme developer who leads such activities. For institutional and budget analysis, the programme developer can consult academics and civil society analysts on appropriate strategies and priorities, and researchers can consult communities about their perspectives on institutions and their priorities for public action.

Throughout the goal-formulation stage, the representatives selected to participate directly should consult the other stakeholders, to ensure that their representation is authentic. Public endorsement of the programme by stakeholders should be based on a community-led ongoing consultation around the planned process, which, if approved, enhances its viability and legitimacy. Consultation with participants on the performance of providers, and on the appropriateness and effectiveness of programme measures, should form the basis for monitoring, implementation and for end-of-programme evaluation.

Consultation, according to Wilcox (1994), is appropriate under the following conditions:

- When you can offer people some choices on what you are going to do, but not the opportunity to develop their own ideas or participate in putting plans into action.
- When the programme developer has a clear vision and plans to implement a project or programme, and there appears to be a limited range of options.
- These options can be set out in terms that community members understand and that they can relate to their own concerns or needs.
- The initiator of the proposals can handle feedback and is prepared to use this to choose between or to modify options.

On the contrary, consultation is inappropriate when the following conditions apply:

- The programme developer wishes to base his or her decisions on the participants' views.
- The programme developer wants to empower community interests.
- The programme developer is not clear what he or she wishes to do and is seeking ideas.
- The programme developer does not have the resources or skills to carry out the options presented, nor any other means of implementing.

Joint decision-making

Joint decision-making is possible at some points of the programme development process. It implies some right to negotiate the content of the programme. Strong stakeholders (for example, local community leaders) can have a determining influence on content. Participants possessing relatively little power can also influence the process by, at the very least, refusing to sanction programme content that they dislike. At goal formulation stage, there is scope for participant representatives to make joint decisions with the programme developer about priority actions and how to execute them. At approval stage, the participants' decision of whether or not to ratify the outcome may prove influential in terms of formal ratification – an example, as we have just mentioned, of the relatively weak being able to impose their will. During implementation, when the roles, responsibilities and entitlements of stakeholders are considered, the programme developer and community actors will jointly decide these issues, as well agreeing upon a definition of performance standards for service provision, budgetary transparency and financial management. These issues will be a central aspect of implementation.

In joint decision-making, different actors always have different levels of authority and control, and the operation of these is not always transparent or vested in formal positions. In a situation where community actors have all the formal authority but are heavily dependent on donor resources, staff from donor agencies may be in a position to dominate the situation analysis and goal-formulation process.

Deciding together is a difficult stance for a programme developer to adopt, as it can mean people have the power to select a course of action that does not bring with it a measure of responsibility, or accountability, on their part. Deciding together means accepting other people's ideas, and then choosing from the options you have collectively developed. Deciding together is appropriate when, (a) it is important for people to own the solution; (b) the programme developer needs fresh ideas; and (c) there is sufficient time to engage in what is often a lengthy process. Conversely, deciding together is inappropriate when the programme developer has little room for manoeuvre and/or the programme content has been determined at a higher level.

Acting together

Acting together may involve short-term collaboration or forming more permanent partnerships with other interests. Acting together in partnership involves both deciding together and then acting together. This means the programme developer and the adult learners have a shared vision of what they want, and the means to carry it out. Partners need to trust each other as well as agree on what they want to do. Effective partnerships take a long time to develop. Each partner needs to feel they have an appropriate stake in the partnership and a fair say in what happens. Partnership, according to Wilcox (1994), may be appropriate under the following conditions:

- When one party cannot achieve what they want on their own.
- The various interests involved all get some extra benefit from acting together.
- There is commitment to the time and effort needed to develop a partnership.

Partnership is not likely to be appropriate under the following circumstances:

- One party holds all the power and resources and uses this to impose its own solutions.
- The commitment to partnership is only superficial.
- People want to have a say in making decisions, but are not committed to carrying out solutions.

Supporting independent community initiatives

Supporting independent community-based initiatives means helping others develop and carry out their own plans. Resource holders who promote this method may decide to place a limit on what they will support. Supporting independent community initiatives is the most empowering method, provided people want to do things for themselves. Using this method may involve people in setting up new forms of organisations to handle funds and carry out projects or programmes. The process has to be owned by, and moved at the pace of, those who are going to run the initiative. This method may be appropriate when, (a) there is a commitment to empower individuals or groups within the community; and (b) where people are interested in starting and running an initiative. On the other hand, use of the method is inappropriate when the following circumstances prevail: (a) higher level authorities impose theoretically sound but impractical community initiatives on those below; (b) where there is no commitment to provide training and support; (c) where there are insufficient resources to maintain initiatives in the longer-term; and (d) where there is limited time available.

Underlying this approach are several assumptions that may be regarded as technocratic, or questionable. Key questions which could be asked are:

- Will the programme developer regulate the process fairly, and include the interests of all key groups within the community?
- How will conflicts and differences of views, priorities and perspectives be mediated and resolved in developing the programme?

- To what extent can individuals genuinely participate in the programme development process?
- If intermediary people or organisations take on the role of representing community interests and views, will they be accountable to the community members that they claim to represent?

There are no easy answers to these and similar questions. What the programme developer can do, however, is provide legitimacy and leadership in these areas. Capacity building in leadership is therefore critical to an effective programme development process.

✳ ACTIVITY

Reflect on your experiences as an adult educator working in a rural community. Consider the different programme situations that you have encountered and match them against the type of participation used, as shown in the table below.

Type of participation	Programme situation
1. Representational participation	
2. Information-sharing	
3. Consultation	
4. Joint decision-making	
5. Acting together	
6. Community initiatives	

INVOLVING PEOPLE IN PROGRAMME DEVELOPMENT

Participation is widely regarded as a desirable and necessary element of the successful development, implementation and participatory evaluation of adult education programmes. The rationale is that people should be involved in making the decisions that affect their lives. This means that they should be able to express their views and make suggestions and requests that can be integrated into the development of programmes. Increased participation will, ideally, raise the level of commitment adult learners demonstrate towards the identified programme. Many adult educators now share the notion that beneficiaries of adult education programmes should be mobilised and encouraged to participate in decision-making.

Participation is viewed by many contemporary adult educators as a means of widening and redistributing opportunities to enable the participants to become involved in decision-making that affects their lives. Adult learners who are beneficiaries of adult education programmes are no longer regarded as objects of educational programmes; instead, they are viewed as subjects capable of thinking and making decisions about programme goals, content, resources and logistics.

Participation in programme development can be considered important for three main reasons. Firstly, it is a means of obtaining information about local conditions, needs and attitudes that will be essential to the success of the programme. Secondly, people are more likely to be committed to an adult education programme if they are involved in its planning and preparation, because they are more likely to identify with it and see it as *their* programme. This commitment is necessary in order to ensure the participants' acceptance or adoption of the programme, particularly if the programme content requires a change in the way a great number of people think, feel and act. It is also important for securing local assistance in the construction or maintenance of the programme. Local contributions in cash or kind may be easier to get for 'self-help' projects if people see these as something they have helped to initiate. The third reason for encouraging participation is that involvement of people in their own development is now considered their basic democratic right. This is considered to be in line with the concept of human-centred development, in which the development process works towards benefiting the participants, rather than regarding the participants as agents of development.

There is sufficient evidence to show that the benefits of the participatory approach to programme development can be profound. Some of the specific reasons why it is crucial to involve people in programme development are outlined below.

Ethical reasons

The contributions people make can improve their self-esteem. The participation process can act as a form of social therapy. New relationships can be developed and feelings of isolation reduced, especially for more disadvantaged participants. It is ethical for providers to take all necessary steps to see that the participants come out of the learning situations with concrete behavioural changes (which is the reason why they enrolled in the programme in the first place). Adult education is not equivalent to indoctrination, mesmerism, hypnotism or head-shrinking. Adult education is for adults: learners as adults are not likely to tolerate moral ignorance or insensitivity in their teaching-learning relationship.

Programme benefits

Programme benefit is measured in terms of financial gains, increase in social prestige, and change in behaviour. However, it is common practice, especially with private providers of adult education, for programmes to place an overwhelming stress upon financial returns. That is, the determining factor or consideration is on what type of programme will make their business a success; and what subject, in case of remedial classes, will be heavily patronised. Some providers will take on one type of programme rather than another for precisely this reason. This explains the profusion of programmes in fields that could easily yield huge returns, such as remedial evening classes and computer literacy courses. The real purpose for mounting adult education programmes, though, should focus on the adult learners. Adults are more likely to participate in and support adult education programmes when they believe that the programme is going to benefit them directly or indirectly.

Goal attainment

The aim of any adult educator is programme effectiveness, which is the ability to achieve programme goals. Programme goals are determined at the onset of programme design by allowing people to participate in programme decisions that will reflect the relevant needs and opportunities of individuals, groups and communities. When people participate and are presented with the accurate intentions of programme effort, they will identify their most critical problems. In the end, programmes developed with the needs and problems of the participants at the centre are likely to succeed. It is also more likely that the participation of people in programme development will facilitate the process of change. The assumption is that those who participate in making programme decisions do not only legitimise the change process, but also serve as agents of change by spreading messages related to the programme.

Efficient use of resources

Participation facilitates the more efficient use of programme resources. This is because decision-making and programme development is based primarily on participatory needs assessment and the identification of local conditions, capacities and priorities.

Cost effectiveness

Participation has a positive impact upon cost effectiveness. This is because programme participants who take responsibility for a programme will require fewer costly outside resources. Instead, local contributions (including labour, materials and equipment) are used to supplement, or in some cases substitute, outside resources.

Self-reliance

Participation generates greater self-reliance by breaking the culture of dependency that characterises much development work in Africa. The influence local people can have on programme development can empower them to seek greater independence and control over their own lives.

Coverage

Participation ensures coverage by opening up access to programme benefits to a larger number of participants. The sharing of costs, especially by those who have the

ability to contribute, is another contributing element towards increased coverage.

Sustainability

Participation is fundamental to developing a self-sustaining momentum of development. In contrast to an externally motivated programme, participatory activities tend to have greater sustainability since the programme participants have a stronger sense of ownership of the programme. This in turn creates a greater willingness to use and maintain the programme on the part of the adult learners. The participants' awareness of the necessity and effectiveness of their active participation in their own development ensures that progress continues even after the programme sponsors pull out.

Learning process

Participation in adult education programmes is a learning experience. As the programme development process unfolds, people continuously learn through their own direct and indirect participation. Through participation, they become more skilled, knowledgeable and creative in problem solving. Participation in programme development promotes active learning. Participation also means that people learn about leadership, group dynamics, cooperation, and conflict resolution. Depriving stakeholders of this learning opportunity may force them into resistance mode.

Local resource mobilisation

Participation is considered as a way of mobilising resources for programme implementation. When people participate in goal formulation and are satisfied that the goals represent their felt needs, they can commit their energy, financial, and material resources to the achievement of goals. It is also true that programmes built on the local resources of participants are more likely to be sustainable than those entirely dependent on external support.

⬚ ACTIVITY

In a group session with your classmates, discuss some of the reasons given in favour of involving programme participants in programme development.

OBSTACLES TO PARTICIPATION

The process of participatory programme development is not without its problems. Stakeholders might agree on their programme's goals, for example, but not on the means for achieving them. Different groups may have different priorities or they may not share the same sense of urgency about different components of their programme. They may disagree on leadership issues, or how resources should be used. Those with overall responsibility for the programme may conclude that involving people in programme development takes longer and is less efficient than doing the job themselves. Also, the people who are invited to participate may be confused and intimidated by the system they have been invited to join.

It is therefore logical to say that despite the importance placed upon participation as a prerequisite for development programmes to succeed, many organisations in Africa still experience poor participation of adult learners in their programmes.

An individual's decision not to participate in programme development activities is not determined by isolated obstacles, but rather by the synergistic action of multiple obstacles. These obstacles, or constraints, can be categorised as dispositional, situational or institutional in nature.

Dispositional constraints

Dispositional constraints present major obstacles to adult learner participation in programme development in Africa. Among the dispositional obstacles are:

1 Scepticism and worries about the success of the programme.
   Scepticism arises from previous experiences of development programmes. Many educational programmes fail because there is a lack of trained and skilled personnel to implement them. As a result, adult learners who have experienced this programme failure will find it difficult to believe in the potential success of any new programmes that are proposed for their benefit. Even with clear and convincing explanations from programme developers, adults with previous experience of programme failure remain very doubtful.
2 Fear of losing customary rights to the government.
   Many development programmes in Africa relate to land usage, particularly in poorer rural communities where agricultural development is often prioritised. Land users in these rural areas seldom hold official title over the land they cultivate; instead, their ownership of the land is regarded as a native customary right. However, because the rural dwellers claim to the land is not officially sanctioned, they believe that the government is using the development programme as a pretext for taking their land, and therefore their livelihood, away from them. Some programmes also take a long time to complete, which means the programme participants will not have land to cultivate during the interim.

3 Lack of clarity surrounding the programme's purpose.
   If programme developers and government officials do not clearly explain the concept and objectives of a project, it is likely that the participants will reject or retard the project's implementation. Because they cannot understand the official explanation of the project objectives, the community may become suspicious of the programme and believe that it will not benefit them in any way.
4 People are comfortable with what they already have and happy with their present way of life.
5 People perceive the programme as a source of problems and not benefits.
6 Exclusion from programme development.
   When programmes are centrally planned, the proposed beneficiaries may think that the programme administrators have no interest in their feelings and desires, or in serving their needs and interests. Marginalised or ignored completely in the decision-making process, potential participants may therefore withdraw their support for the programme.

Situational constraints

Situational constraints include:

1 Lack of resources such as land, time, transportation, capital and labour.
2 Inaccessibility due to remote geographic location.
3 Deterrence due to political influence.
   The opposition party or parties in a community may want the programme to fail for political reasons. If community members can be persuaded to reject the proposed programme, and the programme subsequently collapses, the opposition can blame this failure on the ruling party. This in turn may lead to diminished support for the existing governing body and increased support for the opposition.

Institutional constraints

Institutional constraints are those practices and procedures that exclude or discourage adults from participating in learning activities. Among institutional barriers are:

1 inconvenient schedules or locations for programmes;
2 lack of relevant or appropriate programmes; and
3 the emphasis on full-time study, as opposed to part-time study, in many institutions.

CASE STUDY: DNFE'S LITERACY CLASS

The village of New Xade is one of the Government of Botswana's new initiatives to relocate the Basarwa. The Department of Non-Formal Education (DNFE) has decided to introduce adult basic education in the village for several reasons. One of the main reasons is that many villagers cannot read or write. There is also the problem of a shortage of paid work in the area and many of the youth are leaving the village to get jobs in towns and cities. The youth who migrate, however, do not find jobs because they are illiterate. Mr Dipholo, an employee of DNFE, has started literacy classes in New Xade.

Initially, the class members are very excited and class attendance is good. Villagers say that they enjoy the classes because they give them the opportunity to talk about community issues together, and to learn. They also like the teacher, Mr Dipholo, because he is kind and respects everybody in the village. Mr Dipholo treats the learners as intelligent subjects and not as objects, even when they have difficulties with reading and writing.

However, after the fourth week of classes 70% of the learners have left, which leaves Mr Dipholo wondering what has gone wrong. After speaking to some of the villagers, Mr Dipholo discovers the following reasons for the villagers' defection:

1 They don't see the need to continue literacy classes because they are not sure the effort will earn them employment.
2 There are many other things that the residents of New Xade worry about, including hunting, preparation of food for meals, and getting extra income for *chibuku* (a locally brewed beer).
3 Difficulties in adapting to the new environment, which they find artificial compared to the natural environment where they lived previously.
4 Problems coping with the rules and regulations of modern society.
5 Trying to cope with theft and sexual harassment from outsiders who visit the village while claiming to be petty traders.

Mr Dipholo decides to change his classes. Instead of making literacy the main focus, he tells the villagers that the classes are now about helping people to find solutions to their problems and to cope with the pressures of new life in the village. Mr Dipholo convinces the villagers, including the leaders, that the classes will help individuals and families to solve the problems that affect them. After this, the adults of New Xade resume their classes. Mr Dipholo is very happy to work with the literacy participants in solving their problems.

In the new classes, Mr Dipholo organises participants into groups to identify and prioritise the problems that require attention. The participants also identify the resources that they have and those that they need from

outside sources. The New Xade villagers now have a vegetable garden, two dairy cows, and a good-sized poultry farm. These programmes bring both food and extra income to the participants, who now accept literacy as a component of their income-generating activities.

ACTIVITY

Read the case study above and then answer the following questions.

1 **What were the original reasons for introducing adult basic education in New Xade village?**
2 **Why did the villagers stop participating in the literacy classes?**
3 **What would you have done differently at the beginning of the programme to sustain the interest and participation of villagers?**
4 **How would you relate participation to the needs of programme participants?**

METHODS OF PARTICIPATION

The methods used to involve adult learners in programme development include:
(a) surveys; (b) collaboration/input/sponsorship; (c) community development; (d) organisation; (e) empowering; (f) short-term interventions; (g) longer-term programmes; (h) consultative committees and meetings; (i) established leadership and communication structures; and (j) simulations. We will now look at some of these methods in more detail.

Surveys

Surveys provide an important point for participation processes. Whether they enable people to participate significantly in decision-making, and subsequent action, depends very much on the way they are done. Surveys can be time-consuming and expensive, and should therefore be undertaken only when other means cannot be used. Surveys are appropriate when information is needed from diverse groups, and/or where distance may make face-to-face meetings difficult or impossible. The survey methodology has been discussed in detail in Chapter 5 of this book under approaches to needs assessment. The important thing to note here is that surveys, whether conducted by interviews or completed at home by respondents, may be improved if local groups are involved in the design, collection and analysis of data.

Collaboration

Where this concept is used to encourage participation, there is much reliance on government responsibility and control. The terms 'collaboration', 'input', and 'sponsorship', therefore, reflect a form of participation in which the government is the leading proponent for social change. This form of participation is parallel to informing. The basic decisions that underlie the development process have already been taken and government bureaucracy, in the process of implementation, invites the potential clients to endorse and to collaborate with the decisions taken. It is, in essence, a passive form of participation (Oakley and Marsden, 1984).

Community development

Community participation is defined as the process by which individuals, families or communities assume responsibility for their own health and welfare and develop the capacity to contribute to their own and the community's development. In this type of participation, the voice of the people is to some extent heard. Participation is actively promoted and involves some delegation of responsibility at the community level and the creation of local councils as vehicles for participation. Unlike the more centrally dominated type of community development, local opinions and needs are taken into account. The participation is, however, confined to the task at hand and there is little evidence that the experience is used in order that the participants can tackle their more fundamental problems.

Organisation structures

The argument in the literature on participation follows the trend that, if participants can be brought into some form of organisational structure, their participation would be ensured. Closely associated with the concept of organisation is the assumption that, once such organisations are established, the people will automatically have a voice and can influence decision-making. Unfortunately, for Africa, formal organisations such as cooperatives, rural unions and women's groups have proved inadequate in facilitating the participation of poor people into development programmes. This failure, according to Oakley and Marsden (ibid.), is a reflection of the bureaucratic constraints that limit the successful functioning of the institutions, rather than weaknesses on the part of the institutions per se.

Empowering

The concept of participation as a means for empowerment has quite recently emerged as a dominant paradigm in the literature of adult education. At the core of this concept is the notion of power. Participation in this sense is therefore equated to achieving power in terms of access to, and control of, the resources necessary to protect livelihood.

The following statements illustrate this understanding of participation:

1   Participation is considered as a multi-dimensional social process that helps people gain control over their own lives. It is a process that fosters the capacity to implement in people, for use in their own lives, their communities, and in their society, by acting on issues that they define as important (Page and Czuba, 1999).
2   Participation focuses on the strengths of people, providing opportunities and resources for people to gain experiences and skills while they also gain control over their lives (Horton, 1989).
3   Power is the central theme of participation. Participatory social action entails widely shared, collective power exercised by those who are considered beneficiaries. The people become agents of social action and the power differentials between those who control and those who need resources are reduced through participation.

The understanding of participation as empowering has three main elements:

■   the sharing of power and scarce resources;
■   deliberate efforts by social groups to control their own destinies and improve their living conditions; and
■   opening up opportunities from below.

Established leadership and communication structures

Organisations such as local authorities often favour participation methods that fit with their own way of working. In this scenario, they invite people to join committees, or to set up other structures. Jerry Smith of the Community Development Foundation (quoted in Wilcox, 1994) suggests five main classes of organisations used by local authorities. These are: (i) consultative bodies; (ii) councillor bodies on wards or other local authority administrative divisions (for example, the Kgotla in Botswana); (iii) joint bodies composed of councillors and community representatives; (iv) narrow-range community organisations such as women's groups and youth organisations; and (v) broad-range community associations such as neighbourhood and community councils.

🔡 ACTIVITY

Consider the methods of involving people in programme development and identify the strengths and weaknesses of each method, using the table below.

Method	Strengths	Weaknesses
Surveys		
Collaboration		
Community development		
Organisation		
Empowering		
Leadership and communication		

SUMMARY

Participation in adult education programmes is interpreted differently by different people according to their cultural perspective. At one extreme, participation is perceived as the passive consumer response of receiving services from a development programme. At the other extreme, participation is viewed as the complete ownership of the programme by the community. There are several other interpretations of the concept of participation that are positioned between these two opposing endpoints. As there is no universal agreement on the nature and content of the participation process, a definitive understanding of participation is difficult. However, as a starting point, a programme developer must agree on a working definition with the participants.

There are many types and levels of participation, including representational participation, provision of information, consultation, deciding together, acting together, and supporting independent community initiatives. There are also many reasons for mobilising and encouraging the participation of beneficiaries in the programme development process, including those relating to ethics, programme benefits, goal attainment, gaining of learning experience, and local resource mobilisation. Despite the benefits of participation, there are several obstacles that are responsible for non-participation. These obstacles can be categorised as dispositional, situational and institutional in nature.

There are no 'quick fixes' to participation. The process involves the use of appropriate methods and techniques, which must be carefully selected by a programme developer before engaging in programme development. The commonly used methods of ensuring the participation of programme participants include surveys, collaboration, community development, organisation, empowering, and established leadership and communication structures.

KEY POINTS

- Generally speaking, participation in adult education activities tends to be stronger in theory than in practice. The arguments for enhancing people's participation in adult education is often based mainly on idealistic, humanitarian or egalitarian grounds, while very little attention is given to the practical aspects of participation. There is, however, sufficient evidence to show that the benefits of the participatory approach to programme development can be profound.
- The methods and techniques of participation are numerous and vary from one programme to another. It is important to identify and select the appropriate participatory methods and techniques applicable for each stage of the programme development process.
- The participatory programme development process is likely to thrive in a conducive, caring, democratic environment, rather than in a constraining, highly structured system. Successful participatory programme development will therefore depend on political commitment and genuine interest towards a participatory development process, and confidence and trust in the potential and capacity of the programme participants to learn and develop.

▓ ACTIVITY

Think of an adult education programme that you helped develop and implement.
1 Describe the goals of the programme and its intended beneficiaries.

2 Identify the problems that you encountered in trying to involve the beneficiaries at each stage of the programme cycle.

3 For each of the problems you have identified, suggest an appropriate method(s) and/or technique(s) that would have helped you to ensure the participation of the programme beneficiaries.

FURTHER QUESTIONS

1 What are the distinctive characteristics of participation when conceived of as an empowerment process?

2 Why is it difficult to achieve people's participation in adult education programmes?

3 On what guiding principles would you base people's participation in adult education programmes?

4 What institutions in our country can play important roles in building district and local level capacity in participatory programme development?

SUGGESTED READING

Frankel, Larry. 1981. Small-Small Catch Monkey: Non-Formal Education and Public Health in Ghana. *World Education Reports.* No. 23, April. World Education, Inc., 251 Park Avenue South, New York 10010, USA.

Lewycky, Dennis. 1977. Tapestry – Report from Oodi Weavers. (Working Paper No.11.). National Institute for Research in Development and African Studies (NIR), Documentation Unit, University of Botswana and Swaziland, Gaborone, Botswana.

Masisi, Yohana K. C. 1980. The Chiwanda Nutrition Education Project. *Journal of Adult Education* – Tanzania, No. 2. Institute of Adult Education, Dar es Salaam, Tanzania.

Chapter 10

Programme implementation

OVERVIEW

This chapter provides a systematic appraisal of programme implementation. For the purposes of our discussion, we can refer to implementation as the need to engage in the teaching-learning activities designed to meet programme objectives. This chapter emphasises the following issues: (i) the meaning of implementation; (ii) key features of implementation; (iii) stages of the implementation process; (iv) critical questions on implementation; (v) the administration role in programme implementation; and (vi) the in-programme process.

LEARNING OBJECTIVES

By the end of this chapter, you should be able to:

1 Understand the concept of programme implementation.
2 Specify critical features of programme implementation.
3 Produce plans that lay out how a programme will be conducted and the actions needed to track implementation over time.
4 Identify content, resources, facilities and auxiliary services necessary for the implementation of a specific adult education programme.

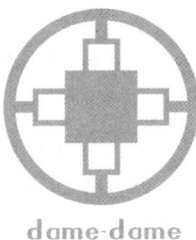

dame-dame

KEY TERMS

implementation   To put into practice planned teaching-learning and assessment exercises aimed at fulfilling the programme goals and learners' desired expectations. It consciously applies adult education principles to explore the social values, problems and needs of adult learners.

methods   The techniques, processes and stages by which adult learners understand programme content in order to attain the desired teaching and learning objectives.

purpose   In an adult education context, this refers to the fact that each programme is executed for specific reasons.

order   In an adult education context, this refers to the systematic structuring of programme development, implementation and evaluation.

utility   This refers to the fact that adult education programmes have real-world applications. Learners in these programmes gain skills, knowledge and attitudes that they can use in real-life situations.

assessment   An exercise in which an answer or rating is given in response to a task or question. For adult learners, this exercise includes undertaking service learning (projects in the community), written tests, school-based projects, oral presentations, storytelling and essay writing.

⊞ BEFORE YOU START

What do you understand by the term 'implementation'? Have you ever attended a teaching-learning activity where you considered the implementation process to be unsatisfactory? If so, can you identify the reasons why implementation was poor?

THE MEANING OF IMPLEMENTATION

In life, people want to accomplish the goals they set. The key to achieving this lies in structuring the way in which these goals are reached. Imagine yourself five years from now – try to think of what you hope to be doing by then. What are your dreams? When you let your mind follow the fantasies you have, you will mentally picture yourself thinking, acting and talking in a certain way. You may even visualise the place or places where you will be. The concept of the dream is used here to refer to things that you aspire to be, to do or to achieve. Implementation may be viewed as a way of making these dreams come true. It is a way of turning dreams (plans) into reality.

In the Random House College Dictionary (1988: 667), implementation is defined as, 'to put into effect according to or by means of a definite plan or procedure'. In the context of adult educational programmes, implementation refers to putting the programme goals and design to work by conducting teaching-learning activities and assessment exercises aimed at fulfilling the desired expectations (Grotelueschen, 1980). It involves two major aspects: (i) developing the implementation plan; and (ii) putting the plan into action.

Implementation within an African context

It is important here to take a closer look at how implementation of adult education programmes appears from an African perspective. A number of writers approaching this topic from an Afrocentric position, such as Ocitti (1973), Pretorious (2002) and Mgadla (2003), see implementation of educational programmes as a step-by-step teaching and learning process through which social values, the survival needs of the learners, the problems and challenges of their lives, and the realities of their African situation are explored. Remember that in Chapter 2 we established that one of the goals of adult education is to help learners to be better prepared for their adult roles in their societies. Thus, implementation should concentrate on ways in which individuals and communities can respond to their present conditions of living. This is a meaningful way of helping learners adapt to their environments and to be better prepared for the eventualities of the future.

One of the fundamental needs of teaching and learning in and for an African context is that the teaching-learning should be functional. This means that what the African learner is taught should be used to address his or her life circumstances. This type of education involves programme content and knowledge that relates directly to the life experiences of adult learners. In essence, the teaching-learning environment is a problem-solving process and one that is concerned with, 'what the learner can do as a result of the entire range of learning experiences' (Pretorious, 2002: 80). Learning, therefore, should be realistic, purposeful and pragmatic rather than theoretical (Ocitti, 1973).

However, the dichotomy between educational theory and practical reality still exists. As one commentator notes: 'many Africans are still unhappy about the gap between what is implemented in formal schools and the life and needs of individuals and society at large' (Busla, 1968: 26). This undesirable situation therefore compels implementers to teach learners in accordance with the principles of functionalism and outcomes-based learning. Learners should explore opportunities in their own lives. Viewed broadly then, implementation is seen as each and every step taken to attain a desirable learning goal or goals.

⚎ ACTIVITY

What should be the main consideration for adult educators implementing programmes for learners in Africa?

KEY FEATURES OF PROGRAMME IMPLEMENTATION

Programmes come in different types and forms and with different purposes. Among different types of programmes are self-help, vocational, compensatory, correctional, adult basic education, literacy, intergenerational, self-enriching, and leisure. These programmes have varied forms of content; they may even employ different approaches to content learning as well as different kinds of resources. However, all programmes share the unifying principles of purpose, order and utility. Table 10.1 below indicates the types and purposes of programme currently available in an adult educational context.

Although markedly different from one another, the programmes are united in their intention to present adult learners with specific programme objectives (purpose), teaching and learning methods (order), and teaching-learning outcomes (utility). Thus,

the presumption is that each programme has a purpose, an order and some utility. These aspects are explained in the discussion that follows.

Programme purpose

All programmes have a purpose. The general purpose of an adult education programme is to transmit the desired knowledge, skills, ideas, attitudes and patterns of behaviours (Mgadla, 2003) that could help individuals to be functional, firstly, in their African societies, then elsewhere. Thus, effective implementation should constantly remind and make learners aware of the problems and challenges of the communities they belong to, and how their learning can be put to good use in their communities. As we know, in the African traditional way of learning, people, 'were educated in and for the community's way of life' (Busla, 1968: 17). That is, the knowledge, skills, and attitudes that are promoted in the programme should apply to the real-life challenges and problems of adult learners. When programmes do not serve the people, there is a reason to be concerned.

A genuine concern amongst many African learners is that formal education does not prepare them properly for the lives

Table 10.1 Types of adult education programmes.

Types of programme	Purpose
Compensatory	To provide remedial learning opportunities for adults to overcome illiteracy
Liberal	To study the humanities, arts, and sciences, with an emphasis on free inquiry, curiosity, and intellectual growth rather than utilitarian purposes or persuasion to partisan points of view
Occupational	To develop job-related knowledge, skills or abilities in order to secure, maintain, or advance employment opportunities in a career
Academic	To teach undergraduate courses, graduate courses, or conduct research in adult learning and instruction
Self-help	To provide knowledge, information, skills or recreational learning in order to adjust better to environments outside the work environment

Source: Birkenholz, 1999

they will lead in their communities. Formal education often ignores the practical elements of community life, where knowledge of the environment, wildlife, farming and craft skills are needed for the community to function properly. Similarly, the importance many Africans attach to inherited values is often missing from adult education curricula. The well-being of a community is dependent to a large extent on each succeeding generation taking on the good practices of the preceding generation, which are handed down in an informal manner from the older community members to the youth.

Programme order

All adult education programmes have order, which means that the implementation process follows some established orientations, philosophies and principles. There are orientations such as constructive learning theories, reflective learning, self-directed learning, problem-based learning, experience-based learning and transformative learning. Each of these orientations has some kind of order. The order is reflected in principles that guide the application of each orientation.

One principle to be applied in dealing with self-directed learners, for example, is that facilitators should avoid highly structured teaching-learning environments when dealing with this group. Instead, two-way (interactive) approaches are recommended. For instance, when a programme is implemented to promote income-generation, analysis of the needs of participants normally starts at the individual level, looking at what has motivated an individual to be involved in an income-generation programme. Thereafter, when teaching, a flow diagram may be used to examine all stages involved in running a business. In short,

implementers normally map out the order that their implementation process will take.

Programme utility

People make efforts to run adult education programmes that are useful. Utility implies an ability to apply knowledge, skills and attitudes gained in the classroom setting in real-life situations (Ocitti, 1973). Traditionally, African people learned by engaging in active and productive learning, such as practical farming, cooking and fishing; in these instances, people learned 'what is of utility to them' (Ocitti, 1973: 93). Learning is largely practical and it enables the learners to live productively in their local environments. For a greater part, therefore, learning in adult education has this utilitarian focus. The performance indicators of this type of learning are: (i) the ability to make rational decisions; (ii) the ability to make judgments; and (iii) the ability to act appropriately when confronted with life tasks. People engage in adult education programmes because they hope to emerge with knowledge, skills and attitudes that they can apply in all functions of their lives (cultural, social, economic and political). It makes no sense, for example, for small-scale rural farmers in Africa to learn about international agricultural trends and markets because this knowledge will have no direct bearing on their working lives.

⊞ ACTIVITY

Imagine that you are an adult educator who has to give a lesson on how to run an adult education programme. Which of the three key features of programme implementation (purpose, order, utility) would you emphasise most, and why?

STAGES OF THE IMPLEMENTATION PROCESS

Successful programme implementation involves developing and putting the plan into action and can be divided into three categories: (i) planning and preparing for the learning activities; (ii) finding and using relevant administration processes; and (iii) the in-programme process (the actual running of a programme), including the use of relevant assessment and follow-up strategies.

Planning and preparing

Adult educators base their teaching-learning activities on sound plans. The concept of a plan has been discussed in Chapter 6 and carries the same meaning here.

Planning is the first thing that facilitators do to prepare for implementation. The plan includes an outline of resources to be used, the learning activities to be done; as well as the time required for each activity. Other factors that need to be outlined in the plan are the use of learning facilities and teaching and learning materials. This question, 'What components are needed for implementation to take place?' can help facilitators decide what should go in the plan. These components are outlined below.

1 Content
   Implementation is about exploring, exchanging, sharing, constructing and gaining new information. In the context of adult education, such information is referred to as 'content'. The content component can be subdivided into several different elements, including:
   ■ Specific objectives. These are carefully stated objectives that capture the essence of the programme content in a clear, concise manner.

■ Learning activities. These are usually step-wise and/or time-bound operations that focus on particular subject matter. Activities are the means by which the subject matter is explored and grasped. Activities such as question-and-answer exercises, group discussions, role-plays, dramatisations, and written work are common learning activities in adult education.
■ Content sequencing strategies. The way the exchange, construction and acquisition of information is sequenced indicates the presumed level of the learners' understanding of the content. Learning for adults is always more effective when the content is organised, guided and sequenced in ways that lead to effective grasping of content. Commonly used sequencing strategies include simple to complex, chronological order, specific examples to general principles (inductive approach), and general principles to specific sequencing (deductive approach).
■ Facilitator's knowledge of the content. Prior to the actual teaching, the facilitator puts together an instructional/implementation plan, which indicates his or her knowledge of the content. Knowledge of the content is an indication of the teacher's preparedness. Qualified and experienced teaching and training staff are required. Going hand-in-hand with knowledge of the content is the facilitator's knowledge of adult teaching and learning strategies.

2 Facilities
During the planning process, facilitators should consider and prepare the facilities necessary for running the programme. Facilities include the physical environment, as well as teaching and learning materials and equipment. The availability

and accessibility of such facilities should be established prior to the actual running of the programme. Because learners learn best in safe, comfortable and healthy environments, proper thought should be given to issues such as seating arrangements, lighting and heating facilities, the availability of fresh drinking water, and so on.

3 Logistics
Logistics covers things such as class organisation (including class size), individual tutoring, group interactions, course length and programme timetable. Again, these issues must be addressed prior to programme implementation.

4 Resources
Resources are used to promote learning. Appropriate resources of personnel, materials, consumable supplies, utilities and other equipment are needed to run a programme. The range and type of resources used will be largely determined by the funding available from the sponsoring organisation.

5 Auxiliary services
Included in auxiliaries are common services such as refreshments, parking and transportation, printing, binding, and photocopying.

6 Administration
Adult educators and/or trainers should decide on the type of administrative functions needed to run the programme effectively and to support the programme participants. Issues of registration, financial management, safety, certification, evaluation and attendance form part of the administrative functions of an adult education programme.

7 Recognition of accomplishments
Adult learners come to the learning environment expecting to accomplish a learning goal. Therefore, the challenging issue of indicating learners' performance standards relative to their learning

goals and potentials using, for example, grading schemes and certification awards, must also be decided upon prior to programme implementation.

8 Programme evaluation
Programme evaluation should be an integral part of the teaching-learning environment. To foster the right climate for evaluation to prosper, it is first necessary to promote a culture of continuous self-assessment among learners and facilitators (Scheirer, 1994). The subject of programme evaluation forms the focus of the last chapter in this book, Chapter 11.

9 Methods
Methods are vehicles through which the objectives of the programmes are realised. Each method entails a set of learning activities, teacher and learner interactions, and the use of resources and facilities, which are all carefully coordinated to lead to the achievement of programmes goals. Assessment, too, is one of the activities included in the method of instruction. Viewed broadly, method is defined as, 'everything that is done, every step that is taken to attain the educational or learning purpose that is desired' (Ocitti, 1973: 102).

CASE STUDY: THE POORLY PLANNED PROGRAMME

Lopang, an adult educator, is given the responsibility of developing an education programme for a small farming community in a remote area of his province. Lopang has three team members to help him and three months to plan the project.

Lopang is extremely enthusiastic about the project and devotes all his energies to it. However, he also believes that he can perform the majority of the work by himself and so only gives the other three team members minor duties to fulfill.

However, with two weeks left of the three-month time schedule, Lopang realises that everything is not going as smoothly as he had anticipated. No programme facilitators have been appointed, transport arrangements for community members have been overlooked, and none of the local farmers have been consulted on the project. Alarmed, Lopang quickly solicits the help of a retired professor of adult education and three agricultural experts.

When the programme is implemented, the farmers are universally opposed to it. They complain that the professor knows very little about the everyday needs of the community and that the farming experts have no knowledge of local soil conditions or weather patterns. Because no transport facilities have been arranged, half the locals invited to the programme cannot get there. The participants were very keen on achieving an accredited certification for their programme work, but because Lopang had not consulted them, nothing of this nature has been arranged. Finally, about half the money that was set aside for the programme remained unused.

⬚ ACTIVITY

Read the above case study on Lopang and reflect on what mistakes he made in planning and implementing the programme for the farmers. If you had been given the responsibility for overseeing this project, how would you have done things?

CRITICAL QUESTIONS ON IMPLEMENTATION

Stufflebeam (1971) suggests a series of questions that can guide adult educators through the implementation process. These questions also explore the factors or elements that need to go into the instructional plan. The questions are as follows:

- What is to be learned?
- What type of facilities will be needed to run the programme?
- What time will the programme begin and how long will each session last?
- On what dates will the programme start and finish?
- What will be the arrangement of the classroom or meeting room?
- What resources will be needed and for what part of the programme will they be needed?
- How will the participants be involved? Will they be used as resources for learning?
- What materials, supplies, equipment and teaching aids will be needed for the programme?
- What type of refreshments will be needed and how will they be provided?
- How will achievements be recognised?

These questions direct the adult educator's attention towards the three principles of good programme design that we referred to at the beginning of the chapter: purpose, order and utility. These also form a useful checklist for the adult educator to refer to during the programme development process.

ADVICE TO HELP EDUCATORS PLAN WELL

Below are some practical suggestions that can help educators check the quality of their plans. The list is not exhaustive and may need adding to, depending on the specific requirements of individual programmes.

- Have a specific objective to be achieved at the end of the programme/lesson/course. For example, for a 30-minute lesson on planning adult education programmes, the facilitator may have an objective such as: 'At the end of the first 30 minutes, learners should be able to list three aspects that are considered important when planning to implement an adult education programme.' With an objective such as this, an educator may assess how effectively the content was delivered and how well the learners grasped this content.
- Have specific learning activities for every session.
  Learners come from a variety of settings. Furthermore, they have different expectations of the course, their learning styles differ, and they have varying levels of understanding. To cater for this variety, different learning activities are required. Activities should be matched carefully to the learners' experiences. A commonly used learning technique is group work. A variety of groupings, such as homogeneous grouping (same learning interests/skills levels/age/job-related experiences), heterogeneous grouping (mixed abilities, different interests/cultural background/gender) or social/peer grouping are used. The groups may engage in different activities, such as oral or written discussion, dramatisation, debate, and field projects. They may perform a number of hands-on activities.

The variety of activities caters for differences in learning styles and needs.
- List alternative procedures for introducing the lesson.
  It is advisable to think of more than one way to introduce the lesson/session. Also, educators must think about how they are going to close the lesson. Closure is the summation of the session/lesson. It is also important to plan alternative activities for the summation.
- Plan adequate breaks.
  After engaging in learning activities for a significant period of time, both the learners and facilitators may need a break. A break helps to refresh the participants. Time may be wasted when learners are denied a break that is necessary. When learners' concentration is weak and feelings of boredom, tiredness, frustration, or lack of motivation are experienced, educators should instigate a break period.
- Plan special rewards, reinforcement or motivating moments.
  Adult learners need to be motivated. Acknowledging responses with positive and encouraging remarks motivates adult learners. Some learning activities have inbuilt rewarding outcomes. Suppose learners are engaged in practical activities such as making a *morula* jam. *Morula* is one of the wild sour-taste berries found in parts of Southern Africa. It is used to make products such as jam, skin moisturising oil and soaps. Learners who are engaged in making any of the *morula* products may have something to take home at the end of the lesson. This would represent a great achievement for the adult learners. It motivates them and deepens their sense of self-achievement by sharing what they do in the classroom with people in authentic community settings. Activities such as this

one create a culture in which training activities are publicly recognised and valued. Facilitators usually plan rewards and motivating and reinforcing effects ahead of time, in order that the learners have something specific (and desirable) to work towards.

✷ ACTIVITY

If you were planning the implementation of an academic programme that aimed to change adult learners' attitudes towards working and living in rural areas, what aspects (name five) would guide your planning?

ADMINISTRATION IN PROGRAMME IMPLEMENTATION

Administration is an integral element of implementing adult education programmes. Administrative functions are those activities that the administrators do in order to make the programme successful (Boyle, 1981). These activities may include: (i) handling participants' registration and attendance records; (ii) distributing programme materials (for example, course outlines, programme packages); (iii) handling financial issues (payment for expenses associated with the programme); (iv) issuing or awarding professional licensure or certification; (v) carrying out evaluation activities; (vi) providing meals and refreshments; (vii) providing additional information; and (viii) programme promotion, marketing and publicity.

Administrative activities differ from programme to programme, especially according to the programme format or type. For example, a programme format such as a symposium or conference will require different administrative functions to, say, a one-year full-time course.

Administrative functions can be performed by a single person or a group of people. A single person, usually the facilitator, is in charge of small-scale programmes such as classroom lessons. In the case of large-scale programmes, a team usually assumes the administrative responsibilities. In large conferences, for instance, handling participants' registration as well as the distribution of information, schedules and other programme documents is done by a group of people, usually referred to as an advisory or planning committee.

Administration is therefore an indispensable function of an adult education programme. Galbraith, Sisco and Guglielmino (1997) suggest that an administrator must be an activist oriented toward designed actions and outcomes. They further advise that the administrator's role should be performed professionally and be considered an important function in the process of planning and implementing an adult education programme.

THE IN-PROGRAMME PROCESS

The term in-programme process refers to what goes on in the teaching-learning environment. The discussion here concentrates on a formal, rather than informal, learning setting.

Most of us have engaged in different types of learning environments and experiences. Despite these differences, however, we can say that all adult teaching-learning environments should follow an andragogical process. This process is explained in the following discussion.

The andragogical process

The concept of andragogy is popular in the field of adult education. While the literature makes it clear that this concept was not invented by Knowles (1968), he has, however, been acknowledged as a theorist who gave it a wider use and popularity in the field of adult education. Knowles used the term andragogy to refer to the systematic way (art and science) of helping adults learn. His main assumption is that while children may learn under the strict direction of teachers, adult learners have unique characteristics that make them unreceptive to such directedness (Knowles, 1996).

Knowles's views have attracted attention from a number of scholars and researchers who have also made significant contributions to the field of adult education from an andragogical perspective. Several of these contributions are outlined below:

1   Learning from life situations is very important for people in the field of adult education. Life tasks, problems, and situations should influence and shape an adult's learning processes because such processes are oriented towards contributing to the learner's social roles. Learning based on life tasks makes sense of learner's experiences and prepares the learner for future life tasks in his or her immediate environment. When, for example, incarcerated women are asked to write stories of the crime they have committed and how they intend to make up for what they have lost while in prison, the programme will be addressing the life experiences of these women and, in this way, learning becomes meaningful to them.

2   A major characteristic that differentiates adults from children relates to experience. An adult learner has accumulated experiences that are excellent resources for learning. Experiences should be integrated with new information through active involvement such as sharing and exchanging information, questioning assumptions and theories, and making use of group interaction techniques. There is great value in considering the context within which experiences are accumulated because it is the same context in which new knowledge will be applied and new experiences gained. There are times when the facilitators may not find relevant information to use when teaching a specific adult group. In this case, the adults may have experiences that they can share and such sharing will help facilitators to provide information or guidelines that can be applied to the adults' local environment.

3   Learning should promote an adult's self-concept, especially the concept of being a responsible, self-directing and independent being. It is therefore necessary that adult learning experiences should use a variety of methods and approaches that promote self-direction and independence in programme participants. Furthermore, different topics should be explored in order to tap into and satisfy learners' diverse interests and needs.

Many of the principles of andragogy can be applied beneficially to African contexts. Practitioners in African settings can benefit a great deal from Knowles' andragogical processes if they make local implications of such processes. Local implication here refers to practitioners' efforts to question assumptions. For example, practitioners can ask critical questions of how experiential learning, self-directedness, problem-based learning and goal-setting may impact on the day-to-day activities of an African adult learner.

One important andragogical principle is that learning activities should grow out of the interests, needs and other life challenges of the learners. The question that African practitioners might want to ask is: 'What are the challenges of an adult learner in an African context?'

Very often, a learner in an African setting is challenged to relate and interact meaningfully with people in the local environment. Community-wide participation has a congenial atmosphere in which each person feels welcomed and at ease. It promotes in an individual the love to work for and with others. For example, when community issues are raised, an educated African is expected to bring different (enlightened) but complimentary perspectives to the issues being discussed. It is therefore important that teaching and learning techniques promote this spirit of open and free communication.

Learning activities would be meaningful for an African adult learner if they emphasised interactive group work, were planned collectively, and directly encouraged open communication. Learning is a way of learning for each other and taking action together (Chamberlain, 1993). Learning is supposed to prepare the learners for the way they live as unitary groups – 'everybody is related to everybody else' (Mbiti 1988: 105). It is therefore important that education should strengthen the collaborative nature of the African people.

While we acknowledge the collective experiences and needs of adult learners, personal gratification is also a goal. There is a basic need in every learner to be personally satisfied that, 'at the end of the day, the inner-self has to be satisfied with the achievement' (Lekoko 2002: 144). The great achievement for the learner in a traditional African environment is to see that his or her accomplishments benefit other people.

In sum, an African model that borrows from Knowles' andragogical perspective would concentrate on processes that:

1 Make an African context a reservoir of learning.
If adult educators believe that the current and immediate situation of the living environment influences what is learned, then the most valuable reservoir of learning is the immediate environment of the learners (Imel, 1990). There is so much happening in African communities that learners do not need to rely solely on books for their learning. Learners in the African settings need to talk about what is happening to them (Lekoko, 2002). When local communities become resources for learning, then local knowledge is respected in formal learning institutions. Local knowledge is something concrete, which helps to engage and stimulate learners. Learning that is abstract in nature is often less meaningful to programme participants.

2 Respect for local knowledge should be encouraged through the use of local facilitators.
Facilitators who are familiar with the local African environments are better prepared to, 'link curricular knowledge (knowledge they gained from reading books) with local knowledge (knowledge of what is actually happening in the local communities)' (Lekoko, 2002: 187). They have great potential to use illustrations that epitomise the problems and challenges of African environments. Case studies, drama, and other representations that are good for depicting real-life challenges are encouraged. High regard should be given to learning activities that are embedded in the day-to-day challenges and problems of the participants. Such activities instil commitment to the development of communities and preservation of local cultures, and encourage a reliance upon local knowledge systems.

3 The inclusion of field-based activities.
This has received widespread acceptance

in the teaching of an African adult learner (Lekoko, 2002). There are a number of benefits to be derived from taking learners to actual life environments, such as workplaces and local community environments. For example, when learners, 'go out in the field and bring field experiences back to the classroom, work responsibilities and challenges are added to the learning environments and training becomes meaningful and challenging' (Lekoko 2002: 190). Another advantage of using field-based activities is that the content of learning will not be solely based on formal written materials that usually overlook, 'the numerous activities that occur through daily interactions and socially embedded arrangements' (Cleaver 2001: 54). Life experiences therefore become part of teaching-learning experiences.

Methods of instruction

Programme implementation is a unified whole of a number of elements, including:

- participants' interactions;
- engagement in learning activities; such as ways of exchanging and sharing information;
- ways of constructing or developing new information or knowledge; and
- ways of monitoring or assessing learning processes.

When these elements are tied together, the resulting process can be labelled a method of instruction. Generally, a method is the means by which the learners learn or grasp the programme content.

Table 10.2 on the next page presents various methods of adult teaching, together with a brief description of each method's purpose as well as suggested implementation strategies.

An important principle of adult education that needs to be remembered here is that of variety. Using different types of methods in a single session helps in a number of ways: (i) it caters for various learning styles; (ii) it breaks the monotony of using a single method; (iii) it offers alternative and alternating roles for both the facilitator and learners; (iv) it exposes learners to different learning environments; and (v) content is learned in interesting and different ways. Therefore, the individual teaching methods outlined in Table 10.2 should not be seen as existing in isolation from one another. Instead, an adult educator can use any combination of methods, or elements of various methods, to meet the unique requirements of the adult education programme he or she is implementing.

SUMMARY

This chapter has raised several important aspects that need to be considered when implementing programmes for adult learners in Africa. We have presented the idea of implementation as a step-by-step teaching and learning process in which the social values and survival needs of the African learner, as well as their real-life problems and challenges, are explored.

We also investigated the key principles of programme purpose, order and utility as well as the various stages of programme implementation. We spent some time looking at the concept of andragogy (learner-centred adult education) and how this concept is useful in the African teaching-learning environment. Critical questions to ask during implementation were put forward, together with a number of helpful suggestions to facilitate the implementation process.

Table 10.2 Adult education teaching methods.

Method	Purpose	Suggested strategies for success
Lecture/ presentation	To provide a large amount of information (knowledge) in a limited amount of time	■ Prepare a detailed outline/plan with key subject-matter ideas ■ Organise and structure the material in a logical way ■ Use teaching aids to add clarity and variability
Symposium	To provide a variety of viewpoints on a particular issue, problem or topic from a panel of experts	■ Clearly define the issue, problem or topic to be discussed, and share this with panelists prior to the symposium ■ Select panelists with a diversity of backgrounds and experiences ■ Have each panelist prepare a brief presentation on the issue, problem or topic ■ After the presentations, let the panelists participate in a panel discussion, question each other, or respond to audience questions ■ Plan for a follow-up discussion during a subsequent session
Panel discussion	To provide an opportunity for experts or a group of learners to present differing viewpoints on an issue, problem or topic to other panelists and the audience (learners)	■ Clearly define the issue, problem or topic to be discussed ■ Select and prepare members of the panel (possibly from the learner group) ■ Designate a panel leader ■ Arrange the learning environment with the audience (learners) in mind ■ Keep the discussion on-task and within a specified time frame
Group discussion	To provide an opportunity for learners to think together constructively for purposes of learning, solving problems, making decisions, and/ or improving human relationships	■ Guide learners into selecting the topic for discussion ■ Prepare a list of leading questions that will stimulate thinking and discussion ■ Establish an atmosphere in which learners have an equal opportunity to participate
Case study	To provide an account of an actual problem or situation an individual or group has experienced	■ Present the case in writing with questions that will generate discussion ■ Establish an atmosphere that promotes an equal opportunity to participate in the discussion ■ Guide the discussion toward the intended outcome
Problem solving	To provide the opportunity for learners to solve a problem through the collection, assessment and application of information	■ Follow a systematic procedure in solving a problem ■ Choose problems that are relevant to the lives of the learners ■ Make problem solving an active learning process that requires learners to inquire into the topic ■ Have learners use a variety of sources to collect information ■ Have learners summarise what was learned from solving the problem

Method	Purpose	Suggested strategies for success
Brainstorming	To solicit creative ideas or to identify possible solutions to problems Allows learners to express opinion and ideas without the threat of being judged by other learners	■ Begin brainstorming session with a specific topic or problem ■ Have the facilitator explain the ground rules of a brainstorming session ■ The more ideas offered the better ■ Have the facilitator keep the group focused on the topic or problem ■ Have a recorder document all ideas
Demonstration	To model the correct step-by-step procedures needed when performing a specified task	■ Involve learners in the demonstration ■ Keep the demonstration simple – do not try to teach too much in one demonstration ■ Outline steps (procedures) using some form of visual aid ■ Provide time for learners to apply and practise the newly acquired skill
Tour/field trip	To provide an opportunity for learners to observe practices, problem situations, or to bring learners into contact with persons or objects that cannot be seen by other means	■ Determine the specific objective(s) to be accomplished ■ Select an appropriate site ■ Plan transportation (include maps if necessary) ■ Explain special circumstances of the site visit ■ Plan a follow-up and summary

Source: Birkenholz, 1999

KEY POINTS

■ The three underlying principles of an adult education programme – purpose, order and utility – differ according to the type of programme being implemented. The adult educator's responsibility is to ensure that these principles are properly identified for his or her specific programme.

■ A critical stage of the implementation process is that of planning and preparing everything that makes up a successful teaching and learning atmosphere, including content, methods, facilities, logistics, resources, administration and evaluation.

■ Implementers ask critical questions to guide their planning for the teaching and learning experiences, such as, 'What is to be learned?', 'How will participants be involved?', 'When will the programme begin and how long will the sessions last?'

■ The andragogical process is presented to shed light on the characteristics and expectations of adult learners as they become involved in a programme.

■ There is variety of teaching methods available and implementers have to choose carefully the ones that meet their learners' needs and the programme goals.

⊞ ACTIVITY

Imagine you are a participant in an educational session in which learners explore the principle, 'Adults learn best when the topic is of immediate interest and value to them'. This lesson has been exclusively designed for you and other adult learners attending an introductory course in adult education. Anticipate the type of learning experience you will go through in this lesson. Share your responses with a co-learner.

FURTHER QUESTIONS

1 What is your understanding of programme implementation?
2 If you have been engaged as a facilitator in an adult education programme, what did you do prior to the actual teaching and learning process?
3 Suppose you meet someone who has not read this chapter; how would you explain the concepts of programme purpose, order and utility to them?

SUGGESTED READING

Pretorious, F. 2002. Changing the curriculum: Outcome-based education and training. In N. Van Wyk and E. Lemmer. *Transforming education: The South African experience* (pp. 77–98). New York: Nova Science Publisher.
Birkenholz, R. J. 1999. *Adult learning.* Danville, Illinois: Interstate Publishers.

Chapter 11

Evaluation of adult education programmes

OVERVIEW

This chapter provides a framework for evaluating adult education programmes. A participatory framework is suggested in which a core team serves to organise, synthesise and coordinate the evaluation exercise in collaboration with other stakeholders. The discussion takes readers through topics such as: (i) understanding the concept of evaluation; (ii) a philosophy for evaluating programmes for adult learners in Africa; (iii) the purpose of evaluation; (iv) the focus of evaluation; (v) evaluation techniques; and (vi) the phases and processes of evaluation.

LEARNING OBJECTIVES

At the end of this chapter, you should be able to:

1 Explain what evaluation means.
2 Demonstrate an understanding of participatory evaluation techniques.
3 State several purposes for evaluating adult education programmes.
4 Distinguish and select evaluation techniques that are relevant to a particular adult education programme.
5 Use a variety of evaluation techniques, such as observation, questionnaires, survey, personal interviewing and role-play to evaluate programmes.
6 Design a participatory evaluation exercise.

dwennimmen

KEY TERMS

participatory evaluation This is a collective and cooperative process that involves programme stakeholders defining and implementing strategies to evaluate the effectiveness of an adult education programme.

programme evaluation This refers to the systematic process of investigating the value and quality of an adult education programme on such factors as accountability, suitability, efficiency and real-world application.

summative evaluation An assessment that takes place either near the end, at the end, or after completion of a programme to assess the merit of a whole programme or some aspects of a programme.

formative evaluation An assessment that takes place during programme development with the aim of auditing the quality and efficiency of input factors, and the processes and the environment (context) of the teaching and learning.

context evaluation An assessment through which evaluators are able to judge the need/importance, suitability and practical realities of a programme.

process evaluation An assessment through which evaluators are able to determine if procedures/actions are/have been done in a manner that leads to the achievement of the desired results.

product evaluation An assessment through which evaluators are able to measure achievements, such as programme objectives, skills, knowledge and attitudes attained, and graduation rate.

⊞ BEFORE YOU START

Adult learners often make statements such as, 'That programme was useful', or 'That programme was a complete waste of time'. What factors influence these types of personal programme evaluations?

THE CONCEPT OF EVALUATION

In life, people like to reflect, ask questions and make conclusions about what they do or what they have done. Actions are proportionally linked to motivation, expectations and outcomes. Behind every programme, there is also an element of motivation that drives what goes on in the programme. Both the learners and facilitator enter the programme expecting to come out with something beneficial or satisfying.

In building a house, for example, the construction process continues stage by stage, with every brick playing its part in the completion of the end product: the house. During building, the construction team will evaluate how the work is proceeding at every stage and take action to correct any errors or lapses that are identified. Likewise, in carrying out adult education programmes, every step taken counts towards satisfying the purposes for which such a programme is run. Evaluation is a way of checking if things are going as planned.

It is normal for people to question if indeed the programme is leading them to where they want to go, because all human actions have a purpose. Thus, people reflect, make judgments and form conclusions about actions taken to see whether their anticipated outcomes have or are being met. Evaluation is all about asking and answering questions such as: 'Are actions generating the desired outcomes?'; 'Have actions generated the desired outcomes?'; and 'Is what is being done relevant, meaningful and appropriate in an African context?'

Asking evaluation questions

Questions are good techniques for evaluating programmes. Practitioners are often asked questions such as:
- How well did learners do?
- How well did the teaching-learning activities go?
- How did learners like the session/class/course?
- How has the programme benefited learners and their community?
- Did learners receive enough support (from administrators, facilitators, auxiliary staff) to enjoy and benefit from the programme?
- Do you think the programme was worth running?

These are evaluation questions. They are asked to determine the effectiveness, impact, achievements, or benefits of a programme.

In general, evaluation questions are asked mainly to gather information that may help practitioners to improve their programmes. It has already been mentioned that adult education programmes are implemented to address the prevailing problems of individuals, groups and communities in African society. Any and all programme evaluations should display this central concern for their programme participants' well-being when the issue of evaluation arises.

A philosophy for evaluating programmes for adult learners in Africa

Evaluation of programmes for adult learners in Africa should be participatory to the greatest extent possible. Participatory is a term that has been used throughout this book to reflect the fact that Africans are collective beings. A core evaluation team is like a traditional African family or a clan. When problems arise, family or clan members join one another to fight the problem, because, '[the] individual does not and cannot exist alone except corporately: He is simply part of a whole' (Mbiti, 1988: 108). That is, at all times, and especially in times of conflict, the family works together. The clan/family analogy is used here to stress the need to carry out evaluation in a collective manner, with respect and recognition being given to the interests of other 'family members'.

The following case study is presented to illustrate the point that evaluation necessitates amalgamating shared interests and opinions.

CASE STUDY: EVALUATING UNEMPLOYMENT

Unemployment is a major problem and challenge for many African countries, which requires our urgent attention. A two-week workshop is planned to evaluate the situation of unemployment since the implementation of an employment policy five years ago. Suppose you are a member of the evaluation team tasked with evaluating activities done do far. Your evaluation will be guided by the following questions:

- Who are the people responsible for tackling the challenge as we see it now? Are they the right people?
- Who are the audience at the workshop? Are they the right audience?
- In the last five years, what has the formal employment sector done to accommodate the increasing numbers of unemployed?
- Who should be responsible for seeing that the sector expands or diversifies?
- Who is hit more by unemployment, youth or adults?
- Who else could join the evaluation team?

In considering the scenario presented in the above case study, you may well have considered the role a participatory approach might play in the workshop on unemployment. Participatory evaluation is fundamentally democratic in the sense that those involved are encouraged to contribute ideas and share tasks. This idea of democratic participation has been discussed previously in Chapter 2.

If community members are involved in programme evaluation, the opportunity for an inclusive analysis of programme benefits, shortcomings and opportunities is afforded. By inviting community participation, the needs of different individuals, groups, organisations and even the community itself can be shared. An evaluation team should, ideally, function as elders in a family, serving as coordinators, synthesisers of information and facilitators for the collaborative process. Importantly, the evaluation team as 'the family' survives through the use of continuous feedback, decision-making, and by having flexible plans and actions. An evaluation team, like a family, should recognise that there are several alternatives or several ways of going about solving a problem. This calls for openness, shared opinions, continuous feedback and modifications to what has been prepared.

🔲 ACTIVITY

How has the analogy of a family or clan contributed to your understanding of evaluation as a participatory process?

THE NATURE OF EVALUATION

Evaluation is a complex activity. It is an outcome or utility-based exercise. To start evaluating, evaluators must first answer the question, ' Why is it necessary to evaluate?'

Evaluation is also a purposeful activity. Systematic evaluation often permits stakeholders to know how to make, 'a weak programme stronger or an effective programme even more effective, or perhaps more efficient' (Scheirer, 1994: 32).

The general notion is that formal and extensive evaluation should be done only when there is the need to do it. Critical questions should be asked to determine if indeed resources should be spent on evaluating a programme. Questions such as, 'Is the programme significant enough to merit evaluation?', 'Can the result of evaluation influence decisions about programme improvement?', and ' Can evaluation be done in time to be useful?' should be addressed (Wholey, Hartry and Newcomer, 1994). In addition, evaluators need to answer the question, 'Can the result of evaluation be used for future offerings of similar programmes?'

Evaluation is not an end in itself. The information obtained during this exercise will guide programmers in making decisions about continuation, modification or termination of a programme. Thus, 'programmes for which decisions must be made about continuation, modification or termination are good candidates for evaluation' (Wholey, Hartry and Newcomer, 1994). To extend this point, the Basic Extension Skill Training (BEST) programme is used to illustrate this point. This programme started in Botswana on a pilot basis in 1996/7 and it brought extension workers from different sectors together to share ideas, learn together and strengthen their coordination strategies. It was through the evaluation exercise that the value of this programme was validated, hence the recommendation for it to continue on yearly basis, as it still does.

Evaluation provides an ideal opportunity for practitioners to learn from their experiences. It provides important information about issues of quality, accountability, practicality, suitability of content and approaches, efficient use of resources, and effective programme management and administration. Experience indicates that,

'the most effective evaluators are those who plan, design, and implement evaluations that are sufficiently relevant and credible to stimulate programme improvement' (Wholey, Hartry and Newcomer, 1994: 9). Evaluation is thus a conscious and purposeful exercise.

There are many purposes for carrying out evaluation exercises. It is beyond the scope of this chapter to address all of these; what follows are examples of the more common purposes.

THE PURPOSE OF EVALUATION

Programme evaluation may be conducted as a means of assessing whether the goals and expectations of participants (individual learners, group of learners, individual facilitators or group of facilitators) have been achieved (Field, 2003).

Programme evaluation may be conducted as a means of justifying resource allocation and use. Budget accountability, for example, is one common ground for engaging in evaluation. Community development projects in some countries are largely funded through government and public expenditure. An evaluation exercise may show how the money was spent. Thus, in this case, evaluation, 'shows value for money and cost effectiveness' (Field, 2003: 2).

There are instances where programmes start off with limited resources. In such instances, programme administrators, who are usually charged with budget accountability, are challenged to exercise their decision-making powers and work out a number of alternatives for effective use of resources. At the end, evaluation may be carried out to check if indeed a programme was run in a cost-effective manner.

Programme evaluation may be conducted as a means of determining effective programme management. The main purpose here is to give an account of the efficiency with which facilities and resources are managed. For example, the programme may be evaluated to determine the extent to which planning was done prior to implementation. This will include such as issues as the learning environment/room arrangement, seating configuration, ventilation/heating facilities, and material and equipment availability being assessed.

Evaluation can be carried out to determine if all of these tasks were done in good time and appropriately. Instructional materials can be evaluated to determine their suitability to the local contexts. They may also be evaluated to determine their suitability in terms of the level of ease or difficulty at which learners understand them.

Programme evaluation may be conducted as a means of determining if the overall objectives of a programme have been achieved (Knox, 1980). One prime area in this type of evaluation is to concentrate on the levels and types of skill attainment, knowledge acquisition and attitudinal dispositions/change. The programme content, too, can be evaluated in terms of its match to the programme objectives. Furthermore, facilitators and planners can be evaluated to determine their knowledge of the content; their ability in communicating the content; and the accuracy with which selected techniques and methods of delivering programme content were used.

In short, evaluation is an assessment of an individual's behavioural change and the programme's impact on the society (Knox, 1980). In adult education, concerted efforts are made to develop programmes that make a maximum contribution to the growth and development of the learner and the society of which the learner is a part (Boyle, 1981).

✥ ACTIVITY

What aspects of a programme evaluation exercise do you think should be addressed in a 'Skills for Livelihood' programme in a specific rural area with which you are familiar?

THE FOCUS OF EVALUATION

There are many forms of programme evaluation. Four of the most commonly used are: i) context evaluation; ii) input evaluation; iii) process evaluation; and iv) product evaluation. These are discussed below.

Context evaluation

Programme implementation does not take place in a vacuum. It is carried out in and to benefit a specific situation/context. Context is a broad concept referring to a whole situation or practice. The word environment is sometimes used to refer to what we here call context. You may therefore come across situations where the term 'environmental scanning' is used interchangeably with the concept of context analysis (Stufflebeam, 1971). Environmental scanning means looking outwardly and scanning the landscape to identify the current situations and emerging trends that will determine the need to embark on a programme, and also looking at the practical realities of such a programme (Stufflebeam, 1971). Context evaluation asks questions such as, 'Did the programme address the real situation or circumstances of the target clientele?'; 'How suitable was the programme to the current situation of the clients?'; and 'How practical is it for trainers to carry out a programme within the current situation?'

These questions indicate that context evaluation is intended to address the needs, importance, suitability and practicality of a programme. A stage whereby such questions are asked can be referred to as the pre-formative (need-assessment). It is carried out to find out the needs or problems of the target group. The information collected from the context evaluation constitutes a basis on which other phases of the programme are built including, for example, the implementation phase.

Input evaluation

The term input refers to everything that is needed for a programme to take off and be completed. One important input factor is resources, including personnel, time and money. For example, a programme has to be well staffed. The staff should display special characteristics, such as a knowledge of programme content, the ability to communicate the content, an efficiency in preparing for the implementation, and the appropriate use of teaching techniques and methods. The major resources allocation categories that are usually examined as part of an input evaluation include funding, time, facilities, personnel, equipment, instructional materials and tools. Effective resource allocation should offer positive conditions for learning. The conditions of learning are evaluated with regard to the appropriateness of the methods used, the effectiveness of supporting materials, the quality of physical facilities, and the proper coordination of the resources used in the programme.

The programme content, too, is an input factor. If, for example, learners came expecting to know how to weave a basket, the content that is explored in the teaching learning environment should provide skills and knowledge in basket-weaving. The evaluation question here is: 'Was the subject matter appropriate?' Overall, input evaluation is directed toward issues of sufficiency and appropriateness (Stufflebeam, 1971).

The primary question for input evaluation is: 'Were the inputs used in the programme appropriate and sufficient to achieve the stated objectives?' (Stufflebeam, 1971).

Process evaluation

There are procedures that are followed in running a programme. Chapter 10, for example, discusses several processes in the teaching and learning of adult learners. The concept of 'andragogical process' was used to help us focus discussion on procedures and elements of design that are perceived important by practitioners in the field of adult education. The term 'andragogical process' is adapted from Knowles's work on andragogy (Knowles, 1968). As already stated, andragogy is a set of assumptions about adult learners, their learning styles, their preferred teaching methods and their relationships with facilitators. In terms of evaluation, educators can set out to assess if the elements of design fit the stated assumptions of teaching adults as defined by the theory of andragogy. Processes such as planning and organisation of learning activities, assessment strategies, teaching procedures, scheduling of breaks, and the process of registration can be evaluated to see if indeed they stand the test of andragogy. The primary question for process evaluation is: 'Was the overall programme design appropriate to achieve the stated objectives?' (Stufflebeam, 1971).

Product evaluation

The word 'product' here refers to the outcomes of a programme. In some cases, product is used to refer to the adult participants who completed the programme. Programme completion is usually measured by the level of achievement, which includes skills attainment, satisfactory ratings, graduation rate, and changes in knowledge, behaviour and attitudes. Thus, product evaluation is a way of assessing the overall results of the programme. Product evaluation seeks to answer the question: 'To what degree did the programme achieve the stated objectives?' (Stufflebeam, 1971).

⬚ ACTIVITY

Think of an adult education programme that you attended. Reflect on your experiences in that programme. Use the following questions to guide your considerations:

1 What were your expectations, goals and motivation in attending the programme? Were these satisfied by the programme?
2 What type of teaching and learning materials and activities were used?
3 What methods did facilitators use to teach the content? What are your feelings about the use of such methods in a programme of this nature?
4 How was the room arranged? What did you like or dislike about the arrangement?
5 Did you observe some undesirable behaviours? If yes, how were they dealt with?
6 What was your overall impression of the programme?

EVALUATION TECHNIQUES

Evaluation is a complex exercise that uses different techniques or tools to collect comprehensive quantitative and qualitative data (Field, 2003). Qualitative data indicates, 'qualities in inputs, processes, outcomes and contexts' (Scheierer, 1994: 69). Quantitative data, on the other hand, indicates measurable amounts, such as the number of participants in a programme, the quantity of programme materials, and the amount of money needed to run a programme. In many cases of programme evaluation, both qualitative and quantitative information are needed.

There is a wide range of techniques to choose from when evaluating a programme. The choice depends on a number of factors, including the sources of data, the context within which evaluation is conducted, the resources put aside for the evaluation exercise, the goals for evaluation, the time-lines, and the type(s) of evaluation engaged in. For example, logistical factors of time, resources, physical environment and facilities, as well as factors such as levels and types of communication and administration, accountability requirements, stakeholders' involvement and input, can determine the methods and techniques to be used for evaluating programmes. Individual interests, preferences, expectations, and organisational and social power, are further determining factors. There are a number of techniques that can be used during the evaluation exercise. The discussion that follows explores some of these techniques.

Documentation review

As the programme goes through different phases, a number of documents are kept as records that might help in the evaluation process. During planning, for example, a number of meetings may be held. Records or minutes of such meetings are kept. These can be consulted during evaluation for a specific purpose. Correspondence regarding previously evaluated programmes may also be evaluated at this stage. At times, the planning process relies on policies and other official documents, which are all essential elements of document review.

Questionnaires

Self-administered questionnaires can be used to collect evaluation data. The structure of the questionnaire can permit evaluators to collect both quantitative and qualitative data. Questionnaires can help an evaluator to gain a good picture of the context, input, processes and products of a programme. Evaluators, for example, can gain insights into what is perceived as good practice as well as the constraining elements to such good practice. Recommendations can then be made to leading policy makers, planners and other practitioners to set priorities and actions for future offerings.

Questionnaires can be used with a number of people, for example, programme participants, volunteers, members of management committees, partners, and other stakeholders. The person designing the questionnaire should ensure that the questionnaire is focused on specific areas. Questions should be structured in such a way that they enable evaluators to gain maximum response from the respondents (Field, 2003). Great care must therefore be taken over questionnaire design.

Chilisa and Preece's book *Research methods for adult educators in Botswana* (2004) is a useful source of further information on the questionnaire as a data-collection technique.

Interviews

An interview can be regarded as a specialised pattern of interaction, initiated for a specific purpose and focused on specific areas (Mathieson, 1999). The interview can allow participants to talk about their experiences and to reflect on their training and other learning situations. Both individual and focus-group interviews are possible. Evaluators are expected to prepare an interview guide. The main reason for using the interview guide is to ensure that the questions asked during interviewing are tailored to the areas or components intended for evaluated. It helps to keep the interaction or discussion focused. There can be different types of interviews conducted – telephone and face-to-face interviews are two options. The use of a particular interview method is context-specific. Interviews may be arranged between the evaluator(s) and the programme participants, volunteers, planners, management committee members, and/or other community beneficiaries.

Face-to-face interviews have the advantage of providing evaluators with the opportunity to visit locations where the programme is being delivered, which may provide additional insights and understanding into the practical circumstances of the programme (Field, 2003).

Discussion

Both individual and group discussion can be arranged. The discussion is specifically structured to focus on specific issues or components of a programme being evaluated. They may address problems or challenges experienced, or look at the effectiveness of particular activities. Approaches such as SWOT analysis (strengths, weaknesses, opportunities and threats) can be used with a group discussion (Field, 2003).

If they wish, evaluators may further concentrate their evaluation on the goals, objectives, achievements, and lessons learnt (GOAL). In using the GOAL approach, respondents may brainstorm about challenges, revise aims and objectives, and set priorities for the improvement of the current programme or projected programmes of a similar nature. The GOAL technique, like SWOT, is an approach that can be adapted for use in different contexts and with different stakeholders.

Story-telling and case studies

Although not commonly used, short anecdotes or stories can be used for evaluation purposes (Field, 2003). These methods provide an opportunity for respondents to paint a picture of a programme in action; they can demonstrate how the programme was planned and implemented. Brief-but-vivid stories can communicate detailed information about the effectiveness or weaknesses of a programme (Field, 2003). The stories can be told during group or one-to-one sessions with the aim of demonstrating the impact of the project. Chilisa and Preece's book *Research methods for adult educators in Botswana* (2004) explores these techniques in detail.

Logbooks

Written notes such as diaries or journals can be used to gather evaluation data. These devices allow respondents to record their experiences and perceptions about the impact of a programme. For example, programme participants (learners and facilitators) may be asked to record activities indicating what they have learned and their feelings about the impact of programme activities on their life tasks. They may record what they would like to do as a result of experiences or knowledge gained from the programme. Logbooks are most effective for recording formative evaluation data and when respondents have been given a framework to guide their responses (Field, 2003).

Message or form analysis

This is an approach to evaluation that requires evaluators to prepare messages or statements that can provoke respondents to talk about the impact of the programme. The messages are prepared specifically to probe respondents for their understanding of and reactions to specified aspects of a programme (Wholey, Hartry and Newcomer, 1994). Messages can be prepared that address the type of materials and activities that were used in the programme, the desirable or undesirable behaviour that were experienced, and the type of communication exhibited. The important issue for evaluators is to take time to prepare messages that will elicit genuine responses from respondents.

Community forum approach

The community forum approach encourages the involvement of the local community members. In the case of evaluation, the perceptions of individuals in the community or a group of community members on the impact of the programme can be gathered. They may be asked to talk about how the programme has benefited or could benefit individuals in the community, or about its impact on the entire community.

The community forum's structure is similar to a brainstorming session in which everyone has a right to express their views and no one's ideas are discounted or discredited (Schierer, 1994). This model is particularly useful in prompting a free-flowing discussion that has the potential to produce the most accurate picture of what community members feel about the programme. However, it is important to bear in mind the logistical problems involved in assembling a disparate group of community members together at a particular time and venue. Involving community members is an ideal that might be difficult to live up to.

⊞ ACTIVITY

Consider the evaluation techniques that have been mentioned in this chapter. If you were a member of the evaluation team for a self-help project – a poultry farm for women outside the formal employment sector – which evaluation technique would you recommend for use, and why?

THE PHASES AND PROCESSES OF EVALUATION

Trainers who are conscious of the importance of evaluation do not wait until the end of the programme to evaluate. Evaluation is inbuilt in all stages of a programme, starting at the pre-planning phase and continuing through to the post-evaluation exercises. In any case, trainers cannot ignore or resist being evaluated. During the process or at the end of the programme, remarks such as 'Good job; well done!' are common. Such remarks give a sense of achievement, positive impact or satisfaction. On the other hand, a trainer may be reluctant to engage in evaluation if they feel that the job was not well done. Regardless of the result of the evaluation, this exercise is very important.

The type of evaluation that we are concerned with here is the formal or systematic exercise. The concept of formal here means that: (i) evaluation activities are planned; (ii) evaluation exercises have specific purposes; (iii) during implementation, intentional assessment exercises are done to monitor progress; (iv) resources are made available to allow evaluation to take place; (v) relevant evaluation techniques, tools or approaches are put in place for carrying out the evaluation activities; (vi) administrative support has to be well defined and readily available for evaluation exercises; and (vii) a post-evaluation plan should be developed.

There is a defined order to the evaluation process and it should be seen as a systematic, professional and formal exercise. Figure 11.1 on the next page depicts the main stages of the evaluation process.

⊞ ACTIVITY

Refer to Figure 11.1. Discuss with a co-learner how the diagram summarises this chapter's consideration of the evaluation process.

THE EVALUATION PLAN

Although there is no universal method for programme evaluation, a general pattern is discernible. The final section of this chapter looks at the fundamental principles and procedural steps that apply to the evaluation process.

Developing a plan for conducting evaluation

In the plan, components or areas needing evaluation are defined. These components or areas can include learning activities, programme content, technology and facilities, as well as broader categories such as context, input, process and product. It is important that evaluators are sure of the areas to be evaluated. In other words, boundaries of evaluation have to be set (Burnham, 1995).

Evaluation can not be carried out without resources. Thus, during the development phase the necessary resources (principally, money, people, and time) should be outlined. A plan for evaluation should also suggest methods, techniques and tools to be used for collecting data. Furthermore, the criteria to be used to collect, record, process, and analyse data should be specified (Kowalski, 1988).

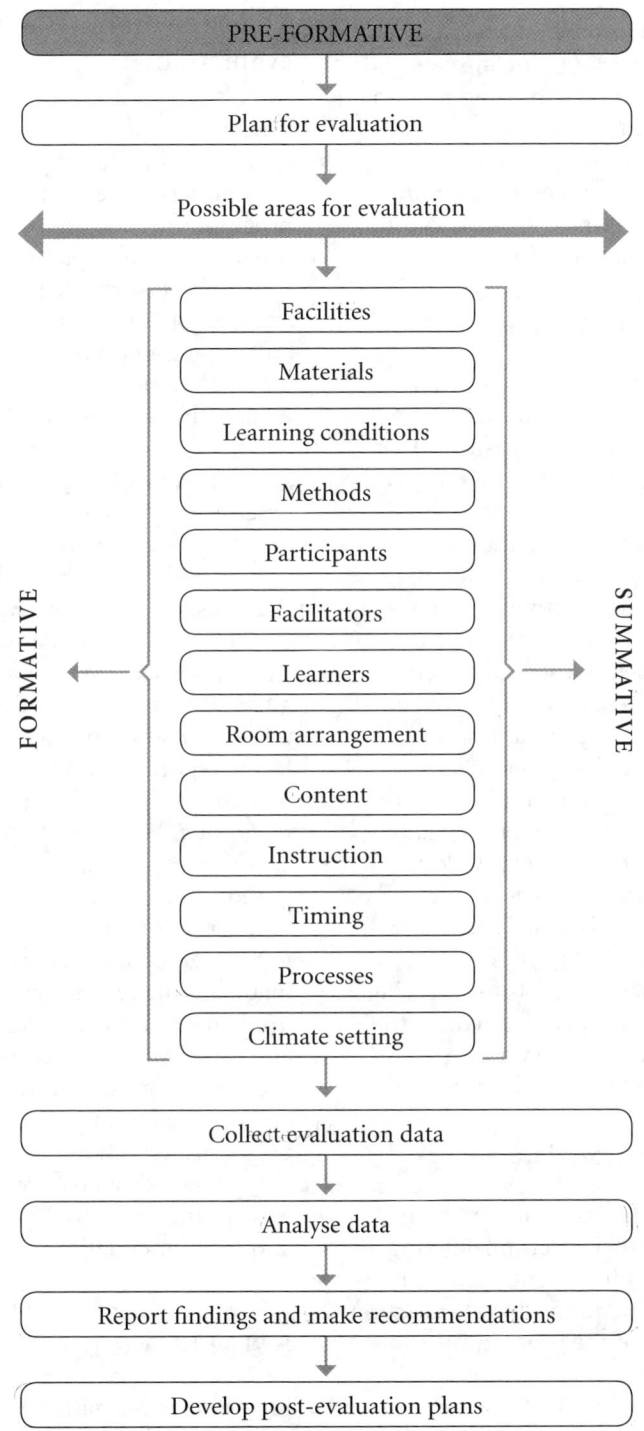

Figure 11.1 Steps in evaluating adult education programmes.

It is important to note that a lack of adequate planning may lead to incomplete and unreliable evaluation activities and information. Poorly planned evaluation activities affect the educator's ability to make accurate decisions on such issues as programme effectiveness, programme discontinuation or future programme intentions.

Executing the evaluation plan

Here, evaluators set out to look at what was done to reach the objectives of the programme. They concentrate on aspects that led to the effectiveness or ineffectiveness of the programme. For example, evaluators could assess programme activities concentrating on issues of what was done to prepare for the learning activities, what happened before the activities were carried out, what happened when the activities were in process, and how these activities were ended.

Specific elements of programme implementation, such as the learners' involvement, participation and interaction in learning activities can also be evaluated. The other area that evaluators may look at is the stakeholders' perceptions of a programme; their needs, concerns and satisfactions (Burnham, 1995). In the plan, the methods, techniques and tools for carrying out the evaluation are specified. This is the phase where evaluators may want to assess how, in practice, such methods were applied.

Analysing evaluation data

Data analysis is an important exercise: it leads evaluators in their decision-making regarding possible adjustments to the programme, recommendations on future action and in their rating of the programme's relative success or failure.

Reporting findings of programme evaluation

The findings of programme evaluation are reported to the relevant authorities. Depending on the nature and status of the programe, results can be communicated to programme participants, policy and decision makers (such as a board of directors, the Ministry of Education or community leaders) and programme administrators. It is important that in the report the evaluators should re-state the original programme objectives and the purpose(s) of the evaluation (House and Howe, 1999). In general, the report describes the major findings and observations resulting from the evaluation activities.

The findings of the evaluation are used as the basis for improving similar programmes; therefore, recommendations to this effect should be made. Where necessary, strategies and reasons for modifying programme plans or operations must also be suggested. In the report, the evaluators can advise the decision makers that action is needed on the recommendations and that feedback should be given to other stakeholders on the proposed action (House and Howe, 1999).

There are occasions where evaluation is carried out and recommendations are made but the recommendations are never implemented. By suggesting some strategies and time-lines for those recommendations, the relevant authorities will perhaps be reminded to implement the report's proposals for action. The evaluation report should include a post-evaluation plan; that is, steps for the utilisation of the findings and recommendations.

SUMMARY

Programme evaluation is a major component of an adult education programme. The position taken in this chapter is that evaluation is a participatory exercise that is best accomplished through teamwork. Evaluation is carried out for specific purposes. To achieve these purposes, the evaluation team, 'like a referee in a ball game, must follow certain sets of rules, procedures, and considerations – not just anything goes' (House and Howe, 1999: 29). We can add to this observation by saying that whatever is done has to be locally relevant within the context of adult education from an African perspective.

Evaluation is carried out, 'within the constraints of the setting and accepted practices' (House and Howe, 1999: 29). Exactly what is to be evaluated is determined by the circumstances of the programme being evaluated, the resources available for the exercise, and the goals of the evaluation exercise.

Furthermore, the position taken in this chapter is that evaluation is utilisation-focused; meaning that the results of the evaluation are directed at programme improvement. The recommendations arising from an evaluation exercise affect decision-making regarding future offerings. For example, decisions can be made about continuation, termination or modifications of or to a programme. If the findings are indeed used to improve programme performance, then the evaluators must understand the bureaucratic and political context of the programme and craft their findings and recommendations in such a way as to highlight their usefulness (Wholey, Hartry and Newcomer, 1994). Evaluation is, to conclude, an important activity that should be done in a professional and responsible manner.

KEY POINTS

- The core evaluation team should be like an African traditional clan/family, in which consultation, shared ideas, and collective decision-making are upheld.
- An evaluation exercise can be focused on a number of elements (input factors, content, process, context, products). Therefore, the area of evaluation should be made clear from the start.
- Many techniques can be used for evaluation purposes, either individually or in combination. The philosophy behind the use of any one or a combination is that the technique(s) should promote the spirit of collaboration and participation.
- Evaluation is done for a specific purpose. Evaluators should therefore be clear about the intended purposes of the evaluation process.

✖ ACTIVITY

From your reading of this chapter, what do you consider to be the main reasons for evaluating an adult education programme?

FURTHER QUESTIONS

1 If you were to evaluate any course or programme, which of the four areas of evaluation would you concentrate on? Give reasons for your answer.
2 Is evaluation something that educators should emphasise? If so, why?

SUGGESTED READING

Busla, K. 1968. *Purposeful education for Africa*. The Netherlands: Mouton & Co.
Scheirer, M. 1994. Designing and Using Programme Evaluation. In Wholey, J., Hartry, H. and Newcomer, K. (Eds.) 1994. *Handbook of practical programme evaluation*, pp. 40–60. San Francisco: Jossey-Bass.

References

Adhikarya, R. 1994. *Strategic Extension Campaign: A participatory-oriented method of agricultural extension.* FAO: Rome, Italy.

Anderson, M.B. and Woodrow, P. J. 1989. *Rising from the ashes: Development strategies in times of disaster.* Paris: UNESCO, West View Press.

Andreasen, A. R. 1994. 'Social marketing: Its definition and domain'. In *Journal of Public Policy and Marketing,* 13(1) Spring, pp. 3–12.

Andreasen, A. R. 1995. *Marketing social change: Changing behavior to promote health, social development, and the environment.* San Francisco: Jossey-Bass.

Apel, H. and Camozzi, A. 1996. *Adult environmental education: A handbook on context and methods.* IIZ/DVV Supplement to Adult Education and Development No. 47.

Bahr, L. S. and Johnson, B. (eds.). 1992. *Collier's Encyclopedia, Vol. 15.* New York: Maxwell Macmillan.

Baker, H. R. 1984. 'The programme planning process'. In *Extension Handbook,* ed. D. J. Blackburn. University of Guelph.

Bellamy, H. Salit, R. and Bell, L. 1997. *Social marketing resource manual: A guide for state nutrition.* Washington D. C.: Health Systems Research, Inc.

Bennet, P. D. 1995. *Dictionary of marketing terms (2nd edition).* New York: American Marketing Association.

Birkenholz, R. 1999. *Adult learning.* Danville: Interstate Publishers.

Bhola, H. S. 1999. Equivalent curriculum construction as situated discourse: A case in the context of adult education in Namibia. In *Curriculum Inquiry, Vol. 29(4),* pp. 459–484.

Blumenteld, P. et al. 1991. 'Motivating project based learning: Sustaining the doing, supporting the learning.' In *Educational Psychologist,* 26, pp. 369–398.

Borg, W. R. and Gall, M. D. 1989. *Educational research: An introduction (5th edition).* New Longman: York and London.

Boyle, P.G. 1981. *Planning better programs.* New York: McGraw-Hill.

Bray, M. Clarke, P.B. and Stephens, D. 1986. *Education and society in Africa.* London: Edward Arnold.

Brown, S. 1984. 'Marketing extension programmes'. In *Extension Handbook,* ed. D. J. Blackburn. University of Guelph.

Burnham, B.R. 1995. 'Program planning as technology in three adult education organizations'. In *Adult Education Quarterly,* 38(4), pp. 211–223.

Busla, K. 1968. *Purposeful education for Africa.* The Netherlands: Mouton and Co.

Caffarella, R. S. 1985. 'A checklist for planning successful training programmes'. In *Training and Development Journal,* 39(3), pp. 81–83.

Caffarella, R.S. 1994. *Planning programmes for adult learners.* San Fracisco: Jossey-Bass.

Caffarella, R. S. 1994. Characteristics of adult learners and foundations of experiential learning. In *Experiential learning: A new approach,* eds. L. Jackson and R. S. Caffarella. San Francisco: Jossey-Bass.

Caffarella, R. S. 2000. *Planning programmes for adult learners: A practical guide for educators, trainers, and staff developers* (2nd edition). San Francisco: Jossey-Bass.

Caffarella, R. S. 2002. *Planning programmes for adult learners: A practical guide for educators, trainers, and staff developers* (2nd edition). San Francisco: Jossey-Bass.

Callaway, B. 1977. *Platform Terms.* Philadelphia: Lippin College.

Central Statistics Office Botswana. 1982. *Guideline for designing and executing small scale surveys in Botswana.* Gabarone: Ministry of Finance and Development Planning.

Central Statistics Office (CSO). 1997. *Literacy Survey Report 1993.* Gaborone: Ministry of Finance and Development Planning.

Cervero, R. M. 1988. *Effective continuing education for professionals.* San Francisco: Jossey-Bass.

Cervero, R. M. and Wilson, A. L. 1994. *Planning responsibility for adult education: A guide to negotiating power and interests.* San Francisco: Jossey-Bass.

Chamberlain, A. 1993. 'Learning from each other – Inspiration and example from Nicaragua'. In *Community Development Journal* 28(1), pp. 31–37.

Chilisa, B. and Preece, J. 2005. *Research methods for adult educators in Africa.* Cape Town: Pearson Education.

Cleaver, F. 2001. Institutions, agency, and the limitations of participatory approaches to development. In *Participation: The new tyranny,* B. Cooke and U. Kothari, London: Zed Books.

Compton, J. L. 1984. Extension programme development. In *Agricultural Extension: A reference manual* (2nd edition), ed. B. E. Swanson. FAO: Rome.

Cookson, P.S. (ed.). 1998. *Programme planning for the training and continuing education of adults: North American perspectives.* Malabar, Florida: Krieger.

Curtis, et al. 1978. Popular participation in decision-making and the basic needs approach to development: Methods, issues and experiences. Mimeographed World Employment Programme research working paper. ILO: Geneva.

Dakenwald, G. and Merriam, S. 1982. *Adult education: Foundations of practice.* New York: HarperCollins.

Diamond. R.M. 1991. *Designing and improving courses and curricula in higher education.* San Francisco: Jossey-Bass.

Dominick, J. 1990. How adult educators make program development decisions in practice. Unpublished doctoral dissertation, Department of Adult Education, University of Georgia.

Donaldson, J. and Kozoll, C. 1999. *Collaborative program planning: Principles, practices and strategies.* Malabar, Florida: Krieger.

Economic Commission for Latin America. 1973. 'Popular participation in development'. In *Community Development Journal,* Vol. 8, No. 3.

Ehiametalor, E. T. and Oduaran, A. B. 1991. *Fundamentals of adult education.* Benin City, Nigeria: Nera.

Ellington, H. 2000. *Producing teaching materials: A handbook for teachers and trainers.* London: Kogan Page.

Ellison, K. H. 1990. Report and recommendations of the District Development Plan 4 Consultancy. Prepared for the Government of Botswana, Ministry of Finance and Development Planning and Ministry of Local Government, Lands and Housing, Gaborone.

Emerton, L. and Mogaka, H. 1996. *PLA Notes,* 26, pp. 6–10.

Exenham, J. D. Katahoire, A. Petkova, A. Mwangi, R. and Sall, O. 2002. *Skills and literacy training for better livelihoods. A review of approaches and experiences.* African Region, The World Bank.

Fardouly, N. 1998. *Learner-centred teaching strategies: Principles of instructional design and adult learning.* Sydney: UNSW.

Field, J. 2003. *Evaluating community projects.* Nottingham: Russell Press.

Finch, C. R. and Crunkilton, J. R. 1993. *Curriculum development in vocational and technical education* (4th edition) Boston, London: Allyn and Bacon.

Fletcher, C. and Ruddock, R. 1986. Key concepts for an alternative approach to adult education. In *Convergence,* 19(2), pp. 41–48.

Freire, P. 1972. *Cultural action for freedom.* Harmondsworth: Penguin Books.

Freire, P. 1990. *Pedagogy of the oppressed.* New York: Continuum.

Galbraith, W. Sisco, B. and Guglielmino, C. 1997. *Administering Successful programs for adults. promoting excellence in adult, community, and continuing education.* Malabar, Florida: Krieger.

Gboku, M. L. S. Mokatse, T. Keletso, K. and Mphahudi, O. 2003. Informatics needs assessment for the development of capacity and establishment of the Botswana HIV/AIDS Response Information Management System (BHRIMS) in the Local Government Institutions. Technical report submitted to the National AIDS Coordinating Agency in collaboration with UNDP/ACHAP/CDC/Ministry of Local Government, Botswana.

Gboku, M. L. S. Keletso, K. and Mphahudi, O. 2004. Feasibility study of the Sekhutlane and Thankane settlements in the Southern District of Botswana. Consultancy report submitted to the Southern District Council, Botswana.

Giroux, H. 1988. 'Literacy and the pedagogy of voice and political empowerments'. In *Journal of Education Theory,* 38(1), pp. 61–76.

Goduku, I. 2000. African/indigenous philosophies: Legitimising spiritually – Centred wisdoms within the Academy. A refereed paper presented at the Australian Indigenous Education Conference, Frementle.

Goody, A. E. and Kozoll, C. E. 1995. *Program development in continuing education.* Malabar, Florida: Krieger.

Grotelueschen, A. 1980. *Developing, administering and evaluating adult education.* Washington, D.C.: Adult Education Association.

Hake, J.M. 1972. *Child reading practices in Northern Nigeria.* Ibadan: Ibadan University Press.

Hamilton, C. Kaudia, A. and Gibbon, D. 1998. Participatory basic needs assessment with the internally displaced using well being ranking. PLA Notes, in *Participation, Literacy and Empowerment.* London: IIED.

Hampton, R. 1994. 'Adult mother tongue literacy as developed by GILLBT'. In *Notes on Literacy,* 20(4), pp. 1–6.

Higgs, P. Vakalisa, N. C. G. Mda, T. V. and Assie-Lumumba, N. T. 2000. *African voices in education.* South Africa: The Rustica Press.

Hinzen, H. 1979. *Education for liberation and development.* Botswana Documents Collection: BAS Printers Limited.

Horton, A. 1989. *The Highlander Folk School: A history of its major programmes.* New York: Carlson Publishers.

Houle, C. O. 1972. *The design of education*. San Francisco: Jossey-Bass.

House, E. and Howe, K. 1999. *Values in evaluation and social research*. London: Sage.

Hoven, D. 1999. 'A model for listening and viewing: Comprehension in multimedia environments'. In *Language Learning and Technology*, 3(1), pp. 88–103.

Imel, S. 1990. 'Transformative learning in adulthood'. In *ERIC Digest*, No. 20.

Imhabekhai, C. I. 1998. *Programme development and programme management in adult and non-formal education in Nigeria*. Lagos: Amfitip Books.

International Congress of University Adult Education (ICUAE). 1969. Report of the first ICUAE, NY: Syracuse University.

Jonassen, D. et al. 1995. 'Constructivism and computer-mediated communication in distance education'. In *American Journal of Distance Education*, 9(2), pp. 7–26.

Kaufman, R. A. 1972. *Educational system planning*. Englewood Cliffs, N. J.: Prentice Hall.

Kemp, J. 1985. *The instructional design process*. New York: Harper and Row.

Kincheloe, J. Steinberg, S. and Slattery, P. 1999. *Contextualizing teaching*. New York: Longman.

Knowles, M. 1978. *The adult learner: A neglected species* (2nd edition). Houston, London, Paris, Tokyo: Gulf Publishing Company.

Knowles, M. S. 1980. *The modern practice of modern education* (2nd edition). New York: Cambridge.

Knowles, M. S. et al. 1994. *A history of the adult education movement in the United States*. Melbourne: Krieger.

Knox, A. 1980. Future directions. In *Developing, administering and evaluating adult education*, A. Knox and associates. Washington, D.C.: Adult Education Association.

Kotler, P. 2003. *Marketing management* (11th edition). Pearson Education International: Prentice Hall.

Kotler, P. and Andreasen, A. R. 1996. *Strategic marketing for non-profit organizations*. Eaglewood Cliffs, NJ.: Prentice Hall.

Kotler, P. and Zaltman, G. 1971. 'Social marketing: an approach to planned social change'. In *Journal of Marketing*, Vol. 35, pp. 3–12.

Kowalski, T. J. 1988. *The organization and planning of adult education*. Albany: State University of New York Press.

Kramish, et al. 1994. 'Improving dietary behavior: the effectiveness of tailored messages in primary care settings'. In *American Journal of Public Health*, 84(5).

Lauglo, J. 1990. 'Factors behind decentralization in educational systems: A comparative perspective with respect to Norway'. In *Comparatives* 20(1), pp. 21–39.

Lekoko, R.N. 2002. An appraisal of Batswana agents' work and training experiences: towards enhanced service coordination. USA: Dissertation Com.

Lele, U. 1975. *The design of rural development*. Baltimore: Johns Hopkins University Press.

Lisk, F. A. N. 1981. 'Popular participation in basic needs orientated development planning'. In *Labour Society*, Vol. 6, No.1.

Long, H.B. 1983. *Adult continuing education*. New York: Teaching College Press.

Mager, R. F. 1984. *Preparing instructional objectives*. Belmont, California: Lakes.

Maruatona, T. 1996. The role of NGOs in literacy activities in Botswana. Paper presented at the Second National Literacy Forum, held at the University of Botswana, June.

Maruatona. T. 1997. Gender perceptions of participation and use of the Botswana National Literacy Programme among the minorities: The case of the Basubiya in the Chobe District. Report submitted to the Gender and Education Committee of the Faculty of Education, University of Botswana.

Maruatona, T. 1998. A critique of centralised curricula in literacy programmes: The case of Botswana. Paper presented at the Africa Literacy Forum, Dakar, March 16–20.

Maslow, A. H. 1970. *Motivation and personality*, (2nd edition). New York: Harper and Row.

Mathieson, M. 1999. *Family and career management: Teacher's instructional guide*. Lubbock: Home Economics Curriculum Center, Texas Tech University.

Matos, N. 2000. The nature of learning, teaching and research in higher education in Africa. In *African voices in education*. eds. P. Higgs, N.C.G. Vakalisa, T.V. Mda and N.T. Assie-Lumumba. Cape Town: Juta.

Mbiti, J. 1988. *African religions and philosophies*. London: Heinemann.

Merriam, S. B. and Caffarella, R. S. 1999. *Learning in adulthood: A comprehensive guide* (2nd edition). San Francisco: Jossey-Bass.

Mgadla, P. 2003. *A history of education in the Bechuanaland protectorate to 1965*. New York: Oxford.

Muller, J. 1998. 'The well-tempered learner: Self-regulation, pedagogical models and teacher education policy'. In *Comparative Education*, 34(2), pp. 177–194.

McGuire, W. J. 1989. 'Theoretical foundations of campaigns'. In *Public communications campaigns*, eds. R. E. Rice and C. K. Newbury Park. California: Sage.

Newcomb, L. H. McCracken, J. D. and Warmbrod, J. R. 1993. *Methods of teaching agriculture*. Danville, Illinois: Interstate.

Namibia. 1996a. Brief report on ABE (Post Literacy) Workshop held at Sandown Lodge, 15–17 April 1996. Windhoek, Namibia: Directorate of Adult Basic Education, Ministry of Basic Education and Culture.

Namibia. 1966b. Pilot curriculum for formal basic education. Windhoek, Namibia: Directorate of Adult Basic Education, Ministry of Basic Education and Culture.

National Institutes of Health (NIH). 1992. *NIH data book 1992*. NIH publication No. 92–1261. Bethesda, MD.

Nkomo, M.O. 2000. African voices in education: retrieving the past, engaging the present and shaping the future. In *African voices in education*, eds. P. Higgs, N.C.G. Vakalisa, T.V. Mda and N.T. Assie-Lumumba. Cape Town: Juta.

Nyerere, J. K. 1974. *Man and development*. London: Oxford University Press.

Oakley and Marsden. 1984. *Approaches to participation in rural development*. Geneva: ILO.

Obi, G. O. 1989. Approaches to programme development in adult education. In *Administration of adult education,* eds. Okafor, et al. Uruowulu-Obosi: Pacific Publishers.

Ocitti, J. 1973. *African indigenous education: As practiced by the Acholi of Uganda*. Nairobi: East African Literature Bureau.

Ocitti, J. 1994. *African indigenous education: As practiced by the Acholi of Uganda*. Nairobi: East African Literature Bureau.

Oduaran, A. B. 1989. Assessment of literacy attainment in Nigeria. In *Approaches to adult literacy*, ed. Doris U. Egonu. Awada Onitsha: Cape Publishers International Ltd.

Oduaran, A. B. 1994. *An introduction to community development*. Benin City, Nigeria: Uniben Press.

Okafor, et al. (eds.). *Administration of adult education*. Uruowulu-Obosi: Pacific Publishers.

Onyemunwa, S. G. 1997. Appropriate adult education programme planning and implementation framework for Nigeria in the 21st century. In *Policy issues in adult and community education*, eds. Ayodele a. Fajonyomi and Idowu Biao. Maiduguri, Nigeria: Mainasara Publishing Co.

Oxenham, J. Diallo, A. Katahoire, A. Petkova-Mwangi, R. & Sall, O. 2002. *Skills and literacy training for better livelihoods – A review of approaches and experiences*. Africa Region, The World Bank.

Page, N. and Czuba, C. E. 1999. *Journal of extension*, Vol. 37, No. 5.

Pearse, A. and Stiefel, M. 1979. *Inquiry into participation: A research approach*. Geneva: UNRISD.

Pesson, L. 1972. Factors associated with farmers' perception of agricultural extension. Unpublished Ed.D dissertation. Louisiana State University, Department of Extension and International Education.

Pretorious, F. 2002. Changing the curriculum: Outcome-based education and training. In *Transforming education: The South African experience*, N. Van Wyk and E. Lemmer. New York: Nova Science Publisher.

Prochaska, J.O. et al. 1994. 'Stages of change and decisional balance for twelve problem behaviours'. In *Health Psychology,* 13(1), pp. 39–46.

Prochaska, J. O. and DiClemente, C. C. 1983. 'Stages and processes of self-change of smoking: toward an integrative model of change'. In *Journal of Consulting and Clinical Psychology*, 51, pp. 390–395.

Rahman, A. 1981. 'Reflections'. In *Development: Seeds of Change*. Rome, SID, No. 1.

Reynolds, M. 1997. Natural resource-use appraisal in Botswana. Preliminary report presented at a seminar at the National Institute for Research and Documentation, 10 January, Gaborone.

Riel, M. 1992. 'a functional analysis of educational tele-computing: A case of learning circle'. In *Interactive Learning Environment*, 2, pp. 9–15.

Robinson, M. 1990. 'The place of local-language literacy in rural development in Cameroon: Presentation of an experimental programme'. In *African Studies Review*, 33(3), pp. 53–64.

Robinson, M. 1992. NGOs and rural poverty alleviation: implications for scaling up. In *Making a difference. NGOs and development in a changing world*, eds. M. Edwards and D. Hulme. London: Earthscan.

Rogers, E. M. 1983. *Diffusion of innovations* (3rd edition). New York: The Free Press.

Ronan, N. 1994. 'A learner-centred approach to training the African manager'. In *Adult Education and Development*, 42, pp. 123–130.

Scheirer, M. 1994. Designing and using programme evaluation. In *Handbook of practical programme evaluation*, eds. J. Wholey, H. Hatry and K. Newcomer. San Francisco: Jossey-Bass.

Seepe, S. 2000. Exploring mathematical and scientific knowledge embedded in African cultural practices. In *African voices in education*, eds. P. Higgs, N. C. G. Vakalisa, T. V. Mda, and N. T. Assie-Lumumba. Cape Town: Juta.

Semali, I. 1999. 'Community as classroom: Dilemma of valuing African indigenous literacy in education'. In *International Review of Education*, 45(3–4), pp. 305–319.

Semali, L. and Kincheloe, L. 1999. *What is indigenous knowledge? Voices from the academy*. New York: Falmer Press.

Simerly, R. G. 1989. A ten-step process to ensure success in marketing. In *Handbook of marketing for continuing education*, R. G. Simerly and Associates. San Francisco: Jossey-Bass.

Sharma, K. C. 1992. Bureaucracy and coordination of rural development policies at the district level in Botswana. In *Bureaucracy and development policies in the Third World*, eds. H. K. Asmerom, R. Hope and R. B. Jain. Amsterdam: Free University Press.

Sisco, B. 1998. Forum, panel, and symposium. In *Adult learning methods* (2nd edition), ed. W. Galbraith. Malabar, Florida: Krieger.

Smith, W. A. 1999. *Dictionary of marketing terms* (2nd edition). Lincolnwood III: NTC Publishing Group.

Songan, P. 1993. 'Obstacles to participation in rural development programmes: A case study of a land development project in Sarawak, Malaysia'. In *Adult Education and Development*, Vol. 41, pp. 163–181.

Sork, T. J. 1982. *Determining priorities*. Vancouver: British Columbia Ministry of Education.

Sork, T. J. 1998. Programme priorities, purposes, and objectives. In *programme planning for the training and continuing education of adults: North American perspectives*, ed. P.S. Cookson. Malabar, Florida: Krieger.

Stein, J. (ed.). *The Random House College Dictionary*. USA: Random House.

Strydom, J. Jooste, C. and Cant, M. (eds.). 2000. *Marketing management* (4th edition). Pretoria: Juta.

Stufflebeam, D. L. 1971. *Educational evaluation and decision making*. Itasca, IL.: Peacock.

Tam, S. W. 2000. Managing learner-centredness: the role of effective student support in ODL. Paper presented at ICDE Asian Regional Conference, New Delhi, 3–5 November.

Taylor, M. C. 2000. 'Transfer of learning in workplace literacy programmes.' In *Adult Basic Education*, 10(1), pp. 3–20.

Teffo, L. 2000. Africanist thinking: An invitation to authenticity. In *African Voices in Education*, eds. P. Higgs, N. C. G. Vakalisa, T. V. Mda, and N. T. Assie-Lumumba. Cape Town: Juta.

Thomas, K. and Mellon, T. 1995. *Planning for training and development: A guide to analysing needs*. London: Save the Children.

UNESCO. 1976. Report of the General Conference of the UNESCO meeting on International Exchange of Cultural Poverty, 19th session, Nairobi, Kenya, 26 October–30 November.

UNESCO. 1993. *Equivalence Programmes*, Vol. III. Appeal training materials for continuing education personnel. Bangkok: UNESCO.

UNRISD. 1981. *Dialogue about participation*. Geneva: UNRISD.

Uphoff, N. T. and Cohen, J. 1979. Feasibility and application of rural development participation: A state of the art paper. Cornell University.

Wagner, E. 1994. 'In Support of a fundamental definition of interaction'. In *American Journal of Distance Education*, 8(2), pp. 6–29.

Weihrich, H. and Koontz, H. 1994. *Management: A global perspective* (10th edition). Hightstown: McGraw-Hill.

Wholey, J. Harty, H. and Newcomer, K. 1994. Improving evaluation activities and results: An introduction. In *Handbook of practical program evaluation*. San Fransisco: Jossey-Bass.

Wilcox, D. 1994. *Participation Guide*. Brighton: Partnership Books.

Williams, S. Seed, J. and Mwau, A. 1994. *The OXFAM Gender Training Manual*. Oxford: OXFAM.

Wilson, A. L. and Hayes, E. R. (eds.). 2000. *Handbook of adult and continuing education*. San Francisco: Jossey-Bass.

World Health Organisation. 1982. *Activities of the World Health Organisation in promoting community involvement for health development*. Geneva.

Youngman, F. 1997. 'Adult literacy and social development in Botswana'. In *Mosenodi*, Vol. 5, no. 2, pp. 15–27.

Youngman, F. 1998. 'Can old dogs learn new tricks?' Lifelong education for all and the challenges facing adult education in Botswana. University of Botswana inaugural lecture series, Gaborone.

http://www.aceproject.org/main/english/ve/ved03d/default.htm, viewed 20 February 2006.

Index

Page references in bold indicate where you can find a definition of key words. Page references in italic refer to diagrams and tables.

programme goals **85**, 89–90
  formulation of 94–96
programme implementation 5, **163**–174, *175–176*
  administration 171
  andragogical process 172–174
  critical questions 169
  features of (*see* programme implementation, features
    of)
  methods of instruction 174
  in-programme process 171–174
  planning 170–171
  stages of 167–169
programme implementation, features of 165–166
  programme order 166
  programme purpose 165–166
  programme utility 166
  types of *165*
programme marketing (*see* marketing, programme)
programme objectives **85**, 91–93
  formulation of 94–96
  sequencing of 97–98
programme planning 4–5, 15, 42, **49**
  action plans 52–53
  as controlled process 54–55
  as process 53–54
  concepts of 53–55
  cultural aspects 55
  pre-planning phase (*see* pre-planning)
  principles of (*see* programme planning, principles of)

programme planning, principles of 55–57
  functionalism 56
  participation and collaboration 56–57
  problem-based 56
programmes **3**, 11
purpose **163**

R
reasoning 7 (*see also* thinking, critical)
reflection 5, 9 (*see also* thinking, critical)
resources and logistics 6, 130

S
segmentation (*see* market segmentation)
social marketing (*see* marketing, social)
stakeholder groups (*see* stakeholders)
stakeholders **123**, 125–126, 133–134
SWOT analysis 140

T
teaching materials (*see* materials, teaching and learning)
thinking, critical 5, 6, 7, 9 (*see also* reasoning; reflection)
top-down approach (*see under* programme development,
  approaches to)
traditional knowledge (*see* knowledge systems,
  indigenous; philosophies, indigenous African)

U
utility **163**

V
values 7–8, 9 (*see also* beliefs)

W
wants (*see* needs)